THE BUDDHA, THE GOLD, AND THE MYTH

How Marcos Looted the Central Bank

Charles C. McDougald

San Francisco Publishers

 Printed in the Philippines by Reyes Publishing Inc. Cover art by Art Esmeralda. For information address San Francisco Publishers, P.O. Box 5282, So. San Francisco, CA 94083.

FIRST EDITION

ISBN: 0–940777–03–7
LCCN: 97–69003

97 98 99 00 10 9 8 7 6 5 4 3 2 1

Publisher's Cataloging-in-Publication
(Provided by Quality Books, Inc)

McDougald, Charles C., 1940–
The Buddha, the gold, and the myth: how Marcos looted the Central Bank / Charles C. McDougald. – 1st ed.
p. cm.
Includes bibliographical references and index.
Preassigned LCCN: 97–69003
ISBN: 0–940777–03–7
1. Marcos, Ferdinand E. (Ferdinand Edralin), 1917– 2. Philippines–Politics and government. 3. Philippines–Economic conditions–1946–1986. 4. Presidents–Philippines–Biography. 5. Treasure-trove–Philippines. I. Title.

DS686.5.M33 1997 959.9'046'092 [B]
QB197–41076

There would be no taker of bribes if there were no giver of bribes.

Ferdinand Marcos

Brass plaque in the arrival area of Manila International Airport
circa 1975

Acknowledgments

So many worked hard and long to keep most of the information in this book away from the public eye. Some wanted to help but said it was too much trouble. Too busy, said others. Few admitted the truth – they were afraid. I found three who were not: Senator Albert G. Romulo, Congressman Bonifacio Gillego, and Presidential Commission on Good Government Chairman Magtanggol Gunigundo.

The courage of their convictions made this book possible. They overwhelmed me with data, provided introductions when necessary, and critiqued the manuscript when it was over. For all this I thank you.

There were others I also owe a debt of gratitude. Mary Jo Agulto and Josie Firmeza on Senator Romulo's staff worked tirelessly in tracking down this memo and that statistic. Sophie Guerrero in Chairman Gunigundo's office did the same. Danilo Daniel, head of PCGG research, made the resources of his office available.

Central Bank Monetary Board Member Guillermo Carague always had the time to see me, usually on short notice, when I had a question. His demeanor and patience in explaining the Central Bank bureaucracy or its accounting system reminded me of my favorite professors at the University of the Philippines.

Many thanks to Dan Cathcart for providing depositions and copies of trial testimony from the golden Buddha trial which were especially helpful.

Contents

Preface

It's been more than a half-century but the rumors persist of a legendary treasure and the dictator that found it. In World War II in the Philippines, General Tomoyuki Yamashita buried thousands of gold, silver, and platinum bars, tons of diamonds and other jewels, and Buddhas made of pure gold. Supposedly. And President Ferdinand Marcos spent a good deal of his twenty-year reign digging it up.

Such stories abound. Some have been embellished in the telling, then exaggerated in the retelling, until today it is hard to separate fact from fiction, legend from reality.

The Marcos years were an incredible era. The Grand Coalition lived in ostentatious splendor while millions starved, billions were stolen, and the Central Bank looted. Marcos got what he wanted. Always. If anyone got in the way, heaven help him.

Rogelio "Roger" Roxas was a locksmith from Baguio. He never wanted trouble but it found him. Or rather, the soldiers found him. His story was not that untypical.

"They beat me up pretty bad. Busted my nose. Broke some ribs. That night they beat me again. I kept passing out. Then they started with the cigarettes. Burned my arms and nipples. That was painful but I was tough. Thought I could take it. Figured they would give up after a while. Then they brought in the car battery. Tied me down and hooked an alligator clip to my finger and testicle. That was the worst. Shock treatment, they called it. More like the electric chair – like a thousand hot needles stuck in me all over. I could smell my burnt flesh. I never screamed so much in my life. I signed the paper."

As Roger described his torture, his good eye blazed with the horror of it all. He chain-smoked, his speech punctuated with a wheezy tubercular cough.

When he was young, Roger was muscular, handsome, with a toothy smile. Now he was gaunt. Part of his face was caved in. His left eye bulged out of its socket. All he needed was a little bulge in the back and he would have made a passable Quasimodo.

The tuberculosis grew worse. He couldn't afford medicine. He was destitute, the cruelest of all ironies.

Roger was a treasure hunter. He found a great treasure and should have lived a long, happy life but Marcos stole it. When Roger protested he was tortured and thrown in prison. He never fully recuperated from his mental and physical injuries.

He stayed in hiding most of the years Marcos was in power. Only after Marcos left did he feel safe. He started again, digging for treasure deep in the jungle or high in the mountains. He had time to think, about the terrible things done to him, and about revenge.

Felix Dacanay was a boyhood friend. He grew up with Roger in San Fernando and Arayat in the province of Pampanga, north of Manila. He left the Philippines and immigrated to the U.S. in 1968, settling in a small town outside Atlanta. For almost two decades the two were out of touch. Then, in 1987, Roger called. Shortly afterward the Golden Budha Corporation was formed. (A golden Buddha was part of the treasure which Roger found.) Dacanay spelled *Budha* wrong in the corporate papers on purpose. It was a backhanded reference to the fact that whoever typed the search warrant and Roger's statement to the police in 1971 also spelled it that way.

Dacanay was a deeply religious man. In addition to his church activities, he belonged to the local chapter of the Wycliffe Bible Translators, which translated bibles into almost every known language and distributed them all over the world. Another member was John P. Tucker, Jr. In 1988 Dacanay asked if he could help Roger on a contingency basis, for free in exchange for a share of the proceeds if they won. Tucker agreed to try. Within a few weeks he knew the case was too big for him and his partner, Michael Butler, but agreed to try and locate someone suitable.

Using the Christian Legal Society Directory as his source, Tucker wrote a dozen or so law firms. Only two replied. Magaña, Cathcart & McCarthy was one. Dan Cathcart, one of the partners, had been a personal injury trial lawyer for forty years. His law firm was eminently successful in the field of aircraft accident litigation. He had the time and the deep pockets to finance a long and drawn out court battle. He agreed to take it.

The lawsuit was filed in February 1988. As it wound its way through the legal system, one of Roger's friends, a judge, arranged a private meeting with former First Lady Imelda Marcos in an attempt to settle the matter. Roger was broke and would have accepted almost anything but Imelda refused.

Shortly afterward, a Filipino movie producer made Roger's story into a movie. He received ₱150,000 (about $6,000). The money was a tremendous boost to the poor man's morale. His story began to attract attention in the States. In January 1993 he appeared in a segment of the *Unsolved Mysteries* television program.

In May he was to fly to Honolulu to give another deposition. He and his common law wife, Rosavilla, were staying at a friend's house in Manila. About eight that morning, emerging from the bathroom after a shower, she found Roger on the floor. He was rushed to Olivarez Hospital in nearby Parañaque but it was too late. The medical examiner said he died of tuberculosis. He was forty-eight. There was no autopsy, leading to speculation he was murdered.

Roger had already been deposed so his death did not impede the lawsuit. It came to trial in July 1996. Cathcart had spent eight years and a fortune, in his words, but he never wavered. He believed if anyone deserved justice, it was Roger. The trial lasted a month. After one day's deliberation the jury agreed with Cathcart. They awarded the Golden Budha Corporation $22 billion in damages for personal injuries, for being falsely imprisoned and tortured, and for theft of the treasure.

Imelda was angry about the verdict. "I intend to use everything that was said and done against us as evidence in all the cases we shall file against those who libeled us, slandered us, stolen from us, convicted us, condemned us and have now convicted even our dead." After all the lawsuits, and there were many, she still would not accept the reality of what she and Marcos did to the Philippines.

The golden Buddha trial provided a glimpse into Marcos' secret passion. He was a treasure hunter – he had the fever. It was more a state of mind than a medical condition. Some people were not affected. Others were, to varying degrees, when old maps were unfolded and the tales first told: "I was there in 1943 when they buried the treasure . . ."

The brain received and processed the information like any other data. But it wasn't like any other data. Here was a riddle, the solution worth millions. Sometimes thinking about the end result caused left lobe lockdown. The brain ceased to function normally. The eyes started to glaze over. The breathing quickened. A little voice inside whispered, "Only sixty feet down . . . a hundred million dollars."

Marcos sent a small army to rob a poor locksmith. That wasn't a rational act. It was the fever. He long had a fascination with the yellow metal. The golden Buddha just proved how serious, how fanatical, this fascination had become. It would continue to get worse.

Marcos stole, no doubt. But after more than a decade nobody still knows how much. Not many people have talked. For some the past was too painful – a loved one lost, a life destroyed. For others it was too sinister – recalling too much might result in a prison sentence, or worse.

Finding the truth was like an old puzzle. You put together what you had. There might be missing pieces but a picture formed.

On a typical day a soldier hunted for treasure in the countryside instead of fighting communists; an official at the Central Bank worked late into the night to keep the dark secrets hidden within; a man was tortured. At the palace Marcos brooded over his enemies, real and imagined; Imelda drew triangles and circles and spoke of a hole in the sky. What madness.

Marcos died in 1989, a broken man. All his life he had sought to achieve the lasting fame that comes with being a hero to his own people. Now the myth he created about himself lay in tatters. But another myth survived. It still survives.

CHAPTER ONE

Exile

On Tuesday evening, February 25, 1986, the last few hours of Marcos' dictatorship were played out at Malacañan Palace in pandemonium. A rocket exploded somewhere on the palace grounds. Inside everyone screamed and rushed around gathering possessions and packing boxes.

Ferdinand Marcos lay on the hospital bed in his bedroom on the second floor. He heard the noise coming from the window. The crowd outside the gates was screaming and shouting. He winced at the crack of a rifle shot.

Down the hall, Gen. Fabian Ver, armed forces Chief of Staff, was busy directing soldiers in one last obscene parting gesture. He had already shown his ugly side the day before when he pleaded with Marcos on national television to bomb and strafe the crowd gathered in front of Camp Crame.

The soldiers plotting the coup against Marcos had fled to Camp Crame. Archbishop Jaime Cardinal Sin, head of the Catholic Church in the Philippines, called for the people to join them. So they came, at first by the hundreds, then thousands. In what was referred to as the Miracle of Edsa – E. De Los Santos Boulevard is the street in front of Camp Crame – more than a million people came to show their support and deliver the message that Marcos must go.

Ver wanted to attack. Marcos had said no then but now he was too tired and too sick to care. "Put the books back," Ver ordered. The men gingerly replaced the books on the shelves in

Marcos' office. Now the bombs were hidden. The soldiers ran the trip-wires across the doorway and finished their job.

Later that evening the crowd outside the gates heard the faint but distinctive whump-whump-whump sound of helicopters landing and taking off. Behind the palace and across the Pasig River was Malacañan Park, the location of Marcos' private golf course and also the home of the Presidential Security Command, his personal bodyguard unit.

As those sounds died away the word spread – Marcos was gone. The crowd moved toward the gates, hesitantly at first. Not meeting any resistance, they surged forward, scaled the fence, and stormed the palace. Their angry shouting reached a fever pitch and drowned out the screams of the few unfortunate loyalists who had not yet scampered to safety. Some were beaten to death. Others were smart enough to hide and melt into the crowd. It was payback time as the poor exacted their own tribute from a tyrant who kept them downtrodden for so many years.

Anything that wasn't nailed down was fair game. Chairs, tables, curtains, rugs, ashtrays, even trash cans were taken. Television camera crews recorded the event and relayed their footage back to the states in time for the six o'clock news. One scene showed a Filipino standing in a window on the second floor wrestling with a large picture of Marcos. He struggled for a moment, then raised it over his head and heaved it out the window. A roar went up from the crowd as it fell to the ground. A picture of Imelda sailed out moments later. The people below rushed to trample, spit on, and curse the pictures. As they took their revenge on two pieces of cardboard, U.S. helicopters sped the real people to Clark Air Base, forty miles north.

The pillaging went on for hours but no one tripped any wires or detonated any explosives. They were at the wrong building. The actual palace, where the first family lived and where Marcos had his office, was next door. The crowd had stormed Maharlika Hall, the executive building, a few yards away. It was more visible from the road and could easily be mistaken for the palace at night. It was a fortunate mistake. While the crowd celebrated, soldiers loyal to President Aquino quietly moved in and secured the palace. They found the bombs and defused them.

Order was restored. Because of the booby-traps that were found, the palace was searched room by room. Downstairs in the courtyard by the fountain another trip-wire was discovered and the bomb defused. Finally the palace was declared safe. Aquino said she didn't want to live there, but, she announced, everyone should come and see the intimate details of the place Marcos called home for twenty years. Soon the world would come to know the wretched excesses of a man consumed by greed and his wife who tried to spend it all.

A doorway separated Marcos' bedroom from Imelda's. Both had triangular-shaped wood parquet on their floors. These shapes also decorated the ceilings of Marcos' bedroom and Imelda's dressing room. They believed, like the Egyptians of old, in the magical properties of the pyramid.

The hospital bed beside his double bed exposed the lie that he was a well man. Nearby were two dialysis machines for his failing kidneys, a portable toilet, and stacks of diapers for his incontinence. There was also a cabinet about ten feet high and twenty feet long full of medicine.

Her bedroom was dimly lit and contained no reading lights. Her oversized bed was actually two queen-size beds side by side on a platform raised a foot off the floor, surrounded by a low balustrade, and crowned by a tulle canopy overhead. The head-board was elaborately carved. The bed cover and pillow cases were made of expensive *piña*, a cloth made from fibers of the pineapple plant. This was supposedly a copy of the bed in which Marie Antoinette slept. Beside it was a cylinder of oxygen. She thought an occasional whiff would make her skin soft. Singer Michael Jackson had recommended it. Doctors didn't agree but no one bothered to tell her.

Off to the left was her bathroom. There were gold plated fixtures and a walk-in tub. Displayed on the shelves were gallon jars of the most expensive perfumes. To the left of this was the sitting room. The centerpiece was a grand piano, especially tuned for her friend, Van Cliburn. He played here often after an evening's performance at the Cultural Center. Seven grand pianos were found in the palace.

To the right of the bedroom was her dressing room. On the shelves were more gallon jars of perfume. Behind was a walk-in closet containing about 200 dresses and some shoes. This was just one week's supply.

Downstairs was a room the size of a basketball court that resembled a smart house of fashion in New York. There were a dozen or so racks of evening wear. Some had the distinct butterfly shoulders of the *terno*, the formal attire favored by the Filipina. Others bore labels of fashion designers in Paris and Rome. There was exquisite hand-sewn beadwork, and gold and silver lamè. Then came the dozens of racks of day dresses of different colors and various styles. Thc numbers were overwhelming – 2,900 gowns and dresses. One person could not have worn all these in two lifetimes. Fifty-four sable and mink coats were found in cold storage lockers of several hotels.

Marcos' clothes occupied a modest corner of the room. There were racks of pants and *barong tagalogs*, the formal Filipino shirt, along with a dozen pairs of elevator shoes. He was a short man, five feet two inches, and vain despite the immense power he wielded.

Of the 122 racks of clothes, sixty-seven were empty. That was all they had time to pack. All of Imelda's bullet-proof bras were still on their hangers. Nearby were her shoes. None were elevated. She was tall for a Filipina, five feet six inches, and beautiful in her youth. But now that youth was gone and what remained was a yearning, for shoes, size eight. Only 1,200 pair were found in the palace. Another 2,800 pair were found in the forty guest houses the Marcoses maintained all over the country.

Next to the wardrobe room was Marcos' private hospital. It contained two more dialysis machines and more medicines – three truckloads were carted away but not before pictures were taken and displayed for the public.

Outside there was a bus equipped as a mobile hospital and containing another dialysis machine. It followed Marcos everywhere during his last run for the presidency. Sometimes after a speech he would have to be carried off the podium to that bus. Now it sat unused, a reminder of a sick president and his last campaign.

Between Marcos' booby-trapped office and the office of his private secretary was the communications room. It was from here that the telexes had been sent in 1983 to the foreign creditors announcing the Philippines could no longer meet its foreign obligations. It was the first inkling that something wasn't right, that dollars were scarce, that somebody was pillaging the Central Bank. Over in the corner were six paper shredding machines, four burned out from overuse. The remains of thousands of pages of documents lay shredded on the floor, a paper trail of hidden wealth now reduced to confetti.

Civilian groups that had assisted Aquino in her presidential bid took on a new role. During the campaign they had armed themselves with hand-held radios and used code names so they couldn't be identified. They organized for a new mission.

Jokingly referring to themselves as the Office of National Revenge, these vigilantes were not seeking vengeance. Their purpose was to try and find the documents that were the key to Marcos' hidden wealth before they could be spirited out of the country. Across Manila, those that had enriched themselves during the dictatorship tried to hide what they could and escape with the rest.

A good example was the raid led by Charlie Avila and Jose Alcuaz. They received a tip in the morning that Marcos' daughter, Imee Marcos-Manotoc, had kept a private office in the suburb of Mandaluyong, Metro Manila, at 82 E. De Los Santos Boulevard. They obtained a search warrant, then rushed to Camp Crame to pick up some soldiers. After devising a plan, they boarded four cars and drove to the premises, arriving around midnight.

The soldiers scaled a fence and sealed off the area. Avila, Alcuaz, and their men moved in and found documents in cardboard boxes, desks, and filing cabinets. Gunfire could be heard outside but it didn't deter the search. The documents revealed the names of offshore companies and overseas investments of Marcos and his cronies – another link in the paper trail.

On February 28, Jim Burke, security expert from the U.S. Embassy, was tapping on the wooden panelling in Imelda's bedroom when he heard a hollow sound. Removing part of the panelling, he found the walk-in vault. Inside were thirty-five suitcases secured with locks and tape. They were removed to a house in Dasmariñas Village for safekeeping, then later picked up by government representatives.

The suitcases contained a treasure trove of documents about Swiss bank accounts, New York real estate, foundations in Vaduz, and some note paper on which Marcos had practiced his William Saunders signature. They also contained jewelry. An inventory placed their value at ₱236 million ($10.5 million).

Finding the vault was not a total surprise. Friends of Imelda had bragged about where she kept some of her favorite jewelry pieces and *objets d'art*. She suffered from insomnia. Late at night she liked to take the pieces out and play with them. She loved the *oohs* and *aahs* of the admiring crowd as she tried on the rings, necklaces, and earrings, and told them where this piece came from or how much that piece cost. A receipt from Bulgari's was found inside the vault for six pieces of jewelry worth $1,431,000.

The wall panel hiding the secret door to Marcos' walk-in vault was also found. Inside were four filing cabinets containing documents, not about affairs of state, but about other matters such as Swiss bank accounts and real estate.

Marcos and his entourage were flown to Clark Air Base. Within hours they were on two U.S. Air Force C-141's heading for Hawaii. The plane landed at an air base on Guam for refueling. While there, they were allowed to shop in the post exchange because, they claimed, they had not had time to pack any toiletries. They neglected to mention what they had packed, however.

The two aircraft touched down at Hickam Air Force Base in Hawaii on Wednesday morning, February 26, 1986. (They crossed the international date-line, gaining another day. Wednesday morning in Hawaii was early Thursday in Manila.) They were coming to the end of a 6,000-mile journey.

George Ariyoshi, the governor of Hawaii and a personal friend of Marcos, was there to greet the former dictator and to give him as warm a welcome as dignity would permit under the circumstances. The whole group, totalling eighty-nine, looked dishevelled. Marcos, his face splotched with purple patches, appeared especially drawn and tired. As he came off the plane he had to be helped by an Air Force captain.

Wearing a windbreaker and a little wrinkled hat emblazoned with the presidential seal, his appearance was almost funny looking. This was in sharp contrast to the imposing figure seen on television just thirty-six hours earlier in crisp *barong*, scowling and haranguing the masses.

A few hours after they landed, their luggage arrived – 300 crates on board a C-141 cargo jet. It took twenty-five customs officers five hours to tag the bags and identify the contents. It was videotaped because of all the money and jewelry found inside.

There were 278 crates of jewelry and art worth an estimated $5 million. Twenty-two crates contained more than ₱27.7 million in newly minted currency, mostly hundred-peso denominations worth approximately $1.27 million. It was illegal for anyone to depart the Philippines carrying more than ₱500 in cash. Marcos' excuse was that the pesos belonged to his campaign fund, but the pesos only served to underscore the double standard of justice that had characterized his version of democracy for twenty years.

The inventory also included various certificates of deposit from Philippine banks worth approximately $1 million, five handguns, 154 videotapes, seventeen cassette tapes, and 2,068 pages of documents. All items were impounded by Customs.

U.S. Ambassador to the Philippines Stephen Bosworth later informed Aquino that the entourage was allowed to keep $300,000 in gold and $150,000 in bearer bonds that they brought in with their personal luggage because they declared them and broke no U.S. customs laws.

The gold, according to a senate investigation report, consisted of twenty-four bars weighing one kilogram each, fitted in a $17,000 hand-tooled Gucci briefcase with a solid gold buckle. The plaque on it read, 'To Ferdinand Marcos, from Imelda, on the Occasion of our 24th Wedding Anniversary.'

Larry Speakes, President Reagan's press secretary, announced the next day that twenty members of the Marcos family "as a courtesy" did not have to go through a customs search so it wasn't known what else of value was carried into the country on their persons.

Aquino acted immediately. The Presidential Commission on Good Government was set up. The mission of the PCGG was to investigate and, where possible, bring lawsuits to prevent Marcos and his family from getting their hands on this vast accumulation of wealth. The documents confiscated in Hawaii, plus those found in the palace, the Mandaluyong offices, and elsewhere were turned over to the PCGG. They were the beginning of a paper trail that would lead all over the world, and reflected a greed obscene in its enormity. Most of all it gave the lie to the constant litany of denials that they owned no real estate in the United States and had no secret Swiss bank accounts. They not only had both, they had them on a scale difficult to comprehend.

A few weeks later, on March 9, a Greek-American, Demetrios Roumeliotes, was stopped at the airport before he could leave with eight large envelopes stuffed with jewelry which he admitted belonged to Imelda. They were valued at ₱104,934,750 ($4.7 million).

According to income tax returns, the Marcoses had a net worth of $7,000 when they became the First Couple in 1965. It was estimated Marcos stole at least $5 billion. He would have had to steal $700,000 a day during the twenty years he was in power to amass that kind of fortune.

On a typical day in the courts, a Filipino might be sentenced to twenty years hard labor for stealing ₱100 (five dollars). For example, on February 8, 1985, the Sandiganbayan, the body assigned to handle cases of corruption in government, sentenced two municipal treasury employees to prison terms of sixty-four and twenty-six years respectively for malversing a few hundred pesos.

In the time it took to sentence these men, Marcos might have received a half-million dollar kickback from a Japanese firm and a cut from one of the monopolies he controlled through his cronies. Whether it was called kickback or bribe, it was still stealing. That's why he was overthrown. After more than twenty years in power, his own people turned against him because they couldn't stomach his last attempted theft – of a presidential election.

He had come a long way. When elected president, he preached reform. Only Japan was better off in terms of economic wealth. The *Far Eastern Economic Review* noted that, "Of the four tigers, Singapore was tied to Malaysia, Hong Kong was a mass of shanty towns, South Korea was reeling from the after-effects of a destructive civil war and the fall of the Rhee government, and Taiwan was a beleaguered outpost." Now in 1986 the four were fully developed countries while his economy lay in ruins and half his people lived below the poverty line.

The *Guinness Book of Records* named him the world's greatest thief and that was based on what they could trace. Papers found in the palace showed he opened his first bank account abroad on July 7, 1967 when he deposited $215,000 in Chase Manhattan Bank in New York. Not yet accustomed to hiding money, he used his own name.

The following year he opened his first Swiss account. The hundreds of millions would begin to pour in and his military would commit one of their first acts of mass murder by killing fourteen of their own. Things started slow at first. Marcos hadn't really reached his stride.

CHAPTER TWO

The Golden Buddha

Nine months into his presidency, Marcos was cast into the world political arena with a state visit to the U.S. In September 1966, President Lyndon Baines Johnson received Marcos warmly and introduced him at a joint session of congress as a war hero. LBJ wanted soldiers from more countries to convince the people Vietnam wasn't just an American war. Marcos paid lip service to the cause but that was it. He sent an engineer battalion – 2,000 men. Korea sent 50,000 troops to Vietnam; Thailand 11,500; Australia 7,500.

His contribution was the smallest, his demands the largest. He walked away with $45 million in economic assistance, $31 million in settlement of Philippine veterans' claims, and $3.5 million from a Special Education Fund which Imelda used to build the Cultural Center.

Imelda, at her beautiful and exquisite best, received rave reviews in Washington and in New York. The couple were the talk of the town. Marcos' popularity abroad was at an all-time high. On October 21, 1966, he made the cover of *Time*.

Later in the year, LBJ visited seven countries in seventeen days, including the Philippines. The Manila slums were hidden by newly erected, whitewashed walls. Marcos waited with his hand out again. That grated on Johnson. His dislike for Marcos grew until eventually he told William Bundy, assistant secretary of state for East Asia, "If you ever bring that man near me again, I'll have your head."

At home, Marcos had done little during his first term to deliver his campaign promises. There was still widespread poverty and extensive unemployment. Graft and corruption prevailed. The newspapers constantly reminded him of the enormous chasm between the lower and upper class.

In February 1968, Imelda was hospitalized. Rumors began to fly she was dying of some dreaded disease. The newspapers picked up the story. Such pronouncements in a predominantly Catholic country where women are placed on a pedestal helped to deflect the biting criticism aimed at Marcos.

If Imelda were sick she apparently didn't feel bad enough to cancel the appointment with her Swiss banker. In March, Walter Fessler, an official of the Credit Suisse Bank in Zurich, came to Manila. He was brought to the palace. Forms were filled out and signatures appended. On his signature verification form, Marcos wrote out " William Saunders (pseudonym)," an alias he had used in his World War II days, and underneath that name he wrote "Ferdinand Marcos (real name)." Imelda did the same, choosing Jane Ryan as her pseudonym. Four bank accounts were opened. Four checks, totalling $950,000, were given for the deposit.

Some of the first payoffs Marcos received came from the U.S. government. After he committed troops to Vietnam, he began receiving quarterly checks of $200,000 each, delivered by the U.S. Embassy, as per a secret agreement "between officials of Department of State and President Marcos that the Philippine Government could conceal the receipt of these payments from the Philippine public in its national defense budget."

While the ink was drying on the Swiss deposit slips, the blood of fourteen soldiers was drying on Corregidor. On March 21, 1968, the *Manila Times* headline was "CAMP MASSACRES BARED." It reported the massacre of fourteen soldiers on Corregidor. Another forty were missing. Code-named Jabida, Marcos had secretly ordered the military to recruit and train a group of Filipino-Muslims. When they found out their mission was to be sabotage and insurgency in Sabah, they rebelled and were massacred. Sabah, formerly a British protectorate in North

Borneo, was primarily Muslim and had joined the Federation of Malaysia in 1963.

The incident was a black-eye for the military and a political bombshell for Marcos. Once again he was on the defensive and once again Imelda came to the fore. The newspapers announced the First Lady had a miscarriage. She was out of danger and resting comfortably but still depressed over her loss. The story helped quiet one more storm of protest.

Marcos continued to plot and scheme his political survival as election year 1969 arrived. As if on cue, President Richard Nixon showed up to praise him. Neil Armstrong, the first man to walk on the moon, splashed down in the Pacific. Nixon was there to welcome him when he landed on the deck of the USS *Hornet*. From there Nixon went to Guam to visit American troops, then to Manila.

The reason for all the attention this time was the bases – Clark Air Base and Subic Naval Base. Strategically they had become two of the most important military bases in the world to the U.S. and Marcos knew this.

Two months after the Nixon visit, Imelda inaugurated the Cultural Center. Representing the U.S. at this occasion was Governor Ronald Reagan of California and his wife, Nancy. It was the beginning of a long friendship.

For the upcoming presidential campaign, Marcos' propaganda machine was cranked up to denounce graft, corruption, and anything else the people were against. It was all a show of course. Winning the election wasn't a problem. The important thing was to look good, especially to the U.S., the IMF, and the World Bank.

Marcos won a second term. The press described him as the most corrupt and ruthless leader the Philippines ever had, and called the election the most corrupt ever held, characterized by fraud, terrorism, vote-buying, and ballot-box stuffing.

Those were serious charges, but what seemed to worry him the most was being called the richest man in Asia. That kind of talk could hurt, especially when it came time to ask for another loan.

Imelda complicated the problem with her spending habits.

When it was time to go shopping any medical problems she had seemed to evaporate. She was well enough at Christmas to go on a huge shopping spree in Hong Kong. The Manila press got wind of it. Once again a strategic move designed to relieve some of the pressure was needed.

On New Years Day 1970, Marcos announced to the nation he was giving up all his worldly wealth. The Ferdinand E. Marcos Foundation was already set up and his possessions being inventoried for donation to the Filipino people. This was in gratitude for electing him to a second term thereby becoming the only president ever to be reelected, he proclaimed.

The announcement raised a few eyebrows at first. Then the reporters started in again. Instead of an outpouring of thanks they just wanted to know what he was up to. They knew the announcement would change nothing, that the corruption would continue.

A few days later, after a round of golf, Marcos met with reporters. It wasn't long before his ill-gotten gains were brought up. "That's unfair," he complained again.

They braced themselves for the usual lecture. Then he did something totally uncharacteristic. He admitted he was rich. This was amazing. Marcos never admitted anything.

He continued while the reporters leaned forward and scribbled furiously, hanging on every word. They had a headline here. Then came the blockbuster. "You know how I made my pile? I discovered Yamashita's treasure."

They stopped scribbling. This was a joke. Marcos was a bit of a wit sometimes. They waited for the punch line. None came. They stifled a collective yawn and put away their note pads.

The Yamashita myth was old hat by then. At the end of World War II, a story was passed around that Gen. Yamashita, commander of Japanese forces, had buried a treasure in the Philippines that rivalled all other treasures throughout history. Since then, treasure hunts were the order of the day especially in the mountains around Baguio. Too many front-page stories had announced that so-and-so had found a treasure, only to announce later that the story was a mistake or a hoax. And now Marcos. What a shabby excuse. It wasn't even original.

The announcement about the Marcos Foundation and then the announcement of his finding a treasure tended to confuse more than enlighten the issue of his wealth. But wealth wasn't the important issue just then, according to the students. A few weeks later 40,000 of them stoned Marcos in front of the legislature building to show their disgust after he delivered his State of the Nation address. They presented him with a mock coffin to represent the death of democracy in the Philippines. In what is now known as the First Quarter Storm, the protest turned violent and bloody when the military were ordered to quell the demonstration with truncheons, water cannons, and guns. Four students died.

While the battle raged, Marcos and Imelda issued handwritten instructions to Markus Geel on February 13, 1970, to establish the Xandy Foundation in Vaduz, the capital city of Liechtenstein. Nestled between Austria and Switzerland, the tiny state was famous for offering a unique form of corporate structure – the *anstalt* – a single-shareholder company protected by the world's tightest corporate secrecy laws. The CIA and KGB hid their covert funds there. Even Swiss bankers who sometimes had the need to hide money used the *anstalten*.

The William Saunders and Jane Ryan accounts were closed and the money transferred to the Xandy Foundation account at Credit Suisse. This would be the first of many foundations set up in this manner with Swiss bankers and lawyers as directors to hide the identities of Marcos and Imelda. Two months later another treasure hunt began on a hillside behind the Baguio General Hospital.

Roger Roxas was a locksmith in Baguio when he started treasure hunting in his spare time in 1962. He searched in the provinces of Nueva Vizcaya, Nueva Ecija, Cagayan, and the mountains around Clark Air Base but never found more than a few old coins and some Japanese weapons and ammunition. In May 1970, Roger got married at the age of twenty-seven. A Japanese, Albert Fushugami, gave him a sketch showing a treasure location. Fushugami claimed to have been with a group of engineers during the war that had buried some treasure during

Yamashita's retreat. The sketch showed where ten truckloads of gold were buried in a tunnel complex in the hillside near Baguio. When asked, Roger could not explain why Fushugami gave him the sketch other than the fact that he was president of the Baguio chapter of the Treasure Hunters Association at the time, and he had just purchased a new metal detector. The brand name was White Electronics. His fellow treasure hunters jokingly referred to it as the White Elephant because he hadn't found any treasure. Then Fushugami gave him the sketch.

Such maps and sketches were not uncommon. In treasure-hunting circles maps were not the problem. There were plenty to go around. The fact that they were all bogus was the problem. Perhaps it wasn't considered polite to ask why anyone would want to give away such a key to wealth, or maybe treasure hunters didn't really care just so long as they had a promise of riches beyond their wildest dreams. Roger had been brought up on stories about the Yamashita treasure. He knew he wasn't the first to search for it in those mountains. When he and his intrepid band began their search, he knew his chances were slim. But like the mountain climber who climbs "because it's there," he had a map, so the hunt was on.

Because of the work required at the excavation, Roger decided more men were needed. In addition to his regular group of sixteen, he hired a dozen Igorot tribesmen who lived in the mountains nearby. They located the hill and began looking for an entrance. It wasn't going to be easy. The tunnel had been blasted shut more than a quarter century before. Now even if there was an entrance it would be covered in dense undergrowth.

After two weeks of sweaty, back-breaking work cutting away trees, bushes, vines, and thick undergrowth they finally spotted the debris of what looked like a collapsed cave. After a few days of removing boulders, rocks, and dirt, they broke through to a tunnel. Cautiously they groped their way, checking for booby-traps.

About a hundred yards inside there was a pile of debris which appeared to be the result of another attempt to blast the tunnel. Roger asked his surveyor to examine the old sketch and determine their location. They made a new shaft at a right angle to the tunnel, dug in that direction for a few yards, turned left again, and dug parallel to the old tunnel. They proceeded about ninety feet and made another left turn to tunnel back to the original shaft. It was still collapsed, so back they went to their tunnel, went another ninety feet, and tunnelled in again only to find another collapse. Their shaft now stretched for about 100 yards.

The surveyor checked again and told Roger the shaft wasn't level. They started angling upward. About ninety feet further on, and at an elevation about fifty feet higher, they finally broke into an open tunnel. They had been digging for four months. It was September.

The air was musty but breathable. Roger stepped through the hole, took one look, and jumped right back out. Laying there against the wall in an eternal sleep was a soldier or rather a skeleton in the rags of a Japanese uniform.

They found more skeletons and all kinds of medical items – old dextrose bottles, syringes, and assorted instruments – indicating this may have been a first aid station. They also found something else – snakes. There were big ones, small ones, all kinds. After trying to kill a few they found out something: if they left the snakes alone, the snakes left them alone. It was a tenuous standoff at best but they managed to concentrate on the digging.

Further on they found the tunnel corkscrewed downward about thirty-five feet, like a spiral staircase, to another tunnel with laterals which contained old kitchen items. Using the surveyor's calculations they walked to the end of this tunnel and began digging. They had only dug about ten feet when one of the shovels broke through to the outside. They were now on the other side of the mountain and could see the hospital. The light poured in and a breeze flowed through. The ventilation cooled the men and propped up their sagging spirits.

In mid-November, Roger called a halt to the digging and told everyone to go home for a two-week rest. He didn't tell them he was almost out of money and supplies. Once again he managed to beg and borrow enough to resume. They were back in operation by the first week of December.

Christmas 1970 was approaching and still Roger and his group had nothing to show for their efforts. Based on the old sketch, he figured the main tunnel was off to the left of where they were digging, so they started excavating in that direction. The work was hard, tedious, and slow but they continued on. They believed the end of their rainbow was somewhere in this labyrinth.

December came and went. While his men were digging the new shaft Roger decided to systematically test the whole tunnel complex with his metal detector. From tunnel to tunnel, going into each lateral and out again he led his machine. Foot by foot, from side to side he swept the instrument, watching for snakes and watching the meter at the same time, listening for that telltale buzzing which would indicate metal below. Occasionally he detected something but all he found was old ammunition or scrap metal. Up and down those dark tunnels he went with his detector. The stride he used made him appear to be skating on the dirt floor.

In late January his men were still digging toward the main shaft. He was in the tunnel where the skeleton was found when the meter began to give off a loud buzzing. He called for a few men and they began digging. Six feet down they struck a heavy solid object. It wouldn't budge so they dug around it. Gradually a head was revealed. The excitement grew as they frantically dug around the object until it was uncovered. They all stood there, staring at their find, at their rainbow's end. It was a gold statuette of Buddha, almost three feet tall and too heavy to lift.

Ecstatic over their find and fearful of another cave-in – they had experienced several during the dig – they decided the ten truckloads could wait. The Buddha was enough treasure for the time being. Using ropes and pulleys they drug it out of the tunnel. On further examination they found the head screwed off. Inside the small space were a few handfuls of diamonds. They borrowed a truck and brought the Buddha back to Roger's house at 47 Ledesma Street in Baguio. It was two in the morning on January 27, 1971.

Scales were found. The Buddha weighed 2,000 pounds. Roger wrapped it in blankets and put it in a sturdy wooden case in the back room. Word of his find quickly spread. Other treasure hunters began to show up to have a look. In order to disguise the location, Roger claimed he found the Buddha in a cave on Mt. Loo, further north.

An Air Force officer at Clark Air Base, First Lieutenant Ken Cheatham, was a part-time treasure hunter. When he heard about Roger and the Buddha, he and some friends came to see it. They took a lot of photos. Each posed with Roger and the Buddha.

A representative from the Treasure Hunters Association in Manila, Louie Mendoza, tested the Buddha and said it was 22-karat, about 92 percent pure gold. At $50 an ounce, the price of gold at the time, it was worth about $1.6 million dollars, and even more as an artifact.

Several offers were made but a price couldn't be agreed upon. Some ladies arrived from Manila claiming to be the personal attendants of Imelda Marcos. They made an offer of ₱3 million ($500,000) but Roger had to bring it to Manila. He knew it was worth a lot more so he declined.

One day in early April a man came to the house. He claimed to represent *Doña* Josepha Edralin Marcos, the mother of Marcos. The Buddha was inspected and an offer was discussed but nothing was agreed upon.

On April 5, Holy Monday in the Philippines, at two-thirty in the morning, Roger was awakened by persistent pounding on the front door. His brother and two cousins had been acting as guards. When they opened it there stood a group of armed men. Four of them in uniform barged inside. One handed Roger a piece of paper, claiming it was a search warrant. He started to read, but it was snatched out of his hands. He did manage to see who signed it – Judge Pio Marcos, an uncle of the president.

Roger's family was ordered into the kitchen and told to lie on the floor. Four men guarded them while the others ransacked the house. When Roger tried to intervene he was clubbed. His wife, who had given birth recently, started to bleed. Despite Roger's pleading, she was forced to remain on the floor. The pillaging continued for half an hour. The Buddha was found in the back room. It was loaded onto a steel handcart and the men departed. Roger took his wife to the hospital.

On April 7 he went to the police and made a sworn statement. He claimed that, in addition to the Buddha, seventeen small gold bars, a Samurai sword, a bag full of foreign coins, a boltless .22 calibre rifle, ₱500 in cash, and some personal photos were taken. He stated the seventeen gold bars were found on another treasure hunting expedition. He did not mention the diamonds because he had already sold them.

After completing the statement, he called Judge Pio Marcos. All the judge would say was that Roger should not have called the police – he seemed upset about that – and that the seizure was legal because Roger had violated a Central Bank regulation. In hindsight Roger suspected the man who claimed to be a representative of *Doña* Josepha Marcos was a spy sent to check out the house and the location of the Buddha.

The newspapers took up the story, screaming government thievery. Three weeks later there was a court hearing. Sgt. Romeo Amansec, a member of the Presidential Security Guards and a "frogman" assigned to Marcos' presidential yacht, was identified as the leader of the party. He claimed he was walking down the street, happened to look in the window of Roger's house and see the Buddha, and concluded there had been a Central Bank violation. He obtained a search warrant and raided the house.

Roger pointed out there was a wall surrounding his house and there was no front window so Amansec could not have seen the Buddha. Roger also identified the police chief, Victoriano Calano, as part of the raiding party.

A Buddha was produced. Roger said it was a fake. It was made of brass and its head wasn't detachable. Also produced at the hearing were fourteen bars of brass, the sword, and the rifle. Calano admitted he was there but he denied taking any gold bars, foreign coins, the ₱500 in cash, or photos.

Once again the theft was reported in the newspapers. This time several senators demanded a hearing. Roger testified. There was no Central Bank regulation violated, the senators concluded, and demanded an investigation. It was established that the Buddha, the rifle, the sword, and some metal bars were taken. Whether the bars were fourteen in number and made of brass or seventeen gold ones could never be ascertained.

A few days later Roger was picked up. The men were not in uniform but he suspected they were military. He was blindfolded and driven to a secret location outside Manila. He thought it was a military camp in Pampanga province. They tortured him until he signed a confession stating Marcos was not involved in the theft of the Buddha and that he was paid a large sum of money to implicate him.

After warning Roger not to talk, they let him go. He went into hiding. It took a long time for his wounds to heal. The more he thought about what they did, the angrier he got. He decided to tell some friendly congressmen. At the time a national election was coming up. Roger was invited to speak at a rally held by the opposition Liberal Party candidates on August 21 at Plaza Miranda. He was to address the crowd right before the principal speaker of the evening, Senator Ninoy Aquino. Before Roger could speak, two grenades were hurled at the platform. The explosion killed nine and injured many others. Marcos decried the incident and ordered an investigation. The perpetrator was never caught.

The personal attacks on Roger continued. He went into hiding while Marcos and Imelda set up more foundations to hide their wealth. Trinidad Foundation was set up in Vaduz on August 26, 1970. Three more were established in 1971: Azio on June 21, Rosalys on September 24, and Charis on December 27.

The golden Buddha discovery created new interest. More treasure hunters headed north to search for treasure. But who was this Gen. Yamashita? And why did he bury a treasure in the Philippines?

CHAPTER THREE

The Tiger

On November 8, 1941, Lt. Gen. Tomoyuki Yamashita celebrated his fifty-sixth birthday. He also received an unexpected present – command of the Japanese Twenty-fifth Army. He had always been a good soldier, ever since he graduated from the Military Academy on June 26, 1906. Japan had been victorious the year before in the Russo-Japanese War of 1904–05. Now the country was going to war again. It was his turn to carry on a proud military tradition. He wound up his assignment as military minister to Germany and Italy and hurried back to Japan to assume his command.

One month later Pearl Harbor was attacked. The world was at war. Yamashita and his army of 30,000 landed in Malaya and charged down the peninsula. His orders were to invade and occupy. He estimated that would take at least three months. To everyone's surprise, including his own, eight weeks after he started he found himself at the end of the peninsula looking across Johore Strait. A twenty yard wide causeway separated his army from Singapore. The island was twenty-six miles wide and fourteen miles long, most of it rubber plantations and jungle with a few scattered settlements. Singapore was located at the southern tip.

Facing Yamashita across the strait was Lt. Gen. A. E. Percival and his 80,000-man army. Yamashita's army stormed across the strait and was on the outskirts of Singapore within a few days. Hoping that Percival was not aware of his own numbers Yamashita massed his troops outside the town in a show of strength and sent a message to Percival calling for a conference.

The meeting took place at a bank in the early afternoon of February 15. The scene was witnessed by dozens of newspaper reporters and observers. In the wire enclosure of a cashier's cage Yamashita and Percival met to decide the fate of the city. Yamashita put on his best poker face and went on the offensive. He offered to spare the city but demanded that Percival surrender at once and order a cease fire for six o'clock.

Percival was still reeling from shock and surprise. A Japanese army had stormed down the impassable Malay peninsula and showed up at the back door of a supposedly impregnable fortress whose big guns were pointing the other way out to sea.

Trying to buy some time, he countered that a cease fire could not possibly be effected that day, that it would have to be at eight the next morning. Yamashita was afraid his numerical weakness might be discovered. He started shaking his head and jabbing his finger at Percival. "Did he agree to six o'clock, yes or no?" Yamashita's verbal barrage was relentless. "Yes or no. Yes or no?"

Percival capitulated. Reporters scribbled furiously in their notebooks. One described Yamashita as a ferocious conqueror and coined a new phrase – the "Tiger of Malaya." The mild-mannered Yamashita was surprised. He had been called many things but never ferocious and certainly not a tiger. Later, in recalling the meeting, he would smile and say "It was a bluff, a bluff that worked."

In Japan, Yamashita was declared a hero and his popularity spread. That did not please the prime minister, Gen. Hideki Tojo. A dozen years before as a colonel, Yamashita supported a move to reduce the size of the army. Ever since he had not gotten along with the military clique in power in Tokyo. Now his popularity threatened to eclipse Tojo's and that could not be.

Yamashita was serving as supreme commander in Malaya when he received his new orders. Instead of an important position due a victorious general, he was transferred to an obscure post in northern Manchuria thousands of miles from the fighting.

He remained in that backwater until October 1944 when once again his talents were called for. By then the tide had turned. Now the Americans moved by leaps and bounds across the vast Pacific, retaking island after island.

When Saipan fell to the Americans in July 1944, Tojo and his cabinet resigned. A new government was formed. A few months later, out of desperation, Yamashita was called on again. This time he was ordered to go to the Philippines and replace Lt. Gen. Shigenori Kuroda, whose notorious predilection for wine, women, and song had contributed nothing toward the war effort.

Yamashita stopped in Tokyo on the way to his new assignment. He saw his family for a few hours and exchanged his winter uniforms for tropical ones. At the briefing he was told the Americans had to be stopped or Japan would be their next landing.

He arrived in Manila on October 7, 1944, and assumed command of the Fourteenth Area Army. Things were not looking good. The Americans had already achieved air superiority and intelligence showed that an invasion force was on the way. His new Chief of Staff, Lt. Gen. Akira Muto, did not arrive until thirteen days later from Sumatra. On arrival Muto was informed that the Americans had just landed at Leyte in the southern Philippines. "Very interesting," he replied, "but where is Leyte?"

That was the almost impossible situation confronting Yamashita. Handicapped from the beginning he set about doing the best he could with what he had. In December he gave the order to abandon Manila after deciding it couldn't be defended. The troop pullout began. The 16,000 naval forces under Rear Admiral Sanji Iwabuchi pulled back to Fort McKinley, Yamashita's headquarters in Manila.

Yamashita pulled out of Fort McKinley on December 22 and headed for Ipo, located twenty-five miles north in Bulacan province. There he set up a temporary headquarters. On January 3 he went back to Fort McKinley for a conference with one of his commanders, Lt. Gen. Yokoyama. He departed the next day and headed for the mountain resort of Baguio.

For some reason Iwabuchi ordered his forces back to Manila. They linked up with 3,750 army security personnel, and within twenty-four hours they were cut off.

There was a lull in the fighting before the American troops arrived. Iwabuchi's troops began pillaging the city. They broke into the warehouses along the waterfront. One was filled with whisky. That was the fuel that sparked one of the worst murderous rampages of the war.

Iwabuchi's demoralized and drunk soldiers set out with a vengeance, raping the women and slaughtering everyone, even babies and children. When the Americans arrived they had to retake the city building by building, block by block. When it was over, Manila was the second most devastated city of the war, behind Warsaw.

Baguio was 150 miles north, high in the mountains. The weather was untropically cool and the scenery magnificent. The city, and the road to it, was built by Americans around 1913 after the American governor of the Philippines, William Howard Taft, made the trek there to cure his dysentery. The U.S. Army had set up a recuperative post, Camp John Hay, situated on a ridge with a panoramic view of the mountains.

From Baguio, Yamashita attempted to coordinate his defense against insurmountable difficulties. Gradually his troops were overwhelmed in the mountain vastness of northern Luzon. As the American troops closed in he retreated.

He was forced to withdraw on the night of April 16, 1945, and retreated westward to Bambang where he set up a new headquarters on April 19. A month later, on May 20, he withdrew again. Once again using the cover of darkness he slipped out of Bambang, passed through Bagabag, and headed north to Kiangan where he set up his headquarters seventy-five miles north of Baguio. On June 18 advancing American troops forced him further north into the mountains.

On August 6, 1945, the world's first atomic bomb was dropped on Hiroshima. A second bomb was dropped on Nagasaki three days later. Emperor Hirohito ordered an end to the hostilities on August 15. Yamashita dutifully received his orders to surrender from the Emperor. On September 2 he and his surrender party, totalling twenty-one persons, made their way back to Kiangan where they had arranged to meet Maj. Gen. William H. Gill, commander of the Thirty-second Infantry Division, and a special detachment of Company I, Second Battalion, 128th Infantry. From there an armed convoy took them to an airstrip near Bagabag. They were flown on a C-47 to La Luna by the Pacific Ocean in La Union province. Another convoy met them and they were taken to Baguio.

The official surrender ceremony took place at noon the next day in the drawing room of the American High Commissioner's residence. Afterwards they were taken back to La Luna and flown to Manila. After landing at Nielsen Field in the evening, they were driven to New Bilibid prison twenty miles outside Manila.

Yamashita went on trial in Manila the next month. On December 7, exactly four years after Pearl Harbor and one month after his sixtieth birthday, he was convicted of war crimes, including the rape of Manila and the slaughter of thousands of innocent men, women, and children in February 1945. It didn't matter to the court that he was 150 miles to the north, that the evidence showed that the atrocities were carried out against his orders, and that he knew nothing about them until they were over. The responsibility was his, they ruled, and he was hung. It was an ignominious end for the Tiger of Malaya. Ironically all his brave deeds on the battlefield were quickly forgotten only to be replaced by a myth.

Stories about Yamashita quickly spread. He had possessed a great treasure but the secret of its location died with him on the scaffold, so the stories went. It seemed that everyone knew somebody that had seen a treasure buried. A lot of digging was going on. Most of it turned up old Japanese garbage pits and latrines. The rumors ebbed and flowed along with the digging over the years.

It took a long time for the Filipinos to get over the war. They had been brutalized by the Japanese forces and they weren't going to forget it anytime soon. Not until December 1951 did the government officially allow a Japanese back into their country. Reverend Goto Mitsuzo, a Protestant minister, was allowed to attend the conference of the Far East Council of Christian Churches held in Manila. There were protests but the visit came off without a serious incident. Gradually the two governments groped toward an understanding as war reparations were worked out and the number of Japanese visitors increased.

In 1953 President Elpidio Quirino announced that some Japanese soldiers, who were still in prison in the Philippines for crimes committed during the war, would be released. In exchange Japan would cooperate in an official inquiry to determine if Yamashita did leave behind a treasure as many people now believed. If there were such a treasure then every attempt would be made to locate and recover it. The investigation was to be headed by Minoru Fukumitsu.

An American of Japanese descent, Fukumitsu's background was as much a mystery as the treasure itself. He claimed that he was born in Salt Lake City, Utah, on March 28, 1918. When the war came he taught Japanese at a U.S. Navy officer's school in Boulder, Colorado. For some reason he was not interned like all other Japanese when the "Yellow Peril" hysteria swept the U.S. at the start of the war. After the war he wound up in Tokyo where he was assigned to work as one of the investigators of the Allied War Crimes Tribunal.

Fukumitsu never explained why or how he was chosen for the task of searching for the treasure but he obviously had connections somewhere. After being appointed he threw himself into his work. From Manila to Tokyo to Washington, he crisscrossed the globe in his search. He was given access to confidential documents in Japan and he sifted through the voluminous documentation in the National Archives in Washington, D.C. More than 300 witnesses were interviewed including former members of Yamashita's staff that had survived the war.

An expedition was planned. Accompanying Fukumitsu was Major Mikiyo Matsonogo, one of Yamashita's staff officers during the war. It began in Baguio and retraced the route of withdrawal of Yamashita and his troops. The group methodically combed the areas where the soldiers had camped. They explored the countryside around each encampment and excavated potential burial sites. Fukumitsu returned to Manila nine months later. All they found, he claimed, were a few old coins. There was no evidence to show that any treasure ever existed. Then he departed the Philippines.

Over the years, whenever the question of the treasure's existence arose he would appear to refute the possibility. In 1977 after rumors of a vast treasure began to fly again, he flew into Manila and held a press conference, proclaiming that there was no such treasure. "I don't want people to waste their time and effort looking for something which never existed," he said, and brandished a few documents and old clippings showing that the gold and silver belonging to the Philippine treasury had been shipped out before the Japanese arrived.

Again in 1978, when the *Philippine News* in the States exposed the Leber Group treasure hunt set up by Marcos, Fukumitsu surfaced to testify that such a claim was ridiculous. Ten years later it was discovered that Americans had been permitted to dig for treasure at Fort Santiago. Fukumitsu appeared once again in Manila. There was no treasure at Fort Santiago, he announced. When questioned, he would not say who sent him to Manila, nor could he explain why he made 600 trips to the Philippines since 1951. He did admit he was a friend of Marcos.

An interesting footnote to the Fukumitsu expedition was that one Filipino who assisted him had been an officer in the army during World War II and served in that area. Venancio Duque was a lieutenant and the adjutant of the Fourteenth Infantry Regiment, the same guerrilla outfit that Marcos joined in the latter stages of World War II. After Marcos joined the Fourteenth, an order came down from higher headquarters to execute him for collaboration. Duque had been one of the signers of a petition attesting to Marcos' loyalty. The petition was then taken to his uncle, Col. Calixto Duque, the operations officer at headquarters. As a result the order was rescinded, Marcos' life was spared, and Duque and Marcos became friends.

Marcos was an influential second-term congressman in 1953. After he was elected president, Duque was appointed to head the commission on elections, a very important post in the Marcos era of voter-fraud and stuffed ballot boxes.

Two years after the Fukumitsu expedition, in June 1955, another joint operation of the Philippine and Japanese governments was begun. This time it was maritime. A total of 269 vessels sunk during the war were to be salvaged by Japan. Their estimated aggregate tonnage was more than 500,000. Of these, 124 vessels were located in Manila Bay and the other 145 were in other parts of the Philippines. According to the agreement, the Philippines would be provided with the "services of the Japanese people including the necessary equipment and supplies" for the project.

The Japanese had pushed this project for years and appeared anxious to start salvaging their own vessels. As soon as the operation began the rumors started – some of these vessels were filled with gold bullion and scuttled on purpose at designated spots for retrieval at some later time.

Once again interest in the Yamashita treasure was renewed, and once again critics came to the forefront. There was no treasure, so stop wasting your time. As further proof they pointed to the fact that several books had been written about Yamashita. Some of the authors interviewed him and others examined his papers rather extensively. None mentioned a treasure.

So what, the believers countered. That didn't prove no treasure existed. After all, if he took the trouble to hide it would he really tell anyone or write about it?

The arguments went back and forth. More convincing proof that Yamashita had little or nothing to do with the burial of a treasure is the historical record. He arrived in October 1944 and was only in Manila eleven weeks. During that time he was busy organizing his defenses at Leyte, planning the evacuation of Manila, and withdrawing his troops into the mountains. But it was still possible he possessed some war booty.

In the American army every soldier strived to collect a personal memento or two, perhaps some Japanese yen, a rifle, or a bayonet. The luckiest might find a Samurai sword. Some soldiers found out in a ghastly way that the Japanese didn't really appreciate this. If they found any Japanese possessions on a captured American soldier it was assumed the soldier killed a Japanese to get it. And that would be the death knell for him.

When the Japanese attacked in December 1941, Gen. MacArthur ordered a withdrawal to the Bataan Peninsular. There they held out for more than three months, but disease, starvation, and the battle finally took its toll. The surrender of these men and their forced march to a prisoner of war camp resulted in one of the cruelest episodes of the war – the Bataan Death March.

During the march the Japanese searched every American and Filipino soldier for anything of value such as a canteen, a watch, or cigarette lighter. If Japanese items were found, the soldier was taken out of the column and beaten to death or beheaded on the roadside. These heads and headless bodies were a far too common scene indelibly burned into the memories of the survivors who could still recall the grisly sight with anguish half a century later.

In the Japanese army it was different. They lived off the land and they pillaged more. It was an unwritten rule that officers had a right to a certain amount of booty and every general officer had a right to even more than that. So it wasn't uncommon for the higher ranks to have their own private stash, maybe even a truckload or two.

It's possible Yamashita possessed his own stash, perhaps a few artifacts and some gold bars, or even a gold statuette of Buddha. And if he buried anything for safekeeping it was probably in the mountains around Baguio where Roger found the Buddha. But it was rather ironic that the few items Yamashita may have buried in those mountains started the legend that would not die. When he was executed the secret of the treasure supposedly died on the scaffold with him. That was part of the legend, told and retold, and reenforced in the telling over the years. But what evidence was there that any treasure existed?

CHAPTER FOUR

The Awa Maru

In 1940 travel brochures touted the Philippines as the Pearl of the Orient. Visitors docking at Pier 7 in Manila unloaded at the "longest and finest covered pier under the American flag," according to Ripley's Believe It Or Not. The heat might be stifling but they could stay in the Manila Hotel nearby, one of the few hotels in Asia to have that new-fangled invention called air conditioning.

There were 5,700 Spanish, 8,500 Americans, 29,000 Japanese, 117,000 Chinese, and 16 million Filipinos. The Chinese had integrated themselves into the population long ago. Only recently, over the last decade, had the Japanese arrived. Some ran shops. Others had menial jobs. Many were fishermen and knew the coastal waters as well as the local fishermen. About 18,000 lived around Davao on Mindanao, the large island 620 miles south of Manila.

There was ominous gossip going around. War was coming. Probably not soon, but it was coming. And probably not the Philippines, since Gen. MacArthur was preparing the defenses. He was in the twilight of his career when President Manuel Quezon visited Washington in 1934 and asked him to come and prepare the country for war, just in case.

Everyday MacArthur could be seen leaving his palatial suite on the top floor of the Manila Hotel and driving over to his "office in the wall" at One Calle Victoria in Intramuros. As long as he was here the Japanese would think twice about attacking this country. That was the talk back then. As the sun set on those halcyon days, the Japanese Rising Sun slowly enveloped the horizon. Pearl Harbor was attacked and soon afterwards the Philippines.

In December 1941 and early 1942 the Japanese Imperial Forces rolled through Asia. Japan had few raw materials of its own. Each country it conquered was systematically pillaged and the raw materials were shipped to Japan to further the war effort. There was tin from Malaya (Malaysia), oil and rubber from Dutch East Indies (Indonesia), rice from Thailand, cotton from India, iron from Indochina (Vietnam), and the mineral resources of the Philippines, rich in iron, chromium, manganese, and copper.

History books neglected to mention the Japanese didn't stop with raw materials. The plunder of each country they occupied was absolute, total. All banks, treasuries, and other depositories of wealth were looted. Even the bodies of the enemy dead were violated. Gold teeth were ripped out and fingers with rings cut off. This macabre booty added considerably to the spoils of war. But that wasn't enough. Museums, temples, and churches were also looted, along with the temples of vice.

Centuries before World War II, in addition to the normal commerce of each Asian country, there was a thriving sub-economy worth billions. It consisted of the usual trades – gambling, prostitution, smuggling, opium, and money lending. When the *gweilos* (foreigners) came to colonize these countries they groped with these problems for awhile then gave up. The heathen was left alone to his own devises and these businesses continued on their thriving course.

The money involved in such activities was considerable. It created a black market where the currency of a transaction might be paper money, jewelry, gold, silver, or anything of value. The preferred currency of the Chinese, who usually ran the commerce and the black market, was precious metals or gemstones.

In preparation for their plan to conquer Asia, the Japanese flooded each country with agents, gathering the most minute detail of advance intelligence that included everything from tidal changes to coastal defenses to who ran the underworld.

When war came, in almost every village there lived at least

one or two Japanese employed as a gardener or driver. After the army was victorious they donned uniforms and marched through town pointing out the black-marketeers. Sometimes they were robbed and executed on the spot or just taxed and retained to help run the local gambling, prostitution, or drug ring, until their usefulness ran out. Whatever the method, each country was methodically looted. Included in this was a considerable amount of so-called hidden wealth. A treasure could have existed.

One story that had been going around for years was that the British, fearing an eminent attack from Hitler in 1940, packed up all their gold bullion and other precious metals, and shipped them to Singapore where they would be safe in that impregnable fortress. A subsequent investigation proved this wasn't true. But it was a fact that Spain, fearing a similar attack, shipped all of its gold reserves to Russia for safekeeping. Guess who never saw their gold again?

Most countries, when they realized the Imperial Army was about to attack, tried to hide their wealth. While the Americans and Filipinos were holding off the Japanese at Bataan in February 1942, President Quezon had twenty tons of the treasury's gold bullion and silver pesos loaded on the submarine USS *Trout* and taken to Australia. Another 350 tons of silver pesos, worth more than ₱15 million (almost $8 million), was dumped in the waters off southern Corregidor in May 1942 and several million dollars in paper currency was burned after the serial numbers were noted and radioed to Washington. During their occupation the Japanese spent a good deal of time looking for the silver and did manage to retrieve about ₱2 million worth. After the war the U.S. Navy recovered ₱5 million worth and the Philippine government ₱6.5 million more, but this still amounted to only 75 percent of what was dumped.

There is no record of Hong Kong, Singapore, and the other occupied countries spiriting their precious metals and financial resources out of harm's way. Only an accidental sinking, on April Fool's Day 1945, uncovered the magnitude of what was plundered by the Japanese.

On April 1, 1945, the war in the Pacific was less than six

months away from its atomic conclusion. The Americans were winning but every battle with the Japanese was a fight to the bitter finish.

Out in the South China Sea a U.S. submarine, the *Queenfish*, patrolled the Formosa Strait 400 miles north of the Philippines looking for Japanese vessels. Around ten in the evening Commander Charles E. Loughlin saw the familiar low silhouette of a Japanese destroyer on his radar scope. After an hour of maneuvering he fired four torpedoes. Cheers of congratulations echoed through the sub as all four found their mark. The *Awa Maru* lit up the evening sky as it exploded and sank in less than three minutes. The *Queenfish* surfaced and lifelines were thrown to those in the water. Strangely no one grabbed hold except a steward.

Soon enough Loughlin found out he was the victim of a cruel April Fool's joke. The vessel he sunk was a hospital ship painted with giant white crosses and guaranteed safe passage by the U.S. It was to deliver Red Cross packages to allied prisoners of war in Hong Kong, Saigon, Singapore, Djakarta in the Dutch East Indies, and Sumatra, and then pick up wounded Japanese soldiers and bring them home. The 11,600 ton vessel was on the return trip to Japan when it was sunk. Of the 2,009 people aboard ship, only the steward survived.

Japan demanded indemnities for damages from the U.S. government. Loughlin was court-martialed. At the trial he claimed he couldn't see the white crosses because of the dense fog and because the ship was so low in the water it looked like a destroyer or destroyer escort. But the lost lives weighed heavily against him. He was found guilty of negligence, the least severe of the charges, and given a letter of reprimand. The incident did not diminish Loughlin's career, however. He was subsequently promoted to the rank of rear admiral.

Later it was discovered the Japanese had taken advantage of its safe passage guarantee and loaded the ship with a cargo which it felt was more important than wounded soldiers. When the ship went down it carried with it 40 metric tons of gold , 12 tons of platinum, 2,000 tons of tungsten, 3,000 tons of tin, 3,000 tons of rubber in bales, 2,000 tons of lead, 800 tons of titanium, 500 tons of brass and bronze, two tons of quicksilver, 150,000 karats of diamonds, forty cases of jewelry, five cases of ivory, an unknown quantity of silver, several large bales of paper currency, and numerous crates of art, all plundered by the Japanese occupation forces.

There were few wounded soldiers on board, but there were a lot of passengers, mostly Japanese VIPs trying to get back to their homeland. Passage was only available to those with enough money or the best connections in government.

The ship was so overloaded it sat low in the water looking, unfortunately, like something else. The estimated value of the cargo ranged from $241 million to $5 billion, making it one of the most valuable sunken treasures in history.

This was a violation of the accords set forth by the Geneva Convention, a dirty trick of the lowest order. The usual protests were filed through diplomatic channels then nothing more was heard of the incident. For a ship flying the flag of the Japanese Imperial Navy to be able to carry off an international crime of this magnitude would require approval at the highest level. One can only wonder. How many other times had the Japanese disguised ships carrying valuable cargo?

Minoru Fukumitsu, he of the first Yamashita treasure hunt, took enough time off from denying there was a treasure to write a book about the *Awa Maru*. Even with his contacts, when he queried the Japanese government he was told there were no documents relating to the case. He thought this was strange, and persisted. Finally he was told that even if there were he could not see them.

In 1976, Loughlin, John E. Bennett, the *Queenfish* navigator in 1945, John Lindbergh, the son of famed aviation pioneer Charles Lindbergh, and former astronaut Scott Carpenter applied to the Republic of China for permission to salvage the sunken vessel. Permission was denied. Fukumitsu also applied and was turned down.

Eyewitnesses claimed a lot of treasure wound up in the Philippines. Since the sea route usually included a stop there, most ships, including the ones carrying treasure, would have docked in the Philippines before proceeding to Japan.

Armchair historians proffer several schools of thought for why it remained. One is that Japan was certain that even if it lost the war it could still retain the Philippines in a negotiated settlement and afterward recover the treasure. (They didn't know the U.S. possessed the atomic bomb.) Another was that the Japanese, in the quest to carve out their Greater East Asia Co-Prosperity Sphere, had chosen the Philippines to be its financial capital and the gold would serve as the standard for its currency.

The main reason the treasure may have stayed in the Philippines was that by the middle of 1942 the tide of battle began to turn. The Japanese forces' invincibility was dealt a shattering blow with the victorious Battle of Midway in June, followed by American victories at New Guinea and Guadalcanal. As a result the Japanese war effort was stepped up. Troop and materiel movements had to take priority over other shipping. If there were any planned movement of treasure back to Japan these plans would have changed. It may have been considered an interim measure at first but later, as victory slipped from their grasp, the powers that be could have made the decision. They would get very few opportunities like the *Awa Maru* to ship their plunder home, so what was already in the Philippines stayed there.

Numerous treasure expeditions were attempted after the Fukumitsu search in 1953 but they ended in failure. The yellowed pages of old Philippine newspapers and magazines are a testament to their exploits. Some lost their money, others lost their lives in the quest for the vast riches of the legendary treasure. Finally in 1970, in the mountains around Baguio, Roger found a golden Buddha. This time Fukumitsu did not make an appearance or make any comment.

Like Roger, some treasure hunters had copies of old maps or sketches. Most, if not all, proved to be fake. There were alleged eyewitnesses to treasure burials. Most of these, too, were fake but some, through hypnosis and detailed debriefing procedures, appeared credible.

Some people believed, and eyewitnesses swore, there was a large and powerful Japanese organization behind the looting. They claimed a group of Japanese officers, assisted by a special engineer brigade, began burying treasure as early as the middle of 1942.

Most of the treasure sites required months of excavation with elaborate tunnel systems. That the Japanese built tunnel complexes in and under their fortifications was no surprise. In every major battle with the Japanese, where they had time to prepare for the American forces, major tunnel complexes were found. The entire atoll of Iwo Jima was honey-combed with tunnels. Biak, in the Mariannas, had five-story caves. The Japanese defense of Okinawa was directed from a vast tunnel complex ninety feet below Shuri Castle. Saipan had its own network of tunnels as did the Philippines. But there may have been one difference in the Philippines. Some of the tunnel systems may have held the immense bounty of Asia.

According to eyewitnesses, all the big sites were at least sixty to ninety feet below ground and a few were even deeper. The larger sites had tunnel complexes large enough to hold trucks. Some were located below the water table. The source of the water was dammed up or kept out with water pumps. The Japanese built the first underwater tunnel from Kyushu, furthest south of the four major islands, to Honshu, the largest island, in 1942. They had the technology.

Marcos believed in the treasure. After he became president he used, or rather misused, his office to search for it. Despite the alleged growing communist insurgency, a large number of military were assigned full time to this task. Their leader was Ver.

Ver and Marcos were related and were from the same home town of Sarrat in Ilocos Norte province. In 1963 Capt. Ver of the Philippine Constabulary was assigned to Marcos, who was then president of the senate. He was intensely loyal, a trait Marcos liked. Ver remained with him, rising in rank and prestige as Marcos rose in power. He would later be appointed armed forces Chief of Staff. Now he was head of the Presidential Security Command and Director General of the National Intelligence Security Authority. NISA, the Orwellian intelligence apparatus designed more for intimidation of anybody considered an enemy of Marcos than for anything useful like fighting communism, had control over all intelligence organizations.

Ver picked a select group of loyal soldiers to assist him. The key members were mostly military, some retired and some still on active duty. Progress reports to Marcos about various treasure site excavations were found in the palace after the revolution. They were on stationery of the Presidential Security Command and signed by Col. Mario Lachica and Brig. Gen. Santiago B. Barangan.

Gen. Onofre Ramos (no relation to Fidel Ramos) and Col. Florentino R. Villacrusis, Jr. had retired in 1971 but they were part of the group. Ramos was the liaison to Ver and Villacrusis was one of the operations officers. The head of the group was originally Ramos but upon retirement he was replaced by Lt. Col. Porfirio Gemoto who had been the chief of operations. Others involved were Brig. Generals Ramon Cannu and Tomas Dumpit, Col. Renato Gemora, who worked with Cannu, Col. Orlando Dulay, Maj. Barangan, brother of Gen. Barangan, and Maj. Patrecio Dumlao. There were two civilians associated with the group – Johnny Wilson, the group's historian, and Venancio Duque. There were other members of Ver's inner circle who were not officially part of the task force but who nevertheless wanted a piece of the treasure-hunting action. Ver did nothing to encourage or discourage them.

While they roamed the countryside pockmarking the landscape, Marcos convened a Constitutional Convention in June 1971 to rewrite the constitution. According to him, the old one had become outmoded since it was American-influenced and written in 1935. The truth was he needed it rewritten so he could run again. He was in his second term. The present constitution forbade a president from serving more than two terms. A new constitution, written according to his guidelines, would change this and, he hoped, make things appear democratic to the U.S., the IMF, and the World Bank.

The delegates were fast at work when one of them exploded a bombshell. As president, Marcos was supposed to remain aloof and impartial to the proceedings, so he had Imelda do his bidding. At first she tried to use his influence to persuade the delegates. When that didn't work she resorted to outright bribery.

Her weekly distribution of envelopes containing cash to delegates who might be receptive to her cause became an open secret and an embarrassment to the entire convention. Finally one delegate reported the bribes.

In what was known as the "Payola Exposè," Eduardo Quintero of Leyte exposed the corrupt practice. The reaction was swift and furious. The opposition newspapers had a field day criticizing Imelda. It was the most serious assault on the presidency since Marcos took over. Now he was angry.

Marcos finalized the top secret plans for Operation Sagittarius. On September 23, 1972, martial law was announced. Marcos called it the birth of a "New Society," set up for the purpose of combating the "awesome communist threat." The bombings in Manila by communists and the ambush of Minister of Defense Juan Ponce Enrile's car proved that things were getting out of control. Later Enrile admitted it was staged. And that set the stage. To paraphrase another Asian leader, the Great Leap Backward was about to begin.

CHAPTER FIVE

Crony Capitalism

Senator Ninoy Aquino was a rising star in politics and considered to be the only one that could beat Marcos in a fair election. On Friday evening, September 22, 1972, he joined two of his aides in a room at the Hilton Hotel for a committee meeting.

At midnight there was a knock on the door. Col. Romeo Gatan stood there alone. He asked Ninoy not to resist, that 200 soldiers surrounded the hotel and he wanted to avoid bloodshed. The two aides were allowed to go home. The word quickly spread – the rumors were true. One of the darkest hours in Philippine history had begun.

Martial law had been carefully planned by Marcos, Enrile, ten military officers, and one civilian. They were General Ver; General Fidel Ramos, commander of the Philippine Constabulary; General Romeo Espino, armed forces Chief of Staff; General Rafael Zagala, commander of the army; General Ignacio Paz, head of army intelligence; Air Force General Jose Rancudo; Navy Rear Admiral Hilario Ruiz; General Tomas Dias of the P.C.; General Alfredo Montoya of Metrocom; Colonel Gatan, who was head of the P.C. in Tarlac; and businessman Eduardo "Danding" Cojuangco, Jr. History would accord them a nickname – the "Rolex 12" – because Marcos gave each a gold Rolex in appreciation of their services.

Under General Order No. 1, Marcos quickly assumed all the powers of government – executive, legislative, and judicial. He padlocked the senate, gave the military pay raises, and threatened the Supreme Court judges who were not in line with his way of thinking.

General Order No. 2 ordered the minister of defense to arrest named individuals who were "active participants in the conspiracy to seize state power." The so-called conspirators were publishers, politicians, reporters, and a few others. Political opponents, like Jose Diokno, Salvador Laurel, Aquilino Pimentel, Tito Guingona, and Ramon Mitra; journalists, like Chino Roces, Armando Doronilla, Ernesto Granada, Max Solivan, Teodoro Benigno, Teodoro Locsin, Renato Constantino, Louie Beltran; and radio commentator Jose Mari Velez.

It was a witch hunt. None of those people were enemies of the state. Nor was Roger Roxas, who was arrested and charged with illegal arms possession. Roger said the only weapon he had was the boltless .22 calibre rifle but that was enough. He was tried and sentenced on January 31, 1973, to a year in prison.

There was some unfinished business. Some of the Constitutional Convention delegates were jailed. Others were threatened. They got the message. Within weeks the new constitution was finished. Marcos now had the kind of absolute power he had dreamed of for so long.

Ver's task force stepped up treasure hunting operations. A letter to Marcos, dated May 2, 1973, told of a group code-named Task Force Restoration that was set up to recover treasure at Fort Bonifacio and Fort Santiago. It stated that "Upon receipt of the signal from Your Excellency as announced by the Chief of Staff, AFP, on 1 March 1973, conferences and preliminary reconnaissances were undertaken."

March 26 was set as "D Day" (Start-of-digging Day) at Fort Bonifacio. The site was in a tunnel system under Gen. MacArthur's old headquarters then called Camp McKinley. In the middle of the fort, next to the officer's club was a circular driveway. In the center was a bomb shelter. When the Japanese occupied the fort they expanded it into an elaborate tunnel system. Part of it had been blown up in the battle for Manila.

The letter went on to state that Lt. Col. Porfirio Gemoto sealed off some of the entrances to the shelter. He then proceeded with "checking the pinpointed areas which were believed to have contained the treasures as indicated on our map. Three sets of detectors and instruments were used and all of them confirmed the locations of at least 16 spots."

The letter ended, "In the meantime the men are acquiring the proficiency and ability needed in working vertical and diagonal excavations. They have been successfully testing their instruments, methods, and equipments (*sic*) and are now ready for Oplan Ligaya."

The letter was signed by Gen. Onofre T. Ramos (Ret.), Col. Florentino R. Villacrusis (Ret.), and Reverend Simeon F. Lepasana. Lepasana wasn't a member of the task force but he had a relative working in the palace so he was allowed to participate.

After Roger served his year in prison, they still wouldn't release him. They finally let him out on November 19, 1974. When he got home, his wife was gone. He discovered she had divorced him, married someone else, and left for the States. He checked his golden Buddha site and found that Marcos had recovered the rest of the treasure in the tunnels. He wondered if that was the reason they kept him in prison the extra nine months. He went back into hiding.

There was no "awesome communist threat." If Marcos had wanted to restore law and order he could have but he had other plans.

After his *enemies* were jailed, he turned to the media. The seventies could have been labelled the Dark Ages for the journalist and reporter. No friend or relative of Marcos or Imelda could be criticized. Other forbidden topics were Marcos' health and Imelda's extravagance. Only government accounts of political and economic news could be reported.

The foreign press was tolerated but occasionally Marcos got angry. In 1976, Arnold Zeitlin, Manila bureau chief for the Associated Press, was barred from reentering the Philippines because he had "carried out activities which endangered national security and public order." All he actually did was catch Marcos perpetrating one of his hoaxes.

There was a front page story, replete with pictures, in all the newspapers about how Marcos had flown into dangerous rebel territory in Luuk, Jolo, and negotiated with the Muslim rebel leader, Maas Bawang, and his band, and convinced them to abandon their jungle hideaway, leave the rebellion, and cooperate with him in pacifying Mindanao.

Shortly afterward, Zeitlin filed his story, stating that this much-publicized meeting could not have taken place "in any spot within the area of Jolo Island on the date officially reported by the Department of Public Information and released through Manila newspapers." For that, Zeitlin was barred.

Later, when Primitivo Mijares published *The Conjugal Dictatorship*, the truth became known. Marcos authorized a former congressman to contact Maas Bawang and ask him and his followers to come to Manila. Financial inducements were offered and their safety assured. The meeting with Marcos took place at Fort Bonifacio in Metro Manila. The pictures were taken near the Malacañan Palace golf course. A few months later Maas Bawang and members of his family were killed in an ambush.

In February 1977, Bernard Wideman's request for an extension of his work visa was denied on the grounds that he was an "undesirable alien" and a security risk. He was Manila correspondent for the *Washington Post* and the American Broadcasting Company. The U.S. State Department inquired about the matter. Wideman was given a public hearing.

Intelligence agents testified he "helped to instigate, and took part in, anti-government demonstrations, and that he was in contact with a man connected with the outlawed Communist Party of the Philippines and the New People's Army." Wideman produced witnesses proving he was just doing his job as a correspondent. The charges were dismissed and he was allowed to stay, but he was warned that he should pursue his profession, "without injury to private reputations or unfair accusations against any public official or public office." What he had done was write some articles critical of Roberto Benedicto.

The control Marcos sought wasn't possible without a loyal group of military officers, cabinet members, appointed and elected officials, relatives and friends, and businessmen who knew how the game was played.

Some of these people were exceptional, gifted with intelligence, education, and the ability to make it on their own in business, government, the military, or whatever profession they preferred. Why they chose to join Marcos and get drawn into a web of intrigue and injustice is inexplicable. Some, to their credit, got out when they saw what was happening. Others didn't. They stayed to the end and contributed to the untold suffering of so many.

Bernie Villegas, head of the Center for Research and Communications, a privately funded think tank and school of economics, coined the term "crony capitalism" to explain the phenomena of so much of the economy being take over by friends and relatives of Marcos and Imelda.

Joaquin G. Bernas, president of the prestigious Ateneo de Manila University, called them The Grand Coalition. Their qualifications were varied but they all shared one common trait – total devotion and unflinching loyalty to Marcos. In exchange, Marcos provided them almost unlimited access to capital and allowed them to take over vast sections of commerce and industry through favorable legislation.

Imelda was a Romualdez. Her family wasted no time in dividing the spoils. Benjamin "Kokoy" Romualdez took over the *Times Journal* newspaper and Manila Electric Company from the Lopez family, one of the richest families in the Philippines before martial law. His brother, Alfredo, forced Enrique Razon, chairman of International Containers Terminal, to give up 60 percent of that company. He also took over the gambling monopoly in the Philippines. An uncle, Eduardo, was named chairman of Philippine Air Lines after it was taken over. He became ambassador to the U.S.

Cesar Zalamea was a close associate of the Romualdez family and served as a director on numerous corporations owned by the family. He was rewarded with the top position at Development Bank of the Philippines.

To take care of his friends in the military, Marcos ordered Minister of Defense Romeo Espino to take over fifteen companies of Fernando Jacinto which included steel, mining, and chemicals.

Another friend, Geronimo Velasco, was appointed chairman of the Philippine National Oil Company, the country's largest business enterprise. Set up by Marcos in 1973 during the oil crisis, PNOC imported more than 50 percent of the country's oil requirements. It was exempt from public accountability.

Jose Reyes' shipping company arranged oil transport for PNOC. His company routinely paid commissions, not to PNOC or the Philippine government, but to Swiss Bank Paribus in Geneva to the attention of Stephen Cattaui, Marcos' banker. The remittances totalled $25 million over ten years.

Bienvenido and Gliceria "Glecy" Tantoco owned Rustans, an upscale department store, and the Tourist Duty Free Shoppers Corporation. Their Sanmar Export Corporation, the import-export firm based in New York, fronted for Imelda for some of her jewelry purchases. They set up several offshore companies as fronts for Imelda's real estate purchases.

J.V. Cruz was a newspaper columnist and Marcos apologist, who later served as ambassador in Egypt. He introduced his brother, Roman, to Imelda. She took him under her wing. He was appointed president of Philippines Air Lines, chairman of the Manila Hotel, chairman of the Commercial Bank of Manila, general manager of the Government Service Insurance System in Manila, and chairman of the Century Bank in Los Angeles. Monies provided by the GSIS helped fund Imelda's projects. He had serious financial problems before he met Imelda. Soon enough he was wealthy and enjoying the good life. When Imelda flew abroad with her entourage, Cruz did not bother to bill Imelda for the planes.

Ricardo Silverio's friendship with Marcos was rewarded with cheap, government backed loans and high level contacts with blue chip foreign firms. He founded Delta Motors Corporation in 1961, which became the sole assembler and distributor of Toyota cars. From this base he expanded to thirty-two companies, including banking, insurance, shipping, and logging.

Antonio Floirendo helped Marcos in the 1965 and 1969 presidential campaigns. His loyalty was rewarded with use of cheap prison labor on his banana plantation and he served as Marcos' agent in the sugar refinery business. His business empire expanded to twenty-seven companies.

Rodolfo Cuenca was a fund raiser for Marcos' presidential campaign in 1965. In 1966 he formed the Construction and Development Corporation of the Philippines. Soon he controlled the construction industry and a diversified conglomerate of seventeen companies.

Herminio Disini was an accountant married to Imelda's personal physician and cousin. He started in business in 1970 with Philippine Tobacco Filters Corporation. Soon he had thirty-three companies in everything from charter airlines and oil exploration to textiles and petrochemical manufacturing. He was the agent for the infamous Westinghouse nuclear reactor deal where the country purchased one reactor for the price of two. Through a maze of corporate cutouts, Disini was paid $80 million in commissions.

Juan Ponce Enrile was already a successful lawyer when he helped Marcos in his 1965 presidential campaign. As a result he was appointed commissioner of customs and later minister of justice. He ran for the senate in 1971 and lost in a close race. Marcos then appointed him minister of defense. He was placed on the board of directors of PNOC. He acquired at least seven lumber or wood-based companies and was also involved with other Marcos cronies in Philippine Communications Satellite, Inc.

Export earnings in 1973 hit $1.87 billion. The major exports were coconuts, logging, and sugar. All earned top dollars. All were nationalized in 1974.

Marcos nationalized everything he could under the guise of improving the economy. The Philippine Cement Corporation regulated that industry; the National Food Authority regulated the rice trade; the Fertilizer and Pesticide Authority regulated those trades; and on and on. All of this was done for profit. None of it had to do with improving the economy. There were sixty-five state-controlled corporations in 1979. There would be more than 300 in 1985.

Danding Cojuangco took over the coconut industry and Roberto Benedicto took over the sugar industry, the nation's two largest dollar earners. They proceeded to run them into the ground while making hundreds of millions of dollars for themselves and Marcos.

Although a first cousin of Cory Aquino, Cojuangco cultivated his friendship with Marcos while serving as a representative in congress. Benedicto was a fraternity brother of Marcos at University of the Philippines. When Marcos opened his own newspaper, the *Daily Express*, Benedicto was the front. He also established California Overseas Bank in Los Angeles for Marcos. He served as ambassador to Japan from 1972 to 1977 and helped administer kickbacks from Japanese firms. Some of these were funnelled through Traders Royal Bank in Manila, owned by Benedicto. Marcos maintained several accounts there.

The Japanese government set up the War Reparations program to indemnify the Philippine government $550 million for losses incurred in World War II. In addition, an economic development loan of $250 million was provided. In Manila, the Reparations Commission selected the beneficiaries of this largesse and chose the Japanese suppliers who provided goods and services. Marcos' friend, Eulogio Balao, secretary of national defense under President Magsaysay and later a senator, was head of the Philippine Reparations Mission in Japan. He collected the kickbacks in Japan in yen, then used his diplomatic status to take the yen out of Japan, go to Hong Kong, and change it to U.S. dollars at Berlin and Company, a foreign exchange dealer.

Rosalys Foundation opened a bank account, number 51960, at Swiss Bank Corporation. From October 1971 to June 30, 1980, Berlin and Company transferred $10.3 million into this account.

After Balao died in August 1977, Andres Genito, Jr., set up the Angenit Investment Corporation to receive the kickbacks and opened an account at Wing Lung Bank in Hong Kong. Berlin and Company transferred HK$44,030,378 from its account in Hang Lung Bank to Wing Lung Bank from 1980 to 1986.

At the same time, Baltazar Aquino, minister of public highways, collected the kickbacks from those funds assigned to public highways projects. The kickbacks ranged from 10 to 15 percent. For example, forty-three road graders and ten road rollers were purchased for ¥77,879,980. Marcos received 15 percent commission. The yen was taken by diplomatic pouch to Hong Kong and changed to dollars at Berlin & Company on November 11, 1978. Then $407,322.07 was credited to his account. On September

25, 1978, thirty road graders and thirty road rollers were purchased, resulting in a kickback of $389,846.91.

Jose Y. Campos was one of Marcos' close friends. He owned a pharmaceutical firm and had the exclusive contract to provide medical supplies to the health ministry. Beginning in 1968 and continuing until a heart attack in 1979, he set up scores of companies to serve as fronts for Marcos' business and financial dealings.

Rolando Gapud, a graduate of M.I.T., was working for Bancom Development Corporation in the late sixties when he served as a financial consultant to Campos. Campos introduced him to Marcos around 1973. After a heart attack, Campos recommended that Gapud take over his job.

In August or September of 1980, Gapud was Marcos' chief financial advisor when he became president of Security Bank and Trust Company. Through front companies, Marcos bought controlling interest in the bank for ₱309 million ($13 million).

On November 21, 1979, two representatives of Standard Chartered Hong Kong Trustee, Ltd. – P.A.L. Vine and Lai Wai Hung – visited the palace. A trust agreement was drawn up. Vine returned to Manila on December 5, 1980, and met with Gapud and Campos. Two trust accounts – a dollar account and a peso account – were opened at Security Bank and Trust Company. Campos was signatory for Marcos. These two accounts were owned by the trust in Hong Kong, which was owned and controlled by Marcos and Imelda.

The trust in Hong Kong also set up ten trust accounts – 7700, 7710, 7720, etc. – at Security Bank and Trust Company in Manila. A deed of trust was executed between Standard Chartered and Security Bank for each account. For example, the deed of trust for account 7730 was between Beneficio Investment, Inc., a Panamanian Corporation, and Security Bank. That account owned Beneficio Investment, whose bearer shares were held by Standard Chartered for Marcos and Imelda.

In addition to the trust accounts in Hong Kong, they maintained other accounts abroad. In Switzerland there were accounts in Credit Suisse, Banque Paribas, Lombard Odier et Cie, Swiss Bank Corporation, Swiss Volksbank, Finanz AG, Trade Development Bank, and Bank Hoffman. There were other accounts in Hong Kong – Wing Lung Bank, Bank de L'Indochine, and Hongkong Bank. There was Barclays Bank in London and offshore banks in the Cayman Islands and the New Hebrides. In the U.S. they had eighty-three accounts in nine banks, including Lloyds Bank and California Overseas Bank in Los Angeles, Redwood Bank in San Francisco, and Irving Trust, Citibank, Chase Manhattan, Chemical Bank, and Manufacturers Hanover in New York.

A few of the aliases used in the financial dealings were Manuel Rodriguez, Armando Martinez, Oscar Marfori, Felisa Grande, Lorna Villa, and L. Virtucio. Other accounts were in the names of friends or front companies, but in Switzerland there was a concerted effort to hide the ill-gotten gains by establishing foundations across the border in Vaduz, then having the foundation open the accounts.

And the money poured in. The *Bulletin Today* newspaper paid Marcos ₱80 million in dividends. (The checks were payable to either Cojuangco, Campos, or Cesar Zalamea, then endorsed and paid into Marcos' account.) Emilio Yap, publisher of the *Bulletin*, also assisted Marcos in acquiring the majority shares in the *Bulletin*.

Lucio Tan, a taipan in his own right, paid him ₱60 to ₱100 million a year. According to Gapud, Tan "belongs to the group that could get presidential decrees and letters of instruction from Mr. Marcos for their joint benefit."

Marcos demanded 60 percent of the shares of Shareholdings, Inc., Tan's holding company that owned Fortune Tobacco, Asia Brewery, Allied Bank, and Foremost Farms. He also asked for and received 20 percent of the capital stock in Silverio's Delta Motors Corporation. He "needed some security for his children," Silverio said.

Gapud received regular sums from Chinese businessman Ralph Nubla but his contributions were smaller than Tan's. Jose Africa, a stockholder in Security Bank and Trust Company, contributed several checks of ₱300,000 each.

Sometimes the mode of payment was unusual. Jesus Tanchanco, head of the National Food Authority once received three large bags containing ₱10 million in cash as kickback from Philippine National Lines for being allowed to import grains. Over the phone, Marcos instructed him to deliver the bags to Gapud at the bank.

Marcos' cronies were allowed easy access to funds with little or no collateral, mostly foreign loans guaranteed by the government. In the mid-seventies Ricardo Silverio applied for and received a $6 million loan for machinery and equipment to manufacture cars. One day Gen. Balao showed up at his office. "I have to receive fifteen percent commission," he said. So Silverio put $900,000 in pesos in paper bags and handed them over for delivery to Marcos.

From ₱2 to ₱10 million in cash were deposited weekly in the accounts at Security Bank and Trust Company. Some ₱500,000 to ₱10 million in checks were received once or twice a month. In addition, $50,000 to $5 million would periodically be received through wire transfers or bank manager's checks. Gapud noted: "Twice a month we would count dollar notes in the basement of Security Bank and then wire transfer them to accounts in Standard Chartered, Hong Kong." From there they were wired to Swiss bank accounts controlled by the foundations.

Gapud helped Marcos acquire hundreds of millions of dollars of shares in a multitude of companies. The shares he controlled were endorsed in blank by the original owner, in effect making them bearer certificates and allowing Marcos to avoid direct involvement. Marcos had a secret interest in almost every industry in the nation – banking, insurance, mining, shipping, oil, sugar, coconut, manufacturing, construction.

As the ill-gotten gains multiplied, more foundations were set up. Rayby Foundation was established in Vaduz on June 22, 1973. Charis was renamed Scolari in December 1974. The purpose behind renaming some of the foundations was never clear. The only plausible motive was to throw investigators off their trail.

This listing of cronies and their deeds is exemplary but not exhaustive. In an article for *Fortune*, Roy Rowan mentioned the sudden affluence of Imelda's relatives and friends. He noted: "Imelda scoffs at these connections. 'I swear to God if I've met

Disini three times in my life I'm lucky,' she says. She observes that in authoritarian regimes, the first family is usually accused of owning just about everything. As for those brothers, cousins, and in-laws, she simply says: 'Sometimes you have smart relatives who can make it . . . My dear, there are always people who are just a little faster, more brilliant, and more aggressive.'"

Were they faster? More brilliant? More aggressive? Could a country base a good portion of its economy on people used to instant gratification and easy money, and who were above the law because they were friends of Marcos and Imelda?

Despite the millions pouring in from illegal tribute, Marcos still had that soft spot for legendary treasure. An event halfway around the world captivated his attention.

CHAPTER SIX

Leber Group

In 1974 Marcos read that treasure hunter Mel Fisher found the seventeenth century Spanish galleon *Atocha*. The gold, jewels, and artifacts salvaged from the wreck were valued at $140 million. The article also noted that psychic Olof Jonsson helped Fisher locate some of this treasure. Jonsson was well known in psychic circles. In February 1971, *Life* magazine reported on some experiments involving ESP (extra sensory perception) carried out between astronaut Edgar Mitchell and Jonsson during the Apollo moon mission. That same year *The Psychic Feats of Olof Jonsson* was published documenting his remarkable psychic powers. Marcos believed in such powers. He sent an emissary to the States and invited Jonsson to the Philippines.

Jonsson and a friend, Cary Calloway, flew there in September 1974. Accompanying them was Norman Kirst, who had just met Jonsson and offered to sponsor the trip. Before receiving Marcos' invitation, an air force officer wrote and asked if Jonsson could come to Clark Air Base and check on a treasure site. As soon as they arrived, they were informed treasure hunting on the base was not allowed. They spent a few weeks searching for treasure off base but found nothing.

They returned to Manila. Jonsson contacted the palace. He was invited to stay in the guest house and treated like a foreign dignitary.

While at Clark, Jonsson had met Vil, a Filipino who had a treasure hunting group called The Professionals. When he mentioned the name, Marcos said he knew him. Vil was Col.

Villacrusis, part of Ver's treasure hunting task force. Marcos suggested they work together. Kirst, not wanting to be left out, presented himself as an international financier who could sell gold with complete secrecy.

Gradually others were added to the team. In December 1974, Kirst called Bob Curtis in Reno, Nevada, and invited him to join the group. In a letter to Curtis dated February 22, 1975, Kirst described the location and value of some of the treasure sites. Eight of the sites were worth more than $5 billion each.

Kirst heard that Curtis possessed a new technology for extracting more gold per ton of material. Such a process would be a convenient cover for any abrupt increase in the quantity of gold going out of the Philippines. Any gold bars recovered would have to be laundered – melted down and reprocessed – in order to eliminate identifying marks and to refine its purity.

Calloway had to return to work in Chicago. Jonsson returned with him, then met Curtis and took him to San Francisco. Kirst met them there and they returned to Manila together. On arrival, Villacrusis introduced them to other members of the team: Cesar Leyran, a friend of Villacrusis; Amelito Mutuc, former ambassador to the United States who had been asked to assist in legal matters; and two eyewitnesses to treasure burials – Ben Valmores and Pol Giga.

Villacrusis had met Ben while treasure hunting. After they became friends, Ben turned over an old leather satchel containing 172 maps. Later Villacrusis befriended Pol, another weekend treasure hunter. Pol soon admitted he was an eyewitness. Such an admission did not come easy. After the war it just wasn't healthy to say you helped the Japanese do anything. To some, this was the same as collaborating and there was still bitter resentment toward collaborators.

Later they met Mario Lachica, another colonel who was part of the team, and Ver, who represented Marcos. They called themselves Leber Group.

Over the next few days, with the help of Ben's maps, they were shown more than two dozen locations in and around Manila. Only a few were excavated. Marcos explained if all the gold were retrieved at the same time it would have to be stored and secured before it was laundered. For this reason he had delayed work at some sites.

That was the purpose of Leber Group. They were going to resolve these problems and in the process make themselves wealthy. The timing of the venture was especially propitious. Effective January 1, 1975, Americans could legally buy and possess gold. Gold markets all over the world were already buzzing with increased activity.

On March 11, Marcos invited Jonsson, Kirst, and Curtis for an overnight cruise on the presidential yacht. Their destination was the summer palace at Mariveles at the southern tip of the Bataan peninsula, the scene of so much suffering in World War II. As the boat approached the dock the guests could see a Spanish hacienda built on the side of a hill overlooking a picture-perfect inlet of white sandy beaches and crystal clear, azure blue water. A few miles out stood the small, tadpole shaped island of Corregidor, from which Gen. MacArthur departed the Philippines with a promise to return.

The group spent the rest of the day like any tourists. Some were taken to Corregidor by helicopter for sightseeing while others chose to go swimming, snorkeling, or waterskiing. That evening after dinner Marcos invited the three to his office. While they talked to Marcos seated at his desk, they kept glancing back over their shoulders. The object of their curiosity was a statuette of Buddha about three feet tall sitting just inside the entrance. It looked like gold.

Marcos told them the Buddha was indeed solid gold, weighed about a ton, and was part of the treasure found at the site at Fort Bonifacio. (Jonsson later said it had a remarkable resemblance to pictures he saw of Roger's golden Buddha.)

Marcos added that part of the gold found at that site was stored right below his office. After the meeting Ver took them downstairs. In a room about thirty feet square gold bars were stacked from floor to ceiling. They noticed the bars had what appeared to be Chinese markings. Ver said this wasn't all, there was more stored at the palace, and this was just the treasure recovered at one site. The group returned to Manila, anxious to get started.

At first they decided to try and recover the treasure on the *Nachi*, a Japanese cruiser sunk at the entrance to Manila Bay. Later it was decided a land site near Teresa, Rizal, would be easier. Excavation began in mid-May. According to the map, the depth was ninety feet. The main tunnel was about 300 yards long, fifty feet wide, and forty feet high. At both ends were side tunnels about 100 yards long. Pol claimed he was present when the treasure was buried. He said several hundred American, Australian, and Filipino prisoners of war excavated the site, then they were killed and buried with the treasure.

The amount of treasure was given in code on the map, but neither Ben nor Pol could decipher it. Pol could only remember that several hundred small crates loaded with gold bullion were placed in the main tunnel, boxes of diamonds and jewels were placed in a side tunnel, and then a few trucks containing more crates of gold were driven into the shelter.

The monsoon season usually arrived in July. The rains came early and slowed the work pace. But on June 8 they broke through the top of the tunnel complex. Everyone smelled a stench. Some became sick and were taken to the hospital. They believed the gases escaping from the tunnel came from the putrefaction of the hundreds of bodies that had decayed long ago and remained sealed until now.

Shortly afterward, a security guard left the site and reappeared a few hours later with a military contingent headed by a colonel known to be loyal to Imelda. He announced that from now on he would provide security. One of Villacrusis' group was able to get a message to Col. Renato Gemora, the military district commander. He returned to the site with reinforcements and demanded the surrender of the Imelda contingent. They gave up without firing a shot. Marcos kept his treasure hunting operations a secret from Imelda. She obviously didn't like this and occasionally interfered.

On the morning of July 6, when Jonsson and Curtis arrived at the site, the workers said they hit some metal and cables during the night. The metal looked like a truck fender. The cables looked suspiciously like a booby-trap. Work was halted. Pol had warned them about two thousand-pound bombs that protected the treasure. Curtis, Jonsson, and the lieutenant in charge of security went to Gemora's office and informed him. Gemora told them to proceed to Quezon City, the large metropolis bordering Metro Manila, to the residence of Gen. Ramon Cannu, Gemora's boss.

They were welcomed by Cannu, who phoned Ver to relay the information. Ver sounded cool over the phone. He told them to go back to the hotel and wait for further instructions. They were about to find out about Primitivo Mijares.

Mijares, the former head of Marcos' Print Media Council, had defected to the U.S. the previous February. Marcos heard he was about to testify before a congressional subcommittee in Washington. Trinidad Algoncel, Philippine consul general in San Francisco, offered him a $50,000 bribe.

He turned down the bribe and went to syndicated columnist Jack Anderson, who announced his defection in June. On the seventeenth he testified about corruption and human rights abuses in the Marcos government. Algoncel then offered Mijares $100,000 to recant his testimony, refute Jack Anderson's story, and retire to Australia. He refused again. Anderson's columns of July 2 and 3 mentioned that Marcos was looking for "buried World War II Japanese treasure in the Sierra Madre." Teresa was in the foothills of those mountains.

A friend in San Francisco, retired Col. Narciso Manzano, financed the publication of Mijares' book, *The Conjugal Dictatorship*, which chronicled the corruption of the Marcos regime. That sealed Mijares' fate.

He was seen on January 7, 1977, at San Francisco Airport in the company of a Philippine intelligence agent, Queruben Makalintal. Manzano received a letter postmarked Honolulu. In it, Mijares said he was going on a "daring foray" to Manila. On January 23 his daughter, Perla, received a cablegram from Guam wishing her a happy birthday. He was never heard from again. Makalintal and Mijares took the Philippine Airlines flight from Guam to Manila. Witnesses claim Ver was on the same flight in the first class section, and that Makalintal and Mijares joined him and stayed there until the plane landed in Manila. Mijares disappeared. Five months later his fifteen year old son disappeared and was later found murdered.

Kirst had returned to the States in March. John McAllaster and his wife Maureen, associates of Curtis, arrived in April. After Anderson's columns in July, everyone was informed the operation would be halted for a week while the Philippine Embassy in Washington assessed the damage Mijares' testimony caused. Jonsson, Curtis, and the McAllasters returned to the States.

Curtis called Mutuc in Manila. He said everything was okay but in a later conversation he warned Curtis not to return. He said they would still get their share when the treasure was recovered.

Curtis tried to phone Marcos and Ver but couldn't get through. He then sent a telex warning them if the agreement were not honored then the secret of the treasure was in jeopardy. The telex was never answered.

Villacrusis wrote Curtis on January 28, 1976, and informed him if he didn't return he would no longer be considered a part of Leber. He also informed Curtis that the check for $2,410.79, which he paid to the Philippine Village Hotel, had bounced and that he should make it good or a criminal action would be filed.

Curtis never responded to the letter. He waited three years before going public. In 1978 he contacted Senator Paul Laxalt, explained his story, and turned over a large array of material to back it up. He had taped all of his phone conversations and also had hundreds of documents and dozens of pictures. Laxalt turned the material over to the State Department. Eventually it was decided no crime had been committed.

Curtis also turned over copies of his material to Jack Anderson, who wrote that the value of the gold at the treasure sites in the 172 maps was estimated at more than $100 billion. As a result of this publicity, a spokesman for the Philippine Embassy issued a statement:

> General Ver has wired me that President Marcos directs that I inform [the reporter] that whatever she has is her own concoction because there is no such plan by the president, General Ver, or Ambassador Mutuc to pick up any Japanese World War II treasures. The allegation about the threat uttered by the president is also denied categorically as a vile and total falsehood.

Curtis claimed that Marcos had threatened his life if he ever said anything about the treasure hunt.

The story attracted the attention of Steve Psinakis, who was familiar with Marcos and his way of dealing with people. The year before, in October 1977, he masterminded the dramatic escape of Eugenio Lopez, Jr. and Sergio Osmeña III. They broke out of a prison in Manila and flew to Hong Kong on a private aircraft. From there they were flown to the U.S. and granted political asylum. Lopez was the brother of Psinakis' wife and the nephew of Marcos' vice-president. Osmeña's father was Marcos' political rival. Both were arrested when martial law was declared and accused of attempting to assassinate Marcos. They were never officially charged but held without bail until their escape.

Psinakis conducted his own investigation into the treasure hunt. The results were printed in a twenty-four part series in the *Philippine News*, a weekly newspaper published in the U.S., beginning in June 1978. Photos and documents added to its credibility. Marcos didn't allow the story to be carried in the local press but copies were distributed anyway via *Xerox Journalism* channels set up to combat the censorship he had imposed on local media.

In addition to Fukumitsu in 1953, Roger in 1971, and Leber Group in 1975, there were two other well known efforts to locate the treasure, both well organized and financed.

An American group, called Nippon Star and led by Gen. John K. Singlaub, searched in 1985, 1986, and 1987. The operation was supposed to be secret but the newspapers found out. They reported Singlaub was CIA. He had developed contacts with allies of Marcos and was also setting up an arms-trading operation in the Philippines. There were some connections to groups which might be considered CIA but Singlaub denied the accusations and distanced himself from the group. They were soon out of business. No treasure was found.

Another American group, International Precious Metals, excavated at Corregidor and Fort Santiago in 1987 and 1988. IPM's president was Bob Curtis. It had the backing of President

Aquino and the national security director, Emanuel V. Soriano. In spite of having maps and eyewitnesses, they walked away empty-handed.

It wasn't until late 1988 that the National Bureau of Investigation, the equivalent of the FBI in the Philippines, found out Curtis was a conman.

Curtis and his partner, John McAllaster, were found guilty in a class action suit in Nevada on December 13, 1976. They induced investors to put nearly a million dollars into a secret formula for the extraction of precious metals. This was the same formula Kirst heard about, and was the reason Curtis was invited to the Philippines.

The court concluded that the so-called secret process was in reality "a farce, a hoax, and a flagrant misrepresentation."

Curtis, McAllaster, their wives, and some others were found guilty and ordered to repay investors $750,000. They were also ordered to pay interest on that amount from July 1, 1974. Curtis had begun perpetrating this fraud before he joined Leber Group.

That was enough to banish IPM from the Philippines. But that wasn't all there was to Curtis. He had also agreed to a Judgment By Consent a month before, on November 16, 1976. After Kirst had contacted him in 1975, he went to Samuel J. Agnew of the John Birch Society and promised Agnew he could launder any gold they found. In return he wanted to borrow money to finance the operation. Agnew loaned him $250,000 in January 1975 and another $125,000 in April 1975. The money was not used to finance Leber Group and Curtis never repaid the loans. Agnew sued him and Curtis agreed to the Judgement by Consent. He, McAllaster, and three corporations listed in the other suit were ordered to pay $443,198.23, which included the loan, interest, attorney's fees, and court costs.

The FBI stepped in and ordered an investigation into Curtis' activities. An indictment was returned on September 15, 1977. His third trial began on August 14, 1978. When he went public with his material in 1978, he neglected to tell Senator Laxalt about his legal problems. This time he pleaded *nolo contendere*. He was sentenced on January 3, 1979, to five years imprisonment, suspended, and placed on probation for five years.

The treasure attracted all kinds – a president, a general who might be CIA, a conman, and thousands of poor like Roger. It still attracts them.

Marcos had the biggest advantage in the search for the yellow metal, so his chances for success would have been greater. He also had the advantage in another quest. This time he robbed a bank. But it wasn't just any bank.

CHAPTER SEVEN

Sleight of Hand

In March 1968 a seven-nation International Gold Pool established a two-tier price system for gold. Under this system there was an official price of $35 per ounce on monetary transactions restricted to government-owned gold, and an open market price for other transactions which fluctuated with supply and demand. Gold bought by private buyers, whether for hoarding or artistic and industrial use, was free to find its own level. During the first year of this new system it hovered between $37 and $43.50 per ounce.

The annual production of gold in the Philippines from primary and secondary sources was between 20 and 30 metric tons a year. Only a third of the production was refined into gold bars. The rest was exported as unrefined copper ore. Any bullion recovered was minted and left abroad in Central Bank gold pool accounts in London, New York, or Zurich, or sold for dollars and remitted back to the Central Bank as reserves.

There had been a steady twenty-year rise in gold reserves up to 1972. When Marcos declared martial law, reserves stood at 1,857,000 ounces (52.75 metric tons). The world average market price on the open market was $58.13 per ounce. In 1973 the price hit $100 and kept rising.

The *Bangko Sentral Ng Pilipinas* was inaugurated that year. Located on Manila Bay diagonally across from the Cultural Center, the new complex consisted of a five-floor headquarters and other buildings. It was Marcos' pride and joy in ways no one could imagine. Gregorio Licaros was the governor. His office was on the far end of the top floor in the headquarters building.

The Central Bank was a powerful entity in the Philippines. It was equivalent to the Board of Governors of the Federal Reserve in the U.S., plus most of the functions of the Federal Depositors Insurance Corporation and various state banking commissions.

As governor, Licaros had complete discretion in the purchase and sale of gold. He answered to no one except the president. In 1973, the Central Bank's gold reserves dropped to 1,057,000 ounces. Licaros claimed that 800,000 ounces (about 22.7 tons) was sold to obtain much needed dollars. This would have brought in $28 million at the official price of $35 an ounce.

But according to one confidential source, the gold was sold at market value which was at least double the official price. No one has ever been able to confirm this information. The Commission on Audit had jurisdiction on all government agencies. All, that is, except the Central Bank, which could not be audited. It policed itself.

The earliest warning that all was not well over there came in 1974. Imelda told *Newsweek*, "I tell him (Marcos) what's the use of building up all those billions of dollars in foreign exchange reserves if you can't spread it among the people?"

She was wiser in the ways of the Central Bank than most people thought. Central Bank letters to Marcos always included a copy to Imelda. The conjugal dictatorship Mijares wrote about was real.

From 1974 through 1977 gold reserves stayed at exactly the same figure of 1,056,000 ounces. This would seem to be a statistical impossibility. A Central Bank spokesman explained that at the time producers could sell their primary gold production directly to the international market, so it was possible for gold reserves to remain at the same level. But they had never stayed at the same level before, not even for two years running.

In December 1975, President Gerald Ford visited the Philippines. Marcos made sure the media interpreted the visit as an endorsement of martial law. In political parlance, he was about to tighten the screws.

Nine months later, on September 22, 1976, he signed Presidential Decree 1033, proposing nine new amendments to the constitution, including the infamous Amendment 6. It allowed him to continue exercising his powers after martial law was lifted "whenever in my judgment . . . there exists a grave emergency or threat or imminence thereof, or whenever the Interim Batasang Pambansa or the regular National Assembly fails or is unable to act adequately on any matter for any reason that, in my judgment, requires immediate action." Despite a petition to the Supreme Court, the amendments were ratified the following month.

In December the midnight oil burned in the office on the top floor at Central Bank. Licaros had a problem – foreign creditors wanted enough international reserves to cover three or four months of import requirements but there was only enough to cover two months. On January 1, 1977, he announced a solution – there would be a new definition for international reserves.

Originally it was "all gold, foreign exchange assets of the Central Bank, and net foreign exchange holdings of the commercial banks." The new definition excluded the net foreign exchange holdings of the commercial banks because it had become an increasingly larger negative figure. Why? Because they were borrowing more and more dollars. In addition, the Central Bank's borrowing would be included as part of its foreign exchange assets. Thus, with the stroke of a pen, the value of the reserves almost doubled, from $844.7 million to $1.525 billion, which was about 4.7 months of import requirements.

It looked good on paper but international lenders, including the World Bank and the IMF, were not impressed with such financial sleight of hand. Foreign borrowing in the seventies were facilitated by a highly liquid capital market flooded with dollars from the Organization of Petroleum Exporting Companies (OPEC). So the government borrowed – from every available source. In 1965, the year Marcos became president, foreign debt was $360 million. By 1976 it was $3.14 billion.

Lenders had another concern – political stability. The people were becoming more vocal about human rights abuses which were getting worse.

Purification Pedro graduated from University of the Philippines in 1968, majoring in social work. She spent the rest of her short life helping the poor. On January 18, 1977, at nine in the morning, she and a group of friends, all unarmed, were on the way to the barrio of Nagbayabas, Abucay, in Bataan province, when soldiers appeared and opened fire. Everyone escaped except Pedro, who was shot in the left shoulder.

She was taken to the provincial hospital and treated without an anesthetic on orders from the soldiers. They claimed they found twenty-four grenades in her handbag. Pedro's friends denied this, and pointed out her handbag had several bullet holes. The family came to the hospital and took turns nursing her. She was under constant guard. One after the other, seven teams of interrogators visited her room. She claimed they tried to bribe her into admitting involvement in subversive church-sponsored activities.

On January 23, Lt. Col. Faustino Sarmiento informed Pedro's family there would be one more interrogation, then she would be transferred to Camp Crame to get better medical attention. About five-forty-five in the afternoon an investigating team headed by Col. Miguel Aure arrived at the hospital and ordered Pedro's sister to leave the room. Less than an hour later, Aure and his men came out. He told the family they could no longer stay in the room. Before leaving he said, "Remember the name Aure."

When a guard brought Pedro's supper tray there was a commotion inside the room. Her sister ran in but Pedro wasn't there. She went into the bathroom and found Pedro on the floor, her body soaking wet. Her face bore signs of a beating. A wire was wound around her neck and attached to the towel holder. A doctor examined the body and declared that she died of asphyxiation by strangulation. She was twenty-eight.

Harsh censorship prevented the media from reporting such incidents. In response, the Catholic Church founded the Task Force for Detainees of the Philippines (TFDP) in the seventies.

It kept records of the torture and murder of civilians by the military.

On April 17, 1978, Marcos signed Presidential Decree 602, ordering all gold producers to sell to the Central Bank. In September he inaugurated the new Central Bank Gold Refinery and Mint in Quezon City.

Gold reserves began another steady annual rise. From 1978 until 1980 they gradually increased to 1,900,000 ounces, or an average of about 8 metric tons a year, which was about the equivalent of local production. The price of gold reached an all-time high of $875 an ounce in January 1980.

That year four chambers of commerce – the European, American, Japanese, and Australian – submitted a position paper under the guise of finding ways to attract new foreign investment. Red tape, corruption, and a flawed infrastructure were delicately criticized. They were trying to send a message: it wasn't easy doing business in the Philippines.

This was quite a change from 1972. Five days after martial law, Marcos received a telegram. "The American Chamber of Commerce wishes you every success in your endeavors to restore peace and order, business confidence, economic growth and the well being of the Filipino people and nation. We assure you of our confidence and cooperation in achieving these objectives. We are communicating these feelings to our associates and affiliates in the United States."

The support was quite effusive for a dictator but Marcos was pro-American. He allowed the bases and even planes with nuclear weapons at Clark Air Base without telling the Filipino people. After the Laurel Langley Agreement, involving trade between the U.S. and the Philippines, expired in 1974, foreigners were not allowed to hold management positions or serve on boards of directors. His new constitution had eased those and other restrictions and even reversed a Supreme Court decision which ruled that U.S. citizens and corporations could not own agricultural lands.

Things looked rosy at first but gradually the foreign business community realized they were not playing on a level field.

There were other indications in 1979. The multinational corporations began receiving negative exposure in pro-government newspapers – a smear campaign. They were blamed for just about everything that was wrong with the economy.

The Technology Resource Center, a government agency, submitted a manuscript to the American Chamber of Commerce. Entitled *Multinational Corporations in the Philippines*, it requested the Chamber to give their comments, which would be published with the book. There were nine chapters, each written by a different author on one aspect of foreign investment such as technology transfer, capital movements, labor, and restrictive business practices. All were critical of the MNC's and their contribution to the economy. The Chamber disproved with facts the manuscript's dramatic presentation. Subsequently the book was never published. The criticism in the newspapers diminished but nothing was done to address the complaints of the foreign businessmen.

Marcos began lobbying for a visit to the Philippines by Pope John Paul II. He knew this would be interpreted as an indorsement of his regime and would be the ideal imprimatur for the Catholic country. The Pope let it be known, however, that he would not visit a dictator. With great fanfare, Marcos announced martial law would end on January 17, 1981.

Licaros left the Central Bank that same month, with one year left on his second six-year term. "I told the president I would like to rest already," Licaros explained. He would be seventy-two in March. Did he really want to rest, or was there another reason?

Licaros was replaced by Jaime C. Laya, the former budget minister. Laya had no sooner taken his oath when the financial crisis began. Dewey Dee, one of the cronies, abruptly left the country in January, leaving behind debts estimated at ₱635 million pesos ($84.7 million). Dee borrowed most of the money using nothing more than his name as collateral. This was the largest financial scandal in history. It wouldn't be the last.

Banks tightened their credit. The cronies were the hardest hit. Some, like Floirendo, Cuenca, Silverio, and Disini, had borrowed way beyond their capacity to repay. Their business empires began to crumble. More than ₱30 billion ($3 billion) in bail-out funds would be provided to them and other cronies over the next two years. It wouldn't be enough.

In the midst of that debacle, Marcos announced his Basic Industries Development Program. Eleven major industrial projects, costing $4 billion over five years, would be launched. These included phosphatic fertilizers, diesel engines, alcogas, heavy engineering, integrated steel, a copper smelter, cement industry expansion, coconut industry rationalization, an aluminum smelter, integrated pulp and paper works, and a petrochemical complex.

Critics charged that all these projects were capital intensive. The country had more pressing needs, such as food production and social services development.

Most of the projects were never implemented, but in hindsight it is easy to speculate that these projects were only intended to benefit a few in the form of large dollar loans and kickbacks from overpriced machinery.

Marcos announced a new constitution, supposedly based on the French model, would better serve the people. A plebiscite was held in April before the June presidential election. The new constitution was ratified. He included some new provisions not mentioned in the French version. One granted him and all government officials lifetime immunity from any legal action. He was elected to a new six-year term. He appointed Minster of Finance Cesar Virata as the new prime minister. That meant nothing. Marcos still ruled.

Former Secretary of State Alexander Haig, in Manila for an Association of Southeast Nations (ASEAN) conference the day after the election, told Marcos, "You are going to find America with you, not in a dominating way, not in a pedantic way, but in a true partnership of equality and friendship."

Vice President George Bush flew in for the inauguration and toasted him. "We love your adherence to democratic processes." Practically the whole democratic world blanched. Newspapers across the U.S. asked, "How could you say that?" Marcos knew the answer if no one else did – the military bases.

He turned his attention to preparing for the Cancun economic summit in October. He wanted an invitation to visit the

States. Even without martial law, his phony democracy and financial policies were wearing thin in the eyes of the World Bank and the IMF. He desperately needed a change of image and more handouts. A slump in world prices was seriously affecting the dollar earnings of the country's major exports.

Foreign business and industry leaders continued to complain about red tape, onerous government requirements, and restrictive policies that made them feel like adversaries rather than partners in economic development. Marcos paid little attention.

On October 1, 1981, the Makati Business Club was formed. Headed by billionaire businessman Enrique Zobel, it was composed of prominent non-crony businessmen. It would become increasingly vocal and critical of Marcos and his economic policies.

At Cancun, eight of the world's richest nations and fourteen less developed countries met to discuss the economic plight of the Third World. Reagan told those gathered that the era of massive American handouts was finished. That wasn't what Marcos wanted to hear. All of a sudden foreign investment suddenly became very important.

Marcos got his invitation. Now he had a year to prepare for the state visit and to make peace with the business community. Business and industry applauded the change in attitude but like so many things in the Marcos government, it was mere window dressing.

As soon as Laya took over, he sold 250,000 ounces (about 7.1 metric tons) of gold. By then most nations conducted gold transactions and valued their gold reserves at market-related prices. The world average market price in 1981 was $459.868. The Central Bank claimed the sale, worth approximately $115 million, was to help with the financial crisis. Gold reserves dipped to 1,650,000 ounces.

Laya's next ambitious project was begun in December 1981, supposedly to optimize the yield of the Central Bank's gold assets. It would exchange good delivery bars in its vault for good delivery bars at a foreign financial institution, usually in London or New York. Called a location swap, a representative of that institution would accept delivery of the bars at the Central Bank and be responsible for shipping them. In return, the Central Bank would pay a swap fee to cover shipping, handling, and insurance costs.

The swap would increase the availability of the gold reserves for investment opportunities in active gold centers. They could be placed on deposit to earn interest. Or they could be used in something more sophisticated, such as a spot sale and forward purchase transaction, or a gold-dollar linked deposit, where the gold earned interest while the counterparty deposited U.S. dollars in the Central Bank to earn interest. Or the gold could be sold. According to the Central Bank, the policy was not to sell gold at all but to stockpile it in the reserves.

Critics scoffed at the whole idea. What was Laya and Marcos really up to? Based on the changes Laya had already made, some expected the worst.

About the same time this program began, a rumor started to circulate. Someone in the Philippines was selling 525 metric tons of gold worth about $5 billion. Journalists tried to trace the seller but were unsuccessful. The deal was never concluded.

The rumor may have started because of the gold leasing program – the 525 tons was supposed to have left Manila on January 4, the same day a legitimate shipment of 100,000 ounces (2.84 tons) left the country. After that, the country's gold reserves stood at 1,550,000 ounces, or 44 metric tons.

In early 1982, Michael Young, a Tokyo-based businessman, claimed a Hong Kong attorney, Tony Grant, informed him that thirty-five 50-kilogram bars of gold were available in Hong Kong and another fifty bars were available in Manila. They were owned by "older generation people, marked AAA, and stamped Sumatra Lloyd." The deal fell through when the sellers refused an inspection without a letter of intent to purchase.

While the rumors swirled, in 1982 Gen. Ramon Cannu, part of Ver's treasure hunting group, met with an American, Ron Lusk, in Manila to arrange the confidential shipment of 50 metric tons to Switzerland. Lusk had been recommended by Credit Suisse Bank. His reputation was well known in Asia and Europe. He could fly anything from a helicopter to a Boeing 747 and could smuggle anything, anywhere.

According to Lusk, the gold Cannu showed him was stored "underground, with a warehouse over the top of it, somewhere outside of Manila." This could have been the summer palace at Mariveles, a few hours drive from Manila. Lusk also said that the gold had Chinese or Japanese markings and was stored in copper boxes. While making the arrangements for the aircraft he was given another tour, this time of a warehouse at Villamor Air Base. Inside were all kinds of military equipment made in the U.S.A. He was told it was all for sale. If he could find a buyer he would earn a commission. A few years later a U.S. congressional report revealed more than $100 million in American military assistance to the Philippines was wastefully spent.

Lusk made plans to fly the gold to Switzerland but all of a sudden the mission was scrubbed. He was never told why. Two years later he was invited back. The plan was canceled again but he did some work for NISA bugging hotel telephones. After the revolution the summer palace and its grounds were searched but no gold was found.

Lusk was not his real name. He was in the Federal Witness Protection Program. Over the years, the information he provided U.S. authorities at the Bureau of Customs and the Defense Criminal Investigation Service in the Pentagon was considered faultless. He had been an informant for seven years and a key witness in the successful prosecution of many drug smugglers.

One of the documents found in the palace after Marcos was overthrown, was a telex sent to Gapud, dated August 12, 1982. It stated in part:

> Further to conversation 130AM this date our time with your office the money has been placed in position by the Saudi National Bank in Madrid to purchase the first 6,000 tons metric of product discussed . . . Bill Erbe, President ITM

The name Bill Erbe could not be traced and was probably an alias. If the product was gold that was the first documented evidence that Marcos had a huge amount, or else he was running some kind of scam on a huge scale.

On September 16, 1982, Marcos arrived in Washington on an official state visit. President Reagan received him with pomp and ceremony. It had been sixteen years since LBJ had handled the honors. Now, five presidents later, Marcos was still in power. He gave quite a performance. "At the risk of our fortunes, our lives, but most important of all, our honor, [we] will stand for the ideals of democracy that is our legacy from the United States of America," he said.

Two days before, the *Seattle Times* announced a $30 million wrongful death lawsuit had been filed against the Philippine government for the killing of Gene Viernes and Silme Domingo. The article noted a motion to include Marcos in the federal civil rights lawsuit had been filed but was turned down because he claimed diplomatic immunity as head of state. It didn't matter. The publicity alone was enough to enrage Marcos.

Also before the visit, Amnesty International released a report documenting hundreds of human rights abuses. When asked, Marcos denied the report and criticized AI as not being an accurate judge.

Marcos wanted to discuss the extradition treaty. Extradition was the formal surrender of a person by a state to another state for trial and punishment. The treaty was proposed in 1973 but the U.S. government suggested that, because of martial law, it wasn't a good time to discuss it. After martial law ended, negotiations were resumed and a treaty finalized and approved. It immediately came under widespread criticism. Influential members of congress knew about his human rights record and that he would use the treaty to eliminate his opposition in the U.S. Congress refused to ratify it. He was told again that now was not the time.

Another item on the agenda was to renegotiate the lease agreement for Subic Naval Base and Clark Air Base. In 1979 Washington signed an agreement to give the Philippines $500 million in compensation over a five-year period. It was due for review in 1984 but Reagan agreed to accommodate his old friend and start negotiations early. The rents were raised to $900 million over a five-year period, beginning October 1, 1984. That would bring in some desperately needed dollars.

Then it was on to New York for an even tougher act. For too long he had neglected the pleas of legitimate businessmen about corruption and red tape. That was why he brought his entire cabinet with him. They had their instructions. Promise anything but attract investors. And hurry. The country was running out of dollars, they were running out of lenders, and they were running out of time.

Laya continued to do his part. In May 1982 the Central Bank had changed the format for reporting the country's external debt. Revolving credits, which were mostly short-term borrowing, would be excluded. Under the old format, the outstanding debt was $16 billion. Under the new, it was $11.5 billion. By a change of definition, it had lowered the country's outstanding debt by $4.5 billion.

Once again, the country's lenders were not impressed. Many had already reached their lending limit. While Marcos was in New York, several international bankers were quoted in the *Wall Street Journal* that they were concerned about the growing size of the Philippines' foreign debt.

Laya was just warming to his task. The Central Bank definition of the debt-service ratio was also changed to keep within the 20 percent lending limit. In 1970 it had voluntarily set a debt-service ratio of 20 percent on the amount it could borrow from abroad. Annual foreign borrowing could not exceed 20 percent of the average annual export earnings over the past three years. This was later changed to 20 percent of the previous year's earnings. In 1982 it was changed again. Short-term loans were excluded (thus decreasing the numerator) and foreign borrowing were added to export earnings (increasing the denominator). Effectively this could allow the government to borrow short term *ad infinitum* without disturbing the ratio. It also made their capacity to repay the loans dependent on their ability to borrow, and not vice-versa, as was normally the case.

In October 1982 the base year for determining the Consumer Price Index was changed. Before, the base year had been 1972. Now it would be 1978. In addition, the composite of the market basket that comprised the index was reduced from 644 to 393 items, with many of the items now under price control. Thus, the C.P.I. for mid 1982 was 28 centavos under the old method and 59 centavos under the new. The purchasing power of the peso was raised.

In 1982 the Central Bank "lowered" the external debt, "raised" the purchasing power of the peso, and changed the definition of debt-service ratio so it could borrow short-term *ad infinitum*, all with the stroke of a pen. It was management by illusion. Looking good became more important than being good. On the positive side, gold reserves continued on their rise to 1,866,000 ounces, but not for long.

In 1983 a Luxembourg bank employee turned over to U.S. authorities photocopies of notarized documents relating to a gold transaction. The sales agreement was dated February 2, 1983, and involved three quantities of gold totalling 4,207,138 bars, each weighing 12.5 kilograms, and hallmarked *Banco Central*. That would have been 52,589 metric tons of gold valued at more than $800 billion.

The documents did not appear to be drawn up by someone comfortable with the English language. Among the terms used were "secret-huge-transactions" and "USBillion dollars loans." Also, the hallmark stated was *Banco Central*. The hallmark of the Central Bank was *Central Bank of the Philippines, Gold Refinery and Mint*.

A memorandum accompanying the agreement was signed by Konsehala Candelaria V. Santiago, "Trusted woman of President & Secret-Seller." The memo forbid the mention of Marcos' name but the sales agreement stated "confidential documents otherwise known as 'notes for the president.'" There were no records of the deal being consummated.

At the Central Bank, reserves dropped to 289,000 ounces, a decrease of almost 1.6 million ounces (44.8 metric tons) from the year before. This was almost twice the amount of 1972. The excuse was the same as before – there was a liquidity crisis and the gold was sold for badly needed foreign exchange.

There was indeed a liquidity crisis. The worst, in fact, in the history of the republic. The stage was set for a monstrous financial disaster.

CHAPTER EIGHT

Disaster

As the country lurched toward the brink of economic chaos in 1983, Marcos was a sick man. He had systemic discoid lupus, a debilitating disease that affected the body's internal organs. His kidneys were failing. Dialysis was needed to filter the poisons from his blood but it was becoming less and less effective. He needed a kidney transplant. Still, he somehow found the strength to negotiate a gold deal. This one was unique because it took place in Manila and included several meetings in the palace.

Michael O'Brien and John Doel were working together on a property development project in Australia. O'Brien flew to Hong Kong to raise capital for the project in 1983. There he met Andrew Tan Beng Chong, a Malaysian, who said he might be able to help. He knew someone "in Asia of large standing" who was offering a commodity for sale at "4 percent below fix" if the transaction were kept confidential. It soon became apparent the commodity was gold. The amount initially discussed was 5,250 metric tons.

Tan flew to Australia. His bona fides included a letter from the Premier of Queensland. Discussions began. At first Tan said the gold was in Hong Kong, then he said it was in Manila. Doel and O'Brien went to work. Using their global connections, buyers were found. One of the agents they used was an American, Joseph Zbin. Before leaving for Manila they set up two offshore companies in the Bahamas – Remington Limited and Bistre Limited – to use during the transactions.

Doel flew into Manila first on April 20, 1983. Tan had given him a letter of introduction to David Sayoc, an American engineer. Sayoc introduced him to Harold Jack Elkins, another American, who introduced him to Domingo Clemente.

Clemente said the gold was war booty that had been buried in tunnels behind the hospital in Baguio. He asked Doel if he wanted to include a golden Buddha in their transaction. Doel said no, he was only interested in gold in traditional format – 12.5-kilogram bars, assayed, and hallmarked.

Doel negotiated nine contracts with Clemente and his associate, Pedro Laurel. Clemente admitted the gold belonged to Marcos but Doel never met with him. The amounts far exceeded the 5,250 tons initially discussed. Doel flew to Hong Kong twice to arrange letters of credit. Everything was arranged and the contracts were prepared. Then one delay followed another. Doel finally gave up and flew home in July.

O'Brien flew to Manila on August 17, 1983, to try and salvage the deal. Accompanying him was Milne Juricich, a Sydney commodities broker and Yugoslav national. They met Norman Lester "Tony" Dacus, who was representing Zbin's interest in the deal.

Dacus was living in Hawaii when he became friends with his neighbor, Zbin. One day Zbin confided he was involved in a gold deal in the Philippines. He couldn't afford to make the trip so he asked Dacus to go and protect his interest. In exchange he would split whatever commissions were earned.

After a few meetings with Clemente, O'Brien suspected a scam. He met with Minister of Defense Enrile and had Clemente and Laurel arrested. Or so he was led to believe. That was the last O'Brien saw the two. He called the palace and tried to secure an appointment to meet Marcos but he was put off.

One night a man called and introduced himself as Ben Cailao. He assured O'Brien the deals were real. To prove it, two men took him to a warehouse. Inside were 300 to 400 weathered wooden boxes, each containing three bars of gold. According to O'Brien, each box was a little larger than a six-pack of Foster's, a popular Australian beer.

Two more contracts were drawn up. Other signatories were

added, including a Col. Pimentel of the Presidential Security Command, identified as the personal pilot of Marcos, and a Mrs. Lazo. Then it happened again. More delays followed other complications. Frustrated, O'Brien left in December 1983.

O'Brien and Doel told their stories when they testified in the golden Buddha trial. Dacus told a slightly different story when he gave a video-taped deposition for the same trial.

He met with Marcos four times but dealt primarily with Ver. He was involved in two gold transactions. The first involved a contract dated May 28, 1983, for the delivery of 60 metric tons a week with a total volume of 15,600 metric tons at a benchmark of $400 an ounce. (The price would be determined by the second fixing of the London Metal Exchange on the Friday before delivery. If that price fell below $400, then the seller could suspend the transaction.) Laurel sat in on all of the meetings, as did Domingo Clemente.

A second contract, also dated May 28, 1983, was for 10 metric tons a week with a total volume of 4,000 tons at the same benchmark price. The same buyers were involved. Laurel and Marcos signed both contracts as sellers. Both contracts stated the bars were 10-kilogram and stamped with the Central Bank hallmark.

The funds for both transactions were to be paid into Hang Lung Bank in Hong Kong, to the account of Pedro Laurel. The bank officer in charge of the transaction was Richard Yap, president and general manager.

The contracts stated that, on the buyer's side, a 1 percent commission was to be divided among four agents: Dacus and Zbin – 25 percent (of the 1 percent); William H. Sener (two-thirds) and David A. Sayoc, Jr. (one-third) – 25 percent; Bistre Limited – 25 percent; Remington Limited – 25 percent.

On the seller's side, 1 percent was due to Domingo Clemente, and 1 percent to a group composed of Enrique Turaray, Rufino Barcelona, Rosauro Webb, Antera G. Clemente, and Yoland Vidal.

The gold for the first transaction, involving 60 metric tons, was already in Hong Kong, according to Dacus. The gold for the second transaction was stored at United Coconut Planters Bank. He earned commissions for both transactions. The first occurred in August 1983. For that, Ver paid him ₱500,000 ($50,000) in cash. He did not see Marcos after the assassination of Ninoy but he was paid another commission, $45,000 in early 1984, which was wired to his bank account in the states.

Dacus said he saw gold bars on two occasions. The first time was in the vault of United Coconut Planters Bank in August 1983. He estimated that 100 metric tons were stored there.

The second occasion was when he flew to Ilocos Norte with Ver and a Col. Fontanilla. On the way the helicopter landed and picked up Bong Bong Marcos. They continued to Ilocos Norte, where Bong Bong showed him an almost completed shrine of Marcos. When he walked in he saw a Buddha about four-feet tall on a pedestal. It was shiny and looked like gold but he couldn't tell for sure. In the rear was a vault about thirty feet wide and seventy-five feet deep. He estimated that 300 to 500 tons of gold was stored there. The bars were larger, about 25-kilogram, than those he saw in the bank in Manila.

They had flown to Ilocos Norte to discuss the logistics of moving gold to Clark Air Base by truck. Dacus learned that CIA pilots were being used to fly it from there to Zurich via Hong Kong and London.

While in the Philippines, Dacus met, courted, and married the niece of Col. Fontanilla, one of the army officers involved with Ver in the gold transactions. "I had seven of the happiest years of my life with her," he said. Through Fontanilla, Dacus became friends with Ver, to the point where Ver personally kept him supplied with his favorite cigars.

O'Brien thought there were nine contracts plus two more arranged by him. Dacus couldn't remember. He said there were five, seven, or nine contracts worth more than $25 billion. He dealt with Ver and sat in on the meetings with Marcos, Clemente, and Laurel. He was paid his commissions. O'Brien went home empty-handed.

In 1985 Dacus returned to his hometown of Las Vegas and contacted U.S. Senator Chic Hecht of Nevada. He showed Hecht the two gold contracts which earned him commissions and explained his involvement with Marcos. He would have earned $600 million in commissions but he left before any other contracts were finalized. All of a sudden he wanted no part of the deals. Not until the golden Buddha trial did he admit he didn't pay Zbin his share. Several times he expressed concern for his life.

At the trial he testified he was present when Pedro Laurel and Marcos signed the contracts he was involved in. The contracts he turned over to Hecht had the signatures. He also had copies but they were turned over to an investigator from Washington and never returned. When he was shown copies of these contracts as evidence, those signatures were missing. They appeared to have been obliterated with typewriter white-out.

On August 7, 1983, Marcos secretly underwent a transplant to replace one of his failing kidneys. The operation did not go well. (He would need another transplant a year later.) He was a very sick man when Ninoy returned to the Philippines.

Ninoy was already a hero to his people that Sunday morning on August 21 as flew into Manila from Taipei on China Airlines. In 1977 he was sentenced to death for subversion. Under pressure from the U.S. government, Marcos released him in 1980 to go to the U.S. for a heart by-pass operation. He could have remained in the States but he heard Marcos was dying. The country would soon need a new leader. It was time to return.

The plane taxied to Gate Number 8. An announcement told the passengers to remain seated. Soldiers boarded the plane and escorted Ninoy out the door. Moments later the back of his head exploded. Within minutes news of the bizarre execution was flashed around the world.

If the murder was intended to frighten the public into submission it didn't work. A million people turned out to bury their fallen hero on August 31. In what must go down as the greatest display of bad taste in all her years as First Lady, Imelda threw a party that evening in honor of Senator Mark Hartfield of Oregon, who was visiting the Philippines. Protocol required Hartfield to appear. U.S. Ambassador Michael Armacost chose not to attend but sent a representative.

Day in and day out there were demonstrations. Businessmen in *barongs* demonstrated alongside taxi drivers in tee-shirts and society matrons in silk, all demanding Marcos must go. Marcos called out his police and military but threats and intimidation didn't work this time.

The international financial community reacted immediately. Banks began asking for full payment of their loans instead of allowing roll-overs. In September, Prime Minister-Finance Minister Cesar Virata announced the foreign debt was $18.1 billion. Lenders wondered, how could that be? By the new reporting format, it was only $11.5 billion in May 1982. Two weeks later Virata corrected himself and announced that it was actually $19.1 billion.

Imelda blamed the media for all the country's problems. Three weeks after the funeral she met with eighty foreign correspondents at the Manila Hotel. Arriving in a black Buick and strolling down a red carpet laid out for her arrival, she lectured them for two hours. "We have lost our credibility because of the media," she said, and called them "racist and sexist." When asked about the protest rallies occurring almost daily, she said they were "politically instigated" and were not signs of a lack of a confidence in government.

President Reagan had planned to visit several cities in the Far East in November, including the Philippines. Marcos had counted on this visit, especially now. On October 3 the White House announced that part of that trip would have to be canceled due to demands of congressional business at home. The Philippines, Indonesia, and Thailand were sent official regrets. There would be no U.S. president to manipulate this time.

Laya and Virata flew to New York to meet with ten of the country's international lenders. On October 14 they told them the Philippines could no longer service its foreign debt. International reserves were not $1.43 billion as reported – they were $430 million. They asked for a moratorium and a rescheduling of their payments.

From Manila, telexes were sent to foreign creditors and to Paris Club, the informal committee of creditor governments that coordinated debt rescheduling and determined the interest rate. The announcement sent shock waves through the halls of international finance. There was more to come.

On October 17, Virata had another surprise. Foreign debt wasn't $19.1 billion after all. It was $24.6 billion. He had neglected to include short-term debt, which had ballooned, from $4.5 billion in May 1982, when the Central Bank started excluding it from it's official report, to almost $10 billion in 1983.

The moratorium was granted but a fraud had been perpetrated. Some of the lenders told Virata they wanted Laya out of the negotiations.

The Bank Advisory Committee, composed of the twelve largest banks representing the 483 commercial lenders, sent an economic subcommittee to Manila to determine the seriousness of the country's financial problems. The firm of Sycip, Gorres, and Velayo in Manila was asked to conduct an audit. It was an odd choice, considering Marcos and SGV were known to have close ties. Virata and Laya had been a partners in the firm. And the *V* in SGV was Fred Velayo, a friend and financial consultant to Marcos.

During the investigation, a senior Central Bank official publicly exclaimed $400 million had been lost because of capital flight. The official also said the other $600 million that was missing never existed. It related to transactions between the Central Bank and the government-owned Philippine National Bank. In December 1982 the PNB had raised $600 million, mostly through financial markets in London. It passed these to the Central Bank, which entered the money into its books as foreign exchange holdings – they became part of the gross reserves. After the Central Bank published its reserves figures for December, it returned the funds to PNB.

The infusion and subsequent withdrawal of short-term foreign exchange holdings through PNB became a monthly exercise – the Central Bank had to submit a monthly statement of its reserves to the IMF. But around April or May 1983, according to the official, the Central Bank started not just window-dressing but creating phony figures on paper.

The IMF had been wary of the Philippines' for a long time. They knew Marcos considered the Central Bank his private preserve. They also knew about a confidential World Bank report not yet made public which stated that $3.1 billion of foreign loans contracted for between 1978 and 1982 had failed to reach their beneficiaries. The money had disappeared.

Before the reserves scandal, the Central Bank stated in a 1983 report the Philippines was "the only country in the world that published accurate information about its foreign debt."

Laya wrote Marcos on December 20, 1983, to explain the problem. The letter stated in part, "The international operations sector of the Central Bank had been gradually reorganized since 1981 (the start of his term as governor) to improve on aspects open to possible abuse."

Like the quote about accurate information, it was so far from the truth as to be mystifying. The Central Bank had been *reinvented*, not reorganized, and not for the benefit of the country but for the benefit of Marcos.

In a private memorandum, Laya accused Fernando Balatbat, head of treasury operations, of masterminding the reserves scam. Balatbat in turn said that Laya was directly involved in the "manipulation" of the balance of payments figures to show lower deficit figures to comply with targets set by the IMF. He said that in order to accomplish such a manipulation, several sectors, departments, and units of the Central Bank had to be involved under the governor's direction and responsibility.

Laya claimed he "could not dismiss Balatbat as would have been appropriate, because he was privy to certain matters that at the time I felt were best left undisclosed. He threatened to blow everything sky high and implicate the Monetary Board and the president . . ."

Composed of seven members, including the governor, the Monetary Board set guidelines and policies for the Central Bank with the objective of providing price stability.

Some of the things "left undisclosed" would stay that way while Marcos was in power. Only later would Laya admit that, on Marcos' instructions, he ordered the falsification of documents regarding a loan of $30 million to Razon, the illegal purchase of $8 million in foreign exchange by CDCP, and the diversion of $70 million by PNOC, all in direct violation of Central Bank regulations. Laya was relieved of his duties and later appointed the minister of education.

About a month before the moratorium, on September 9, 1983, 247 400-ounce gold bars were flown from Manila to London via Amsterdam on KLM flight 864. A KLM employee obtained a copy of the air waybill and made it available to the press. According to the waybill the gold was shipped in sixty-two crates and weighed 3,020 kilograms (3.02 metric tons). Morgan Guaranty Trust Company of Manila was listed as the shipper, and Morgan Guaranty Trust Company of London as the consignee. The gold was purchased for $39 million and the proceeds deposited into the Central Bank accounts at Morgan Guaranty and Citicorp.

The shipment appeared to be legitimate and was relatively small compared to the sale of 60 metric tons witnessed by Dacus the month before.

Also in September, the local news in Manila reported that a Korean Airlines scheduled flight from Manila to Zurich via Bahrain failed to achieve lift-off and ran off the runway. Under a promise of secrecy the pilot said the plane's cargo shifted and couldn't lift off "because of the weight of the gold." After Marcos fled the Philippines there was an investigation of this incident, but the control tower could find no records of this flight. They had disappeared.

A month later, a 707 from Amsterdam was chartered to carry "flowers" from Manila to Zurich via Hong Kong and Karachi. The plane had a diplomatic air waybill and also nearly crashed into the sea on takeoff because of the weight. Bong Bong was reported to be on this flight. The gold was supposedly strapped in individual seats to distribute the weight. The PCGG attempted to confirm this flight but these records had also disappeared.

On November 24, Jose Cruz-Cruzal was arrested when he arrived at Seattle-Tacoma International Airport from Manila. Customs inspectors found a plastic bag he tried to conceal in the small of his back. It contained documents which stated that Marcos wanted to borrow billions of dollars from banks through an American, Frank B. Higdon, living in Virginia. The collateral, according to the documents, was "four floors of gold" stored underneath a bank in Manila.

Cruz-Cruzal carried an identification card showing he was

an agent of the Presidential Security Command. He was accompanied by a Filipino-American, Clarence E. Decker. When a customs agent called, Higdon asked that the two men be allowed to depart without further delay. He stated that Cruz-Cruzal's mission was sanctioned by U.S. government officials and that pursuit of the matter would prove detrimental to the government. An argument ensued and Higdon hung up.

Shortly afterward, Higdon's lawyer called back and said a government official would soon advise customs to discontinue the investigation because national security was involved.

No official called back. Cruz-Cruzal and Decker's passports were taken and a case was filed against them. The case was later broadened to include possible foreign corrupt practices violations and gold smuggling.

Higdon, age sixty-seven at the time, was a certified public accountant with strong government connections. He had tried before to arrange the shipment of a large quantity of gold from Manila to the States. That fell through when Wells Fargo, the bank that was asked to handle the delivery, advised him it would not deliver to a private residence or non-financial institution.

Higdon's phone records were subpoenaed. They showed he made a number of calls to Col. Florentino Villacrusis, Jr. and his attorney, Jesus M. Capilli.

Brian Lendrum, head of American Express Private Bank in Hong Kong in 1983, recalled that two men, Florentino Villacrusis, Jr. and Domingo Clemente, approached him about a large amount of gold for sale but nothing happened. Lendrum said the name of Jaime Laya was mentioned but Laya wasn't there.

Nothing came of the investigation. The charges against Cruz-Cruzal and Decker were dropped.

The Philippine economy began to collapse. Dollar allocations needed by industry to purchase raw materials and supplies from abroad became almost non-existent. Many major manufacturers, whose very existence depended on raw materials from abroad, could no longer obtain them. Factories began to close. The domino effect began. Other companies dependant on the manufacturers for business began to close. The unemployment rate skyrocketed. The numbers of the poor and starving increased by leaps and bounds. The Catholic Church began to complain. Businessmen and academics joined in, voicing their own complaints. Public furor increased.

As the economy crumbled, capital flight was at an all-time high. An estimated $5 million a day was leaving the country. The Central Bank had another problem. They were such a bad credit risk that banks wouldn't lend to them. A scheme was hatched to borrow from individuals, corporations, and various entities abroad. Marcos called Velasco at the PNOC and asked him to draw $200 to $250 million against its short term credits and deposit them in the Central Bank to ease the dollar crisis.

Multinational corporate heads and local businessmen were summoned to the palace. Imelda pleaded with them to come to the aid of the country. Laya was more specific – he asked them to make private placement loans to ease the difficulty. Their timing was terrible. In the business community, Laya had lost all credibility and Imelda's spending habits were front page news all over the world.

The Central Bank announced it would issue $125 million in dollar denominated two-year Treasury Notes. Marcos wanted to offer them to thirty of his friends. Laya called back and said no one was buying. Marcos said he would take care of it.

At the time he had $115.5 million in two Avertina Foundation accounts in Credit Suisse Bank, just two of the dozens of accounts he maintained. Seventy-five-million dollars worth of the Treasury Notes was bought by the Avertina Foundation in the names of three Swiss banks: Bank Hoffman – $50 million; Swiss Bank Corporation – $10 million; and Paribas – $15 million. Three Manila banks purchased $41.4 million: Security Bank and Trust Company – $14 million; United Coconut Planters Bank – $26.4 million; and Philippine Bank of Communication – $1 million. Antonio Floirendo purchased $2 million.

The sale occurred about the same time the Central Bank announced it was selling more gold – 1.577 million ounces – to alleviate yet another liquidity crisis.

Early in November, Marcos spoke at a televised meeting of 350 business leaders at the palace. He angrily accused them of contributing to the nation's economic ills through tax evasion, hoarding of foreign exchange, and illegal practices like "double bookkeeping."

Viewers only saw the Marcos speech – they did not see the first part of the meeting. The businessmen had presented Marcos with a six-page pamphlet entitled "Mandate for Economic Survival." They had labored long and hard for several days to present what they considered a rational plan for the country's economic survival. It called for sweeping political changes to restore confidence in the economy. Political stability was the key. Among other things, it urged a return to an unfettered press, an independent and honest judiciary, the restoration of public constitutional rights, guarantees of free elections, and a clearly defined system of presidential succession.

Marcos' reaction should not have been a surprise. He had never listened to them before and he wasn't going to listen now. During the state visit a year earlier he had paid lip service to them but all he wanted was their investment.

What little hope these captains of industry had was lost that evening. From that day on, they knew it was only a matter of time. Instead of planning for the future, some began packing up and searching for a better business environment. Others adopted a siege mentality and prepared to hold out until the worst was over.

The demand for dollars pushed the peso farther out of sight. In October the peso had been devalued, from ₱8.83 to ₱14.00 to the dollar. Even so, the black market rate zoomed to ₱27.00. At the height of the frenzy, someone in the palace came up with an idea.

In November, Ver issued an invitation to the heads of the eight money changing syndicates – Jimmy Chua, Raffy Chua, Benito Peñalosa, Go Pok, Catalino Coo/Lito Lliege, Peter Uy, Sio Lim, and Wilson Chua. The names were no big secret. A significant portion of the police, military, and others received payoffs from them to insure a peaceful coexistence.

They were asked to meet Ver at the Elks Club in Makati, which implied a social gathering. They accepted, knowing they didn't have a choice. When they showed up they were arrested. While incarcerated the problem was explained – the peso had to be controlled. At first they rejected all suggestions outright. But after two months of incarceration they accepted the offer. Thus was born the Binondo Central Bank.

Created by Executive Order No. 934, the Presidential Anti-Dollar Salting Task Force (PADSTF) was set up and run by Bobby Ongpin, minister of trade and industry. Code-named Luntian, the syndicates were permitted to continue their operations and keep their profits provided they cooperated with the government by buying and selling foreign exchange at government-dictated rates. The participants organized the corporation and ran it themselves. Ver's NISA provided security.

On December 2, Foreign Minister Carlos P. Romulo resigned. He was eighty-four. In his letter to Marcos, he claimed ill health. There were other reasons also. "I am heartsick," he said. "My work of forty years to build up the prestige of our country internationally has been spoiled and torpedoed by events beyond my control."

One of the last living framers and signatories of the United Nations Charter, a Pulitzer Prize-winning author, an aide-de-camp to Gen. Douglas MacArthur, Romulo was a man of enormous credibility. The cabinet lost what little prestige it had left.

Marcos' propaganda machine was cranked up. A three-part series, prepared by "the Domestic Information Service of the Bureau of National and Foreign Information based on a report by the National Economic and Development Authority to the President," was published in the newspapers explaining how the financial crisis happened.

Using economic buzz-words – like rising interest rates, recession, current account deficit – coupled with financial double-speak, the report explained how all those factors contributed to the country's present predicament.

It was a masterpiece of deception, concluding no one was to blame and everybody else was at fault. In street parlance, it was absolute doggerel.

And if the public only knew what Imelda was doing during the crisis, with her husband's cooperation and assistance, they might have brought down the Marcos government two years early.

CHAPTER NINE

The Wandering Wastrel

During the economic crisis, when dollars were sorely needed, Imelda spent millions on herself. For starters, she purchased four New York properties, paying out a total of $181.5 million. The last sale occurred after the Central Bank admitted it couldn't pay its foreign debt obligations. On November 18, 1983, Imelda made a down payment of $50.5 million for 200 Madison Avenue.

At the same time she spent millions on jewelry and other frivolities. On one trip during the crisis she paid $200,000 for a diamond bracelet, $360,000 for antique jewelry, $19,400 for towels, bed sheets, nightgowns, and table cloths at Bloomingdales, and ran up an $18,400 bill at the Waldorf Astoria. She used very little of her own money. Most of the dollars were provided by the Philippine National Bank and the Central Bank.

To spend so much so quickly required a special knack. It had to be acquired. She started slowly. In September 1976 the Marcoses bought their first property in the U.S. – a condo in the exclusive Olympic Towers on Fifth Avenue in New York. Five months later they bought the three adjoining apartments, paying a total of $4 million for the four. Antonio Floirendo's company, Theaventures Limited in Hong Kong, was the front for those purchases.

While the Central Bank broke new ground in creative accounting in 1977, Imelda began to express herself in an art form as unique as it was outrageous. She was a spendthrift. Like the original NASA astronauts who "pushed the envelope" by flying higher and higher, Imelda wandered the globe and pushed her own envelope, only it was full of cash for purchasing jewelry, antiques, and even a few bed sheets. *People* magazine called her a "one-woman balance-of-payments problem, a seemingly psychopathic buyer who squandered her country's treasury on everything from Bulgari baubles to macadamia nuts." She was notorious for being a wastrel in a country famous for being desperately poor.

In October 1977 she addressed the United Nations General Assembly, then she went shopping. On October 13 she spent $384,000, which included $50,000 for a platinum bracelet with rubies; $50,000 for a diamond bracelet; and $58,000 for a pin set with diamonds. The day before, Vilma Bautista paid $18,500 for a gold pendant with diamonds and emeralds; $9,450 for a gold ring with diamonds and emeralds; and $4,800 for a gold and diamond necklace. Bautista was employed by the Philippine Mission to the United Nations but also functioned as Imelda's private secretary.

A few weeks later, on November 2, Imelda paid $450,000 for a gold necklace and bracelet with emeralds, rubies, and diamonds; $300,000 for a gold ring with emeralds and diamonds; and $300,000 for a gold pendant with diamonds, rubies, and thirty-nine emeralds.

On October 27 the Marcoses donated $1.5 million to Tufts University in Boston, endowing a professorial chair in East Asian and Pacific Studies at the Fletcher School of Law and Diplomacy. The gift was kept secret from students and professors. When they found out, the outcry forced the university to reject the donation. To save face, the Marcoses were allowed to finance several seminars and lectures.

The real estate purchase for that year was a house at 2338 Makiki Heights Drive, Honolulu, for $717,000. The Tantocos did the honors this time. In 1983 they transferred the property to a Panamanian corporation, New York Financial, Inc. In March 1980 the Marcoses bought the estate across the street at 2443 Makiki Heights Drive for $1 million. Floirendo's name was on the deed.

In July 1978, Imelda arrived in New York after a sojourn to Russia. This time she paid $193,320 for antiques, including $12,000 for a Ming Period side table; $24,000 for a pair of Georgian mahogany Gainsborough armchairs; $6,240 for a Sheraton double-sided writing desk; $11,600 for a George II wood side table with marble top. The purchaser was listed as the Philippine consulate, thereby exempt from New York sales tax. Did the consulate of a poor country really need antiques?

That was just a warmup. A week later she spent $2,181,000 in one day. This included $1,150,000 for a platinum and emerald bracelet with diamonds from Bulgari; $330,000 for a necklace with a ruby, diamonds, and emeralds; $300,000 for a ring with heart-shaped emeralds; $78,000 for 18-carat gold ear clips with diamonds; $300,000 for a pendant with canary diamonds, rubies, and emeralds on a gold chain.

When she couldn't make it to New York, there were jewelers closer to home. In Hong Kong, a Cartier representative said Imelda had put together the world's largest collection of gems. That was in 1978.

They did not neglect their annual real estate purchase. In 1978 and 1979 they purchased two properties in New Jersey. One, at 3850 Princeton Pike, Princeton, was a 13-acre estate used by daughter Imee when she attended Princeton. The other was a house at 19 Pendleton Drive in Cherry Hill for Bong Bong when he attended the University of Pennsylvania. A second house, at 4 Capshire Drive, was purchased on November 23, 1978, for use by servants and Bong Bong's security detachment.

In Vaduz the names kept changing. In August 1978 the Azio Foundation was renamed Verso, Scolari was renamed Valamo, and Xandy was renamed Wintrop.

And Imelda continued spending. In two days in New York in April 1979 she spent $280,000 for a necklace set with emeralds and diamonds; $18,500 for a yellow gold evening bag with one round cut diamond; $8,975.20 for 20-carat gold ear clips with twenty-four baguette diamonds; $8,438.10 for 18-carat gold ear clips with fifty-two tapered baguette diamonds; and $12,056.50 for 20-carat gold ear clips with diamonds.

In June 1980, Marcos and Imelda were principals in a partnership which included several doctors connected with the Heart Center. They purchased the Webster Hotel on West 45th Street in New York for $1.577 million. One of the limited partners, Gen. Romeo Gatan, was a colonel when he arrested Ninoy Aquino at the beginning of martial law.

In February 1981 the twelve acre Lindenmere estate at Center Moriches on Long Island was purchased for $550,000 by Luna 7 Development Corporation of New York. Ownership was transferred to Ancor Holdings, a Netherlands Antilles corporation controlled by Floirendo, in December 1982.

Also in 1982, actor George Hamilton, a close friend of Imelda, purchased a mansion on Summit Drive in Beverly Hills for $1.5 million. After the purchase, it was refurbished at Imelda's request by a Filipino architect. The money for the purchase came from a loan from Ancor Holdings. After Hamilton came under media attack for the property's connection to Imelda, it was sold to the daughter of Adnan Khashoggi for $6 million. Khashoggi, international businessman and jet-setter, was well known in Imelda's circle of friends. The title was later voluntarily relinquished to the Philippine government.

Imelda travelled extensively, supposedly on official business. One document found at the palace, a memo to PNB president Panfilio Domingo, dated September 30, 1981, and signed by Marcos, authorized the disbursement of $200,000 from Intelligence Fund Account No. 2 for "expenses incurred in connection with the official trip of the First Lady to Iraq."

Another document showed that in 1981 the PNB disbursed $200,000 on August 10 for Imelda's trip to Nairobi; $200,000 on September 30 for her trip to Iraq; $200,000 on October 29 for her trip to New York; and $200,000 on December 2 for another trip to New York.

She visited New York three or four times a year from 1980 to 1984. While there she stayed at the Waldorf Astoria Hotel in the $1,800 a day presidential suite. On each visit she called the PNB in New York four or five times and ordered vice president Oscar Cariño to deliver $100,000 to her at the hotel. The amounts totalled $22 million by 1983 when the New York state bank examiners threatened to close the bank. One U.S. Attorney said, "Imelda treated the New York branch of the Philippine National Bank as her personal piggy bank."

The paperwork at Vaduz increased. On March 10, 1981, Imelda issued handwritten instructions to liquidate the Rayby Foundation and transfer its assets to Trinidad. On the same day, in an apparent change of mind, she ordered Trinidad dissolved and the assets transferred to Fides Trust Company at Bank Hoffman in Zurich. The next day Marcos issued written instructions – liquidate Valamo and transfers its assets to Fides. Then another – liquidate Verso and transfer its assets to Fides. Rayby was dissolved in April. In May four more foundations were established – Vibur, Avertina, Spinus, and Palmy. In June, Valamo was dissolved. In November, Maler Corporation, which had been purchased from Swiss Bank Corporation, Geneva, in 1968, was transformed into a foundation.

On August 25, 1981, a month after Marcos' inauguration, Imelda, through Bautista in New York, purchased a heart-shaped necklace with pearls and matching earrings for $1.1 million; a necklace and matching earrings with rubies and diamonds for $130,000; a necklace of Egyptian coral and onyx for $255,000.

Two days later it was $610,640 worth of antiques, including a rare mahogany China cabinet for $100,000; a pair of eighteenth century carved and gilt wood Georgian armchairs for $41,600; an eighteenth century red lacquer grandfather clock for $12,000; an eighteenth century English cut glass chandelier for $33,600.

Three weeks later, through Glecy Tantoco, she bought the entire estate of Leslie R. Samuels, a New York philanthropist, for $5.95 million. This included rare books, paintings by the Old Masters (the great European painters before the eighteenth century), and stately furniture. The paintings she purchased may have been her introduction to the world of art. Cariño provided $5.45 million of those funds from PNB.

About this time Imelda's appetite for real estate increased. On September 15, 1981, Cariño made out two checks totalling $4.45 million as a down payment on the Crown Building in New York. Domingo, in a memo dated September 4, authorized the payment.

Despite the shortage in dollar reserves, Marcos instructed the president of Razon International Stevedoring Corporation,

Enrique Razon, through its chairman, to submit a $30 million loan request to purchase cargo handling equipment for their project in Saudi Arabia. Razon said he didn't need the $30 million but he complied.

Laya was out of the country at the time attending a meeting of the IMF and World Bank in Washington, D.C. Gabriel Singson, the deputy governor, called him at three in the morning at the Watergate Hotel. Singson had received a note and a phone call from Marcos regarding the $30 million. What should he do, he asked. Laya told him he had full powers and was in charge while he was away, so take care of it. "Take it to the Monetary Board," said Laya.

Singson followed Laya's instructions. The request was approved by the Monetary Board upon recommendation by the Management of External Debt and Investment Accounts Department (Mediad). Razon never received the money. It was wired to New York in September 1981 as part of the $43.5 million purchase price of the Crown Building. The sale closed on September 30, 1981. The buyer was Lyra Corporation, a Netherlands Antilles corporation. That's how easy it was to steal $30 million from the Central Bank. How many more times did they do this?

Gapud supervised this and other real estate purchases with the assistance of a few pricey lawyers knowledgeable in the wily ways of offshore banking.

Lyra was one of a network of shell companies that were set up to conceal ownership of the New York properties. Lastura Corporation was formed and the Crown Building assigned to it. Then shares of Lastura were pledged to three Panamanian companies – Yewell, Panelpor, and Trade and Commodities. Later these companies would pledge their shares to a bank for a loan. It was all a maze, cleverly designed to hide the true owners. It was also illegal. Under U.S. law, moving ill-gotten wealth through the mail or wire transfers was classified as mail fraud, a federal offense.

Imelda was just getting warmed up. On November 17, 1981, she purchased the Herald Center for $17.4 million. The sale closed on February 17, 1982. The buyer was listed as Voloby Corporation, another nonentity. A total of $19.43 million was wired from Philippine banks to U.S. accounts. She used the difference to pay her jewelers.

Laya received a note from Marcos. This time the Central Bank approved a request for $8 million for a construction project in Iraq for Cuenca's Construction and Development Corporation of the Philippines in December 1981. Gapud provided the pesos for the dollars from the 7700 accounts at Security Bank and Trust Company. Cuenca purchased the dollars and Gapud took it from there. The money was wired to New York as part of the purchase price of the Herald Center. Benedicto wired money from his Traders Royal Bank. Genito wired money from Angenit. It was a team effort with three of Marcos top cronies committing wire fraud and the Central Bank violating its own regulations.

Imelda's personal secretary at the palace was Fe Roa Geminez. She handled Imelda's affairs. This included keeping up with her purchases which were itemized in notebooks. When Geminez hurriedly left with her boss on the night of February 25 she forgot to pack these. Seven were found in the palace after the overthrow.

An entry on December 30, 1981, showed that Geminez made three fund transfers: the first was $100,000 to Hanover Trust bank account of Danaos, the corporate name of jeweler Bulgari; the second transfer consisted of three checks – $830,000, $90,000, and $150,000 – payable to Mario Bellini, an Italian art dealer; the third transfer was two checks for $80,000 and $51,350 to jeweler Isi Fischzang at National Bank of North America.

Tantoco had already given Bellini two checks totalling $1 million on December 26. Geminez' entry on December 30 stated, "A. Bellini – balance of $1,070,000 for Flemish paintings." These paintings were shipped to the palace on January 12, 1982.

From January 22 to 28 a total of $5,021,136 was disbursed to pay Imelda's outstanding accounts. On January 22, $220,000 was paid to Helen Chen, a Hong Kong jeweler; a $76,000 partial payment was paid to A La Vielle Russie, a shop specializing in fine works of art; $830,000 was paid to the same shop a week later; $191,500 was paid to Milan dress designer Renato Balestera a week after that; $350,000 was paid to Mila Schon, dress designer;

a one-year balance of $500,000 paid to Van Cleef and Arpels; another unpaid balance of $500,000 was paid to Bulgari's Danaos account.

In February part of the money wired to New York by Security Bank and Trust Company and Traders Royal Bank went to Glecy Tantoco. She received $4.65 million and purchased a Flemish painting for $4 million and a silver service for $428,000.

On another occasion, she and Imelda visited New York art dealer Jack Tanzer where later Tantoco purchased three paintings for $2 million. Tanzer said the bill of sale was first made out to Gallery Bleue of Rustan's Department Store, then changed to the Metropolitan Museum of Manila.

Andres Genito withdrew $1 million from Wing Lung Bank in Hong Kong and brought it to Marcos on August 19, 1982, before the state visit to Washington. Danding Cojuangco gave Imelda $500,000 and Domingo at PNB provided $200,000. Lucio Tan, J.Y. Campos, and Nemesio Yabut, mayor of Makati, frequently gave money to Imelda when she took trips.

In New York on September 14 she purchased a black fox-trimmed stole for $3,500. On September 25 she bought $133,500 worth of jewelry from Fred Leighton, $52,000 worth from Cartier, and paid Ralph W. Cowan $62,000 for portraits of her and Marcos and President and Mrs. Reagan.

The following month, more monies started moving – from Switzerland, Hong Kong, and Manila – through dozens of corporate bank accounts and back again, sometimes twice, for the biggest purchase of all. In December 1982, 40 Wall Street was purchased for $70,126,228. The money came from two accounts managed by Gapud, from Traders Royal Bank, and from funds of the Philippine National Oil Company.

Geronimo Velasco, on Marcos' instructions, instructed the PNOC treasurer to wire dollars earned from oil exports to PNOC's account at Chemical Bank, New York, then transfer them to Security Bank and Trust Company's account in New York. Gapud reimbursed him in pesos from the 7700 accounts. A total of about $70 million was wired between November 1982 and Spring 1983. Those dollars should have been surrendered to the Central Bank.

The official buyer of 40 Wall Street was Nyland Corporation, a Netherlands Antilles offshore corporation, which had three shareholders – Beneficio Investments, Inc., Excelencia Investments, Inc., and Bueno Total Investments, Inc. All were Panama companies set up by Gapud in 1980. The two Hong Kong trust accounts at Standard Chartered Hong Kong Trustee Ltd. owned the corporations.

Imelda bought twelve paintings in one day from the Hammer Galleries owned by Armand Hammer, chairman of Occidental Petroleum, for $3 million. Altogether seventy-seven paintings were purchased at the Hammer Galleries for $5 million. On May 16, 1983, Imelda paid $273,500 for fifty-two paintings by a little known French Impressionist Paule Gobillard. This caused a few snickers in art circles. Nobody had collected him before.

Geminez signed checks on May 30 for jewelry totalling $577,920. Two weeks later she signed checks worth $635,000. In one two-month period in 1983, Imelda bought $2 million worth of jewelry. In July she made a $1 million down payment to her friend Bellini on a $3.5 million Michelangelo painting. Bellini would eventually sell her $8.3 million worth of art.

The next real estate purchase was 200 Madison Avenue, for $50.5 million. At least $49 million in loans were used for this purchase. The sale closed on November 16 during the international reserves scandal at the Central Bank. Glockhurst Corporation purchased it from real estate tycoon Harry Helmsley.

Glecy Tantoco handled the offshore manipulations for Imelda. Rico, her son, held the bearer shares of Glockhurst. Later, when things got dicey, she asked her Panamanian lawyer to make it appear that the offshore companies in Netherlands Antilles and British Virgin Islands were owned by Khashoggi.

Gimenez had an account at Bankers Trust Company in New York. A certified public accountant at the PCGG later reconciled this account with other documents and pieced together a six-year period of Imelda's clothing and jewelry purchases:

JEWELRY PURCHASES

From Philippine National Bank records:

Paid to - J.S.S. Young	$825,000
- Van Cleef & Arpels	$623,000

- Canabrican	$324,895
- Danaos Ltd. (Bulgari)	$100,000
- Others	$179,256
From Philippine Treasury records:	
Paid to - Van Cleef & Arpels	$400,000
- Canabrican	$172,843
- A La Vielle Russie	$157,721
- Fred Leighton	$151,139
- Others	$264,999
From anonymous Manila bank accounts:	
Paid to - Fred Leighton	$864,108
- Gaston Issert	$668,923
- Van Cleef & Arpels	$552,213
- Cartier	$355,451
- Isi Fischzang	$314,550
- Bulgari	$244,250
- Others	$473,571
TOTAL	$6,671,919
CLOTHING	
From Philippine Treasury records:	
Paid to - Renato Balestera	$300,000
From Philippine (anonymous) Bank records:	
Paid to - Renato Balestera	$188,616
- Mila Schon	$121,673
TOTAL	$ 610,289
GRAND TOTAL	$7,282,208

The total amount of jewelry she purchased from Van Cleef and Arpels in New York while she was First Lady amounted to $16 million. Of this, $623,000 was paid by Philippine National Bank; $400,000 came out of Central Bank treasury warrants; and $552,213 from the 7700 accounts at Security Bank and Trust Company. That was just one jeweler.

There were 328 pieces of jewelry found in Imelda's baggage in Honolulu valued at $3 million. The jewelry recovered in the suitcases in the palace was valued at $10.5 million. And the jewelry confiscated at the airport on March 9, 1986, was valued at $4.7 million.

She bought paintings the way she bought jewelry – in reckless sprees. At least one was fake and others were overpriced. The PCGG compiled a master list of 182 paintings. The artists included Picasso, Francis Bacon, Paul Cezanne, Marc Chagall, Francisco Goya, Edouard Manet, Grandma Moses, Auguste Renoir, Andres Segovia, Paul Signac, Vincent Van Gogh, and Andre Wyeth.

Immediately after the overthrow, Aquino supporters raided Imelda's East 66th Street townhouse but the walls had been stripped clean. Nameplates left behind suggested seven Old Masters had been there, including Picasso's "Head of a Woman." Van Gogh's "Peasant Woman Winding Bobbins," and another by Brueghel the Younger. One painting was found at her Olympic Towers condominium wrapped in a white blanket and stuffed under the bed of the maids' quarters – "Sweet Peas In a Vase" by Henri Fantin-Latour. It was later auctioned at Christies for $440,000.

Before the raid, thirty-eight paintings were crated, taken to the airport, and loaded into the DC-8 of Adnan Khashoggi. Imelda claimed she sold them before the injunction freezing all of the Marcos accounts. Khashoggi delivered a check in the amount of $5.8 million, followed by $700,000 in cash. He admitted making the payment by bearer check and cash because the Marcoses could not collect money by check or by transfer. Seventeen of the paintings were seized in a Paris warehouse and the rest in Cannes in 1987.

Experts examined twenty-six of the paintings and said their total value in 1986 would have ranged from $1.7 to $2.7 million. Khashoggi said he did not have the paintings appraised because the Marcoses were friends and he trusted them. He and Imelda signed a quit claim, turning them over to the U.S. government. They were sold at auction for $5.3 million.

Seventy-eight lots of silver and seventy-one Old Masters, including paintings by Raphael Titan, Tiepolo, Tintoretto, and El Greco, were auctioned by Christies in January 1991 and grossed $20,287,355. One Tintoretto was determined to be fake. In February twenty-six more Old Masters sold for $4.8 million.

After a while the numbers begin to blur. This is not even a complete list but the point has been made. There is no way to exaggerate the amount of money Imelda spent abroad. But she squandered more at home.

CHAPTER TEN

The Needs of Man

The anniversary of Gen. Douglas MacArthur's return to the Philippines during World War II was celebrated every year. Imelda usually presided over the ceremonies since he had landed in Leyte, her home province. The year 1974 was the thirtieth anniversary. She decided the occasion would be special. All members of the diplomatic corp were invited. Her desire for public acclaim got out of hand sometimes. This was one of those times.

In anticipation of the event, she acquired some beachfront property at the town of Olot. She built an "ancestral estate" and proceeded to claim she was born there. U.S. Ambassador William Sullivan was in attendance. He described the estate as "a large, colonial-style house, with proper antique fixtures, a guest house, a swimming pool, a large coconut-log reception hall-cum-chapel, and a number of bamboo and coconut wood cabanas, all set among the palm trees. It was so new that the grass in front of the house was literally painted green."

Imelda had always felt like an outcast in society because of her poor childhood. To reassure herself of her position, she drafted a group of thirty wealthy matrons. Know as the Blue Ladies, they served as her assistants at official functions and traveled with her on trips. They were present for this occasion and pointed out to everyone the First Lady's "birthplace" at every opportunity. Most of those in attendance were aware of the charade. They also knew to keep quiet. Imelda was already a formidable force.

On January 17, 1975, Marcos signed a secret decree not made public until after the revolution. It stated in the event he became incapacitated or passed away, power would be turned over to Imelda. On June 7 in his own handwriting he amended the decree. He clarified her role as chairperson of a committee with presidential powers. Other members on the committee would be the secretaries of defense, finance, foreign affairs, industry, local government and community development, and an executive secretary. This was the first sign Marcos was propagating a dynasty.

Imelda began her political career that year. Marcos appointed her governor of Metropolitan Manila. He said the residents clamored for her appointment to "save the metropolis from the fate of other 'suffering' cities like New York."

That same year *Cosmopolitan* listed her among the world's richest women. It mentioned her world-class shopping sprees and the large entourage that usually travelled with her. She usually took two jets from the Philippine Airlines fleet and on at least one occasion took four.

Herb Caen, renowned columnist for the *San Francisco Chronicle*, attended the coronation of King Birenda in Nepal in 1975. Imelda was there. Caen wrote, ". . . the Marcos group arrived in four government jets, one of which flew back to Manila to pick up food for her group."

Other appointments followed. In 1978 she was appointed minister of human settlements, which the *New York Times* described as "a newly created post, whose functions she devises as she carries them out."

She ran against Ninoy Aquino in the elections for representatives of the Interim National Assembly. Ninoy was in prison. On election eve, April 6, 1978, at a predetermined time almost every street corner in Metro Manila overflowed with people beating on cans, pots, and frying pans, shouting the name of his political party. "LABAN! LABAN! LABAN!" There was massive voter fraud. Imelda won by a landslide.

That November, Panorama, the Sunday magazine of the *Bulletin Today* newspaper, published a poll of campus heroes. Marcos came in second, Ninoy fifth, and Imelda sixth. As a result, all

300,000 copies were confiscated. She out-polled Jesus Christ, who came in ninth, but that did not appease her.

In February 1979 she was named chairman of the Cabinet Committee, composed of all ministries, to launch the BLISS (Bagong Lipunan Site and Services) program, an ambitious attempt to centralize control of all economic and social development. Her Ministry of Human Settlements assumed responsibility for the "11 Needs of Man," providing water, power, food, clothing, work, medical services, education, culture and technology, ecological balance, sports and recreation, and shelter and mobility.

The Cabinet Committee would oversee its implementation. The undertaking almost defied description. The "Ministry of Human Settlements Multi-Year Human Settlements Plan, 1978–2000," was geared toward "improved quality of life, sustained economic growth, balanced ecology, and enhanced cultural heritage that underlie the formulation of the physical framework plan for the country."

For all its lavish descriptions, the only comments the BLISS project elicited were in purple prose. Little was accomplished. The real reason for such verbal obfuscation would become known later. Because of BLISS, Imelda had considerable influence over the allocation of economic development funds. She regularly encroached on other ministries and took money from their budgets in the name of her basic needs program. But she didn't let those needs get in the way of her social life.

In 1979 she hosted the opening of the Marbella beach resort. Her usual coterie of European royalty and movie stars were flown in for the party. She didn't like the color of the beach so a plane was sent to Australia to fetch a load of white sand.

In May she and Marcos celebrated their twenty-fifth wedding anniversary. The party cost $5 million. There was a silver carriage drawn by eight white horses. There was another planeload of European royalty. Trumpeters announced the arrival of each of the 500 guests. *Life* magazine did a spread on the affair. The issue was banned in the Philippines. The party was not reported in the local media.

For the Pope's visit in February 1981, Imelda spent $13 million on a new statehouse made of coconut products. The Pope did not appreciate such an ostentatious display in a country of abject poverty. He declined her invitation to stay there.

The BLISS program should have been enough to keep her busy and to satisfy all the country's social and economic needs. But while it was still ongoing she launched another program in July 1981. Called the Kilusang Kabuhayan at Kaunlaran, or KKK, she was appointed its head as Secretary-General. She called the KKK a movement of "national livelihood." Its aim was to give economic opportunities to the most disadvantaged people, and to help raise the standard of living of the country's poor. It was a huge venture costing billions of pesos.

When discussing the KKK and her formula for development she liked to sketch: a political triangle, an economic rectangle, and a circle representing the attainment of social goals equalled a big heart-shaped figure – happiness.

It was a vast undertaking launched on the heels of another vast undertaking very similar in concept and run by the same people. Like BLISS there was a predominance of officials at every bureaucratic level who had a reputation for bypassing normal channels of budgeting, auditing, and fund disbursement. Like BLISS, misuse of funds abounded. And, like all her projects, there was no public accountability of funds.

Later a government commission uncovered some of the results. Fictitious contractors were paid ₱198 million ($10.5 million) for work done on non-existent "ghost" projects.

She managed to keep up her travels. That year she traveled to Kenya, Iraq, and New York, spending like crazy along the way.

Almost since the beginning of martial law Marcos had been criticized for not having a vice-president. In August 1982, in preparation for his state visit, he defused some of that criticism by announcing the set up of an Executive Committee. Comprised of ten members, primarily cabinet ministers, including Imelda, it resembled the secret decree signed in 1975. In the event of his death or incapacity, the committee would run the country until a new president was elected.

After the state visit, the Ministry of Human Settlements was appointed to implement the Economic Support Fund (ESF), which totalled in excess of $200 million and was part of the military bases rental agreement. Although the funds were a grant from the U.S. Agency for International Development, and its counterpart was the Philippine National Economic and Development Authority, Imelda was appointed chairperson of a new inter-ministerial body to advise on all ESF projects.

In 1982 Marcos, under pressure from the IMF, slashed all government ministry budgets by 18 percent and announced a freeze on all government spending, which had ballooned from ₱1.1 billion ($114 million) in 1980 to ₱12.1 billion ($1.36 billion) in 1981. Imelda's KKK program was exempt from the slashing and the freezing. That was a mistake. Government spending jumped to ₱14 billion ($1.6 billion) in 1982.

In January 1983, Imelda hosted her pet project, the Manila International Film Festival. The first festival was held the previous year. She had constructed a new film center at a cost of $21 million. An additional $4 million had been contributed by government ministries, agencies, and the Central Bank for festival costs, which included flying in 300 of her jet-setters and serving $100-a-bottle champagne. This frivolous display led the World Bank to caution Marcos during the state visit against wasting public money and specifically mentioned the film center.

Left to her own resources, she violated film censorship laws and allowed thirteen soft-core pornographic films to be shown uncut at local theaters which generated huge profits and helped defray the festival's expenses. Cardinal Sin criticized the showings. The incident exemplified Imelda's frivolity, power, and adversary relationship with the Catholic Church.

It also pointed out what everyone already knew. There were two sets of laws in the Philippines – one for those in power and one for the others. Lino Brocka, film director, was a good example of the others. He was under constant attack by government officials for attempting to portray slum life as it really was.

In what palace observers believe was an overreaction to her being denied an invitation to the 1981 wedding of Prince Charles and Lady Diana Spencer, Imelda decided the wedding of daughter Irene would be a full-blown state occasion. It took place in June 1983 in Sarrat, Ilocos Norte, the home town of Marcos and Ver. This time she transformed an entire town.

Sarrat was made over to look like a seventeenth century Spanish colonial town. Ver's home and the homes of Marcos' relatives were taken apart and reconstructed to give the impression they came from the aristocracy. Native huts were replaced by European houses. Some were liveable. Others were just facades. The landscaping was enhanced by freshly planted flowering trees, from which paper machè blossoms bloomed. In addition, a Spanish colonial-style hotel and international airport were constructed for the occasion. An ocean liner was moored offshore to accommodate more guests.

The cost amounted to more than $10 million and was shared by the government. During the seventies Marcos had banned town fiestas as being too frivolous and costly.

Her penchant for lavish building projects led some critic to say she had an "edifice complex." In 1976, she had spearheaded the building of fourteen luxury hotels in preparation for the International Monetary Fund conference held in Manila. Critics charged that the $200 million in foreign loans they required could have been better utilized to fight poverty. They were proved right. Most were bankrupt within a few years.

She built numerous estates all over the country for herself and her family. She spent $40 million on a "University of Life," a school with an ultra-modern campus but whose purpose was never made exactly clear. She built the Heart Center, the Kidney Center, the Eye Center, and the Nutrition Center, when most hospitals could not offer basic services due to a lack of medicine and medical supplies.

She was also the driving force behind the Cultural Center and the National Arts Center. Her particular fund-raising style earned her the nickname, "The Iron Butterfly." She had a reputation for getting her way, telling one interviewer, "I'm like Robin Hood. I rob the rich to make those projects come alive . . . not really rob. It's done with a smile."

After the international reserves scandal, Imelda resigned from the powerful Executive Committee because of pressure from creditor banks. They were very aware of how she handled money.

By the end of 1985 her Metro Manila Commission had managed to accumulate debts of ₱1.99 billion (which included $100 million in foreign loans) in its ten years of existence.

Imelda did more damage than she ever imagined. The communists were never a threat until after martial law, when she and Marcos became their best recruiters.

There were serious problems in the rural areas caused by hard economic times. Instead of attending to them, she ran around the countryside claiming to be their savior, dreaming up exotic schemes with grandiose names, all in front of the television cameras. In reality she accomplished nothing and left the people embittered and even more disillusioned.

They became fed up. They saw no end to the abject poverty. The Communist Party saw an opening and took advantage. They pointed out the lack of government concern for their hardships. Then they terrorized the abusive landlords and gained the people's sympathy. Such tactics made recruiting easy. They joined by the hundreds, then the thousands. Party ranks grew by twenty percent a year during the Marcos regime. Most were not communists in the classic sense. Their motives for joining were related more to injustice than to ideology.

Soon they were big enough to form a fighting arm. The New People's Army, the NPA, was created. At its height in 1977 they had 25,000 soldiers in the field. The government had a military force of 200,000 of which about 60,000 were combat troops, but this was misleading. The NPA were better trained and had the dedication and willingness to put their lives on the line for what they believed in.

On the government side, morale was low due to Marcos' penchant for promoting friends over more deserving officers. Poor leadership resulted. In addition, chronic equipment shortages plagued the field troops. Many units lacked uniforms. Equipment that did arrive was shoddy. Boots fell apart after a month. By the time Marcos was overthrown, the NPA had begun to confront the military in company-size and even battalion-size strength.

One of Imelda's last official acts was to give a speech before the U.N. General Assembly on October 10, 1985. Resplendent in a yellow and orange dress, she called for international relations founded on "moral principles accepted by all mankind – justice, equitable sharing of resources, mutual understanding and cooperation, tolerance, the protection of the weak, and freedom from domination by the strong . . ."

How she said such things with a straight face was "astonishing," according to one newspaper. But she had better speeches, like the one she delivered on several occasions to businessmen about the "hole in the sky." She believed there was a hole in the sky over the Philippines from which God looked benevolently down on her people.

In November 1985, Senator Edward Kennedy, citing numerous reports of corruption at the highest levels of the Philippine government, asked the U.S. General Accounting Office to investigate economic and military assistance programs to the country.

The GAO sent a team to the Philippines in December 1985. Their report stated that $92.5 million of non-project ESF aid could not be accounted for. There were other anomalies. In addition, the team also reported they could not state that $227 million in ESF funds were not misused. The funds had been commingled with other government funds in such a way as to make it impossible to track.

Numerous cases were filed against her for crimes committed during her tenure as First Lady (sixty-six as of December 1991). In September 1993 she and transportation minister Jose Dans were found guilty of two charges of entering into contracts that were "grossly disadvantageous" to the government. In 1982, when the Light Rail Transit Authority was constructed, it leased property to the Philippine General Hospital (P.G.H.) Foundation at rates way below the market level. Imelda, as head of the P.G.H. Foundation, then signed sublease agreements with various entities providing for much higher rents and made millions of pesos as a result. She appealed the conviction.

And her "11 Needs of Man?" When she departed in 1986 the number of Filipinos living below the poverty line had almost doubled, from 18 million in 1965 to 35 million. In the province, the farmer still plowed with his water buffalo, women still washed clothes in streams. There were few paved roads, no irrigation, no doctor or dentist. In most homes there was no running water, no electricity, no indoor toilets. There was malnutrition, especially among infants.

And the ecological balance of the country? In the fifties, 75 percent of the country was covered in forest. In 1986 only 27 percent remained. Thirty-nine million acres of forest disappeared, mostly due to rampant logging during the Marcos era.

She left behind a legacy, of sorts. Four-thousand outhouses were discovered in isolated areas outside Manila. There were no houses, just outhouses. Jose Conrado "Jolly" Benitez, her deputy, was dubbed the Toilet King for this misadventure. In a way, this project provided more for Man's Basic Needs than just about anything else she did.

For the town fiesta in her hometown of Tacloban, Leyte, in 1979, Imelda had a building constructed that was supposedly modeled after a palace in Versailles. Palatial in size and opulent in furnishings, it was a beautiful showcase for whatever its intended purpose. As one entered, the focal point was a huge mural of Imelda, larger than life, ascending into heaven as other smaller figures, resembling her family, looked on. Perhaps this was her ultimate fantasy – the dream of a little girl who grew up poor and achieved more fame and more wealth and rose higher than any Filipina ever before. That she had done, but probably not in the way she wanted.

CHAPTER ELEVEN

Big Bird

Late in the evening of January 10, 1984, Marcos summoned Jose Fernandez, head of the Far East Bank and Trust Company, to the palace and offered him Laya's old job. "Non-acceptance would be tantamount to treason," Marcos said to Fernandez. The comment was in jest. Fernandez was part of the Old Boy network. He could be trusted to carry on where Laya left off.

Tall, gray haired, and dignified, he preferred business suits. This was quite a contrast to the previous governor, a boyish-looking brunette who preferred the *barong*. Virata called Fernandez "The Englishman" because of his suits, his mannerisms, and the pipe he smoked. He was a vigorous man, adept on the golf course as well as the tennis court, and he played a fair game of chess. He was good at other matters also.

In August 1984 the IMF reported the Central Bank had overstated its reserves by $264 million in 1981, $823 million in 1982, and $1.2 billion in 1983. Gross reserves had fallen $1.4 billion between June and December 1983. That left the Central Bank with practically no usable reserves. It could no longer pay its foreign debt. That was what brought on the financial crisis and resulting scandal.

What about the Central Bank officials' claims that the reserves were only overstated in 1983, and that $600 million never existed and $400 million was lost to capital flight? What did the new numbers mean? This time no one from the Central Bank came forward to explain how much of this amount was window dressing and how much was capital flight. The term *capital flight* began to sound more sinister, like a euphemism for the world's largest bank heist. Other than the announced figures, no other information was given out.

Rumors were rampant all across Manila. Billions of dollars were being salted abroad and Imelda was buying real estate in New York. To quell the rumors, Marcos appointed Minister of Trade and Industry Roberto V. Ongpin to head a seventeen-member task force to investigate the dollar salting. He reported back an estimated $2 billion had flown the country in 1984 and $1 billion the year before.

Back in the States, three reporters – Pete Carey, Lew Simons, and Katherine Ellison – went to their boss, Jonathan Krim, and asked if they could look into the real estate rumors. He gave the go-signal.

On June 23, 1985, the *San Jose Mercury News* published the first of a three-part series entitled "Hidden Billions: The Draining of the Philippines." It focussed on ten people and their investments abroad – Marcos and Imelda, Benedicto, Campos, Cojuangco, Enrile, Velasco, Floirendo, Cuenca, and Roman Cruz.

Copies of the articles were published in Manila. One newspaper, *Malaya*, was threatened with libel but nothing happened. Marcos, his cabinet ministers, and cronies all denied the allegations. Minister of Labor Blas Ople noted: "After all, this is not a court of law that has convicted him. These are the findings of a small regional newspaper in California." (The paper had a daily circulation of 265,000.)

Others had written about the hidden wealth before. The *Far Eastern Economic Review* wrote numerous articles about corruption at home and investments abroad. In the U.S., Jeff Gerth and Fox Butterfield of the *New York Times*, Barry Kramer of the *Wall Street Journal*, and Brennon Jones of the *Nation* all contributed to exposing the Marcoses and their cronies.

But the *San Jose Mercury News* caught the perfect wave. The floodgates were opened. Every week brought another revelation. Marcos and Imelda denied everything. One cabinet minister, Velasco, wanted to resign but Marcos talked him out of it.

The three reporters would ultimately win a Pulitzer Prize for International Reporting.

While Marcos battled the hidden wealth scandal, a gold deal was being offered in Israel. In August 1985, Lt. Col. Oliver North was trying to find ways to fund the Contras, who were attempting to overthrow Nicaragua's Sandanista government. Congress had cut off U.S. military aid but North and a few others in the National Security Council didn't let this dissuade them. Richard Miller, formerly with the Agency for International Development but now assisting North in his escapades, called from London. The Israelis had 40 metric tons of gold for sale for $465 million, with a possible 20 more tons if the first deal went through. If Miller brokered the deal, he could earn a commission and net $5 million for the Contras. When they found out the seller was Ver, they approached him directly to cut out the Israeli middlemen.

Ver had befriended the Israelis when they used him to sign fake end-user certificates for arms shipments destined for Iran. This made it appear the weapons were bound for the Philippines. The Israelis didn't want the White House to find out where the weapons were going. Ver turned to them when he needed to find a buyer for his gold. When Miller and North contacted Ver, he got angry and accused the Israelis of telling everybody. The deal fizzled when the buyer wanted to view the goods before posting a bank guarantee.

There was some reported smuggling going on during this period, on a very high level. Johnson Matthey was one of the London Five, the five-member gold pool which sets the daily price of gold. It was also the company that assisted the Central Bank in setting up its gold and silver refinery in 1976. Dr. David Owen, leader of the Social Democrats, and Brian Sedgmore of the Labour Party charged in the British House of Commons that gold worth approximately 7.25 million pounds had been smuggled into England by Johnson Matthey without payment of taxes from April 1985 until February 1986, and that these activities ended only days before Marcos fled the Philippines. They demanded a tribunal of inquiry be set up. The prime minister refused.

In October or November 1985, Interpol sent a cable from Manila. It began, "A Philippine national within *(sic)* direct access to the information reported herein who has reported reliably in the past . . ." The cable went on to state that three suspicious shipments – one of gold and two of silver – had been made by the Central Bank in 1985. The informant speculated that the Marcos family diverted the precious metals to Switzerland and put them in their personal accounts. The only proof the informant had was a Bill of Lading from one shipment which showed that 244 silver bars, weighing 8,202 kilograms, were received by First United Transport on October 11, 1985, and moved to the docks escorted by the Presidential Security Command. They were loaded onto the USS *President Kennedy* for shipment to Los Angeles, and then on to Drexel, Burnham, Lambert Trading Corporation in New York via Alba Forwarding Company of New York.

This information jibed with a secret U.S. Treasury report, which reported that in the fall of 1985 American President Lines, which owned the *President Kennedy*, made three shipments of gold and silver bullion whose worth was estimated at between $12 and $36 million. The bill of lading for 244 bars of silver was also contained in this report. On investigation, Drexel Burnham stated the gold sale was legitimate and the shipment was routine. The proceeds were deposited in the Central Bank's account in the Federal Reserve Bank in New York.

The last days of Marcos in power were marked by fraud and murder. On November 1, 1985, Potenciano Baccay's body was found in the back of his own van with twenty stab wounds. Baccay was one of Marcos' doctors and vice president of the Kidney Foundation of the Philippines. Marcos secretly had another kidney transplant in November 1984. When the news leaked out the palace adamantly denied the rumors the same way they had in 1983. The *Pittsburgh Press* ran a story which included interviews by Baccay and another doctor, Enrique Ona. They revealed Marcos had indeed had two kidney transplants. Two weeks later Baccay was dead. Ona quickly retracted his statement.

One thing was certain. No one could second-guess Marcos. When the economy was in a tail-spin to certain destruction, most thought he would listen to the titans of business and industry.

And most thought he would try and ride out the political storm raging around him until 1987 when the next presidential election was scheduled.

Two days after Baccay was murdered, Marcos appeared on the U.S. television program *This Week with David Brinkley*. Commentator George Will asked him if he had considered moving up the election date. Marcos dropped a bombshell. "Well, I understand the opposition has been asking for an election. In answer to their request I announce that I am ready to call a snap election perhaps earlier than eight months, perhaps in three months or less . . ."

Everyone of his advisers, including Imelda, had warned him about the dangers of such a move. "You're not in the best of health." "The people are angry." "A campaign could turn treacherous." On and on the admonitions went. To no avail. The election was scheduled for February 7, 1986.

In December 1985 the Central Bank wired the Federal Reserve Bank in New York to pay $15 million to First Chicago International, for account of Lombard, for redemption of U.S. dollar Treasury Notes. The Fed wired back on December 20 that there was only $6 million in the account. Then $45 million earmarked for USAID projects in the Philippines was released by the U.S. Part of this money was used to redeem the Notes.

Such illegal use of aid funds was the norm and not the exception. Whether the monies were earmarked for the military, the Economic Support Fund, or other projects, the abuse persisted. The U.S. General Accounting Office investigation in 1985 had also revealed that $18 million earmarked for building typhoon-resistant schools was invested in a money market instead. USAID had already stopped giving financial assistance to the National Electrical Administration after an audit discovered the NEA padded a $1.45 million disaster relief fund for the rehabilitation of typhoon-wrecked power lines. They had submitted false vouchers amounting to $108,441.

Fe Roa Geminez kept a record of monies paid out during Marcos' last campaign. A fifty-six page ledger listed the expenditures from September 1, 1985 to February 22, 1986. One unusually large item, for ₱1 million, was authorized by "FL" (First Lady) and paid to Assemblyman Arturo Pacificador on February 16.

A few days after the election, two carloads of men drove into San Jose, the provincial capital of Antigue. Evelio Javier, the former governor and head of Aquino's campaign in the area, was watching the votes being counted. The men opened fire, wounding him in the shoulder and hitting two others. Javier managed to get away. He was chased through town, cornered in a public toilet, and gunned down in front of shocked townspeople. Pacificador was later convicted of the murder.

After the election, President Reagan told a televised news conference there had been "fraud on both sides." Official observers from the U.S. thought otherwise. So did the international press, who were aware of Reagan's friendship with Marcos. Cory Aquino wasted no time in telling the media what she thought of Reagan's comment.

That was Reagan's last effort to help his friend Marcos. Within days, he sent Senator Laxalt to the Philippines with a personal message to "cut and cut cleanly." It was a shameful end to U.S. support of a corrupt and tyrannical dictator. Aquino never forgave Reagan for accusing her of fraud.

Marcos fled the Philippines leaving behind a foreign debt of $27 billion and a bureaucracy gone mad. During the two-month period before the election, ₱3.12 billion ($150 million) was withdrawn from the treasury as "cash advances," presumably to pay for his re-election campaign.

Growth of money supply was important in any banking system. It helped maintain a stable currency by controlling inflation and expanding or limiting credit. Disregarding this economic safeguard, the Central Bank Mint printed millions of peso bills, many with the same serial number. After Marcos fled, sixty-million pesos in newly printed bills was found in a vehicle belonging to Alfredo "Bejo" Romualdez, Imelda's brother, in the Port Area of Manila. In Leyte, another ten crates and six sacks of newly printed bills, amounting to ₱100 million, were found aboard the MV *Legaspi*, also owned by Romualdez.

Gold deals continued to emanate from all over the world. On March 17, 1986, the Archdiocese of San Francisco released a bulletin. It announced they had:

> . . . notified Filipino and U.S. authorities of a telex brought to its attention describing a transaction involving 5,000 metric tons of gold bullion allegedly connected to the government of deposed president Ferdinand Marcos.
>
> The 2-page telex is a copy of a purchase order addressed "To: owner/seller, Manila Philippines, c/o Mrs. Alejandria Pineda Caldona" in Manila and calls for the transfer of 160,750,000 troy ounces of gold bullion from a non-specified bank in Europe to a servicing bank in Hong Kong.

One of those involved, who requested anonymity, had contacted the Archdiocese and asked for help in advising the proper authorities because of the possible link to Marcos. Once again, the name given on the telex couldn't be traced and was probably an alias.

In April 1986 an Australian broker in Sydney told the *Sunday Telegraph* newspaper that T.C.B. "Andrew" Tan had telexed him an offer to sell 2,000 tons of gold worth nearly $22 billion just before Marcos' downfall. The broker said Tan claimed to be a friend of Bong Bong. The gold was "24-carat, 999.95 percent pure gold, 12.5 kilograms per bar," and that it had been stashed in Hong Kong, London, U.S., Singapore, Switzerland, Panama, and the Netherlands Antilles. Tan told the broker the gold was part of the spoils of war taken by the Japanese in World War II.

The broker couldn't handle the sale because of its size so he passed it on to an Arab consortium located in London. They were asked to deliver $1 billion to the Central Bank in the Philippines and exchange it for U.S. Treasury Notes. The Treasury Notes were to be swapped for gold bars at a bank overseas. Negotiations had just started when Marcos was ousted.

The Sydney broker sounded suspiciously like Milne Juricich and T.C.B. "Andrew" Tan was Andrew Tan Beng Chong, who had started Doel, O'Brien, and Dacus on their adventure in 1983.

A representative of the Great American Management Corporation from Houston, Texas, met in Hong Kong with someone from Manila to discuss the sale of "12,000 pieces" of gold. The size of the pieces were not clear. Both 12.5 and 75-kilogram bars were mentioned. Negotiations with various agents from Athens, Zurich, Capetown, and the U.S. began before the revolution and continued until May 1986. No deal was concluded.

In Tokyo an estimated 20 metric tons of gold, worth about $330 million, was sold beginning in the spring of 1986 shortly after Marcos' overthrow, according to the English-language daily newspaper *Yomiuri Shimbun*. It said its investigation revealed the bullion was sold in Tokyo for cash at unregistered precious metal stores where records were not kept. Japanese traders and mining company sources claimed that, before the gold was sold, people identifying themselves as Marcos aides offered to sell to them. They refused, so it entered the black market.

On his arrival in Hawaii, Marcos was housed on Hickam for almost a month. U.S. officials feared he might be assassinated so he and his party were isolated on one part of the base guarded by military police. In addition to his own bodyguards, Marcos was protected by Secret Service agents and the Coast Guard patrolled the Pearl Harbor Channel. Only those closest to Marcos were allowed past this security to visit him.

Marcos phoned Reagan but he couldn't get through. Imelda tried to call Nancy but she wouldn't take the call. Reality slowly set in.

On March 19, Michael de Guzman flew into Honolulu and checked into the Ilikai Hotel. He called Irwin Ver, the son of Gen. Ver. A meeting was arranged with Gen. Ver. De Guzman asked to meet with Marcos and Imelda.

About seven the following evening, March 20, Irwin and a bodyguard picked up de Guzman and took him to Marcos' duplex. There he met with Marcos, Imelda, and Bong Bong for several hours.

After the meeting Bong Bong and de Guzman drove to Honolulu International Airport where Bong Bong used a pay phone to call Ernst Scheller of Credit Suisse Bank in Zurich. They drove back to Hickam and told Marcos it was arranged. Later, about two in the morning, Bong Bong made one more phone call to Zurich from de Guzman's hotel room. At two that afternoon, March 21, Bong Bong delivered some documents to de Guzman in his hotel room. More papers were delivered that evening. The next morning de Guzman departed for Zurich. Accompanying him was Ibrahim Dagher, a Lebanese businessman who reputedly had substantial banking connections in Switzerland.

The reason for the meeting and the secret phone calls was hidden wealth, the kind Marcos had been vehemently denying. He had already contacted Gapud and asked him to wire funds but Gapud said he could not because a global injunction froze all his bank accounts. At the time there was ₱1.2 billion (about $60 million) and between $5 and $6 million still on deposit at Security Bank and Trust Company. On March 21, Marcos tried to transfer his Credit Suisse accounts but he was prevented because of the freeze order of the Swiss authorities.

De Guzman appeared to be their only hope. He was given two letters of authority, one signed by Marcos and the other by Imelda. They both were dated March 21, 1986, and stated "Please hold all securities and cash at the disposal of Michael de Guzman who will present this letter to you in person. He will identify himself by presenting his passport."

In addition Imelda had given him $300,000 in travelers' checks for safekeeping, and Ver gave him a cashier's check for $150,000 with instructions to cash it and send him the money. In a portent of what was to come, de Guzman cashed the travelers' checks and cashier's check and kept the money.

De Guzman and Dagher flew to Zurich. On March 24, de Guzman presented the letters of authority to the bank to release the first batch of deposits in the form of cash, bonds, securities, real estate certificates, and gold deposit certificates. They amounted to approximately $213 million.

The bank refused because of the freeze order. De Guzman tried again on May 7, 1986, and was turned down a second time. Only then did he turn to the Philippine government and offer to help them get the Marcos deposits in return for a 20 percent fee. He claimed that, in addition to the $213 million, he had identified eleven foundations set up by Marcos to hide his wealth.

They held a total of $4.5 billion in deposits in nine different banks. He also claimed there was an additional $3 billion in precious metals and securities on deposit, but these were subject to final verification. That would bring the total to $7.5 billion. The amount of gold included in the precious metals was not identified.

In a secret operation code-named Big Bird, the government cooperated with de Guzman at first, but gradually that cooperation ceased. There were too many gray areas. De Guzman had first tried to get the money without the help of the government. Then after seeking their help he was insistent in his demand that whatever was recovered be first transferred to his bank, the Export Finanzierungsbank, in Vienna, and then later to wherever the government requested.

The bank's board of directors included Marcos' former executive secretary Alejandro Melchor and crony Herminio Disini. The government considered the situation. If the money were transferred, de Guzman could divert it to other destinations and the money would be beyond their reach. That was enough to torpedo the deal. De Guzman's bank declared bankruptcy a few years later. The Philippine government proceeded through legal channels to demand the Marcos deposits. A subsequent accounting of the foundation bank accounts could only locate a total of $250 million in deposits.

The global freeze was not totally effective, however. On August 12, 1986, P.A.L. Vine, who managed Marcos' two trust accounts at Standard Chartered Hong Kong Trustee Ltd., received instructions from Marcos and remitted $708,000 to the law firm of Anderson, Hibey, Manheim and Blair, Marcos' attorneys in Washington, D.C. How much more Marcos was able to move after the freeze may never be known.

Meanwhile, back in Honolulu, Marcos settled down in what many called paradise. But Hawaii quickly became a living hell for him. He plotted and schemed and came up with another idea.

CHAPTER TWELVE

I Shall (Try to) Return

The legal battles started immediately. It was an emotional roller coaster. On June 5 a judge ordered the Bureau of Customs to release Marcos' money, jewelry, and belongings. The family rejoiced, then a timely government appeal prevented that. The attorney general in New York announced Marcos and Imelda were being investigated for alleged violations of the RICO (Racketeering Influenced Corrupt Organizations) statute. The Philippine government followed suit by filing several civil cases in the U.S. Subpoenas began to arrive.

Marcos' legal mind told him that as a former head of state he should be immune to prosecution. But his political savvy told him it would be unwise to hang around to argue the point.

Quietly he put out the word. Find another safe haven. It was an exercise in frustration. One by one, the replies came back. Couched in diplomatese, Spain, Mexico, Singapore, Panama, Ghana all said he wasn't welcome. A few countries were more receptive but they were more interested in his money than in him or his family. There was nowhere to go.

Ver decided it was time to leave. He said goodbye and slipped away one night in June, flying out of the country on a fake passport.

On Sunday, July 6, in Manila heavily armed Marcos loyalists, led by Marcos' vice president elect Arturo Tolentino, occupied the Manila Hotel. Tolentino declared himself acting president in Marcos' absence. He had hoped that this would spark a revolt and that millions would rise up across the country and demand

Marcos' return. In Honolulu, an excited Marcos was constantly on the phone with Tolentino keeping abreast of developments. But the millions never materialized and the revolt fizzled.

Lawyers representing the Committee for Justice of Viernes and Domingo arrived in Honolulu to take Marcos' deposition. When the wrongful death lawsuit was filed, Marcos claimed diplomatic immunity as head of state. That defense no longer held. Now his lawyers had a battle on their hands. The court ordered Marcos' deposition could be taken. He spent an uncomfortable two days dodging questions about Philippine government involvement.

Marcos became a natural target for con men. They came from all over suggesting grandiose schemes costing huge sums of money for his return to the Philippines. Dulay came in August 1986 with two former CIA employees. They made a lot of promises and asked for a lot of money. Neither were delivered. Two retired Philippine colonels showed up in October. All they needed was ₱400 million. They were shunted aside but others with bigger and costlier schemes were waiting in line to replace them.

On September 30, Marcos was questioned by Philippine and American lawyers representing the Philippine government about his hidden wealth. He took the Fifth Amendment (the right against self-incrimination) 197 times. The next day Imelda followed suit, taking the Fifth 200 times. Despite having the best lawyers money could buy, it was obvious that sooner or later they would wind up in court.

In January 1987 they were subpoenaed to testify in the investigation of kickbacks paid in the sale of weapons to the Philippine military. Marcos' lawyers claimed he was too sick to travel. He agreed to produce documents in his possession without having to go before the Grand Jury. While this was going on he rented a rather large airplane.

In the pre-dawn hours of Tuesday, January 27, 1987, 500 heavily armed rebel soldiers loyal to Marcos fanned out over Metro Manila. Headed by a general and seventeen officers, they intended to take over three key military facilities and two television stations, then announce over the airways Marcos had returned. Unfortunately things didn't quite work out that way.

Of the five targets the rebels were routed at four within hours: the Channel Four television station; the Operations Center at Villamor Air Base; Sangley Point in Cavite, base of the Fifteenth Strike Wing; and Camp Aguinaldo, headquarters of the National Defense Ministry. The attack on the Channel Seven television station took a little longer to repulse. A colonel and 150 soldiers took hostages when they saw their efforts were futile but released them and surrendered two days later. Just as the siege was ending, rumors swept the country that Marcos had returned to the Philippines and landed in Ilocos Norte.

At the same time, it was reported that the mother of Marcos, *Doña* Josepha, disappeared from her hospital room at the Philippine Heart Center just before the rebel soldiers began their attacks. In Honolulu, Marcos left his home and couldn't be found for twelve hours, fueling the rumors of his return to the Philippines. Tomas "Buddy" Gomez III, then Philippine consul general in Hawaii and later President Aquino's press secretary, announced Marcos had not returned to the Philippines, he was still in Hawaii although that wasn't where he wanted to be.

Gomez explained that he and his intrepid band of "Marcos-watchers," a volunteer group of Filipinos loyal to President Aquino who kept a close watch on Marcos and Imelda, had uncovered a plan by Marcos to secretly fly back to the Philippines and land on Bugsuk Island off Palawan. He had chartered a Boeing 707 from an aviation company in Miami headed by a Lebanese arms dealer close to Adnan Khashoggi, a frequent visitor to the Marcos home in Hawaii. He once admitted that Marcos promised him 10 percent of a shipload of gold if he could find a safe port for the vessel, preferably an Arab country. Khashoggi never saw the ship or the gold. Later Marcos told him he made other arrangements.

Gomez reported Marcos' plan to the State Department. He told them the aircraft was parked at a private airfield near the Honolulu International Airport ready for takeoff. They visited Marcos and told him they knew about the 707. They advised him he could not leave the country. As usual he denied all knowledge of the incident.

Marcos had other schemes prepared, just in case. In 1986 three Filipinos in Hawaii – Francisco S. Ugale and Alfonso Adeva, businessmen, and Jiamil Dianalan, a Muslim Filipino who had served in parliament under Marcos – hatched a plan for Marcos' return. It was code-named Sheraton Project. After the failed coup in January 1987, Sheraton was given added prestige in February when Hawaiian Senator Daniel Inouye agreed to meet with Marcos after the negotiating points had been agreed upon. The meeting never took place, however. Marcos was caught attempting to implement yet another scheme.

On July 9 former Representative Stephen Solarz, chairman of the House Foreign Affairs Subcommittee on Asia and the Pacific, convened hearings in Washington, D.C. Richard Hirschfield and Robert Chastain testified that Marcos had planned to return to the Philippines in June 1987 and link up with a 10,000 man army to retake the Philippines. Their testimony was based on three and a half hours of tapes played at the subcommittee hearings. In May they had secretly recorded their conversations with Marcos using a voice-activated tape recorder hidden in a briefcase. Marcos said he would try to take President Aquino hostage, by force if necessary. "This is a go-for-broke deal," he said on the tape.

Richard Hirschfield was a Virginia attorney who claimed to have as clients Muhammad Ali and a billionaire Saudi Arabian businessman by the name of Mohamad Al Fassi, known for his penchant for painting the private parts of the nude statues that adorned the walls of his Beverly Hills mansion.

Hirschfield called Marcos in the fall of 1986 and wangled an appointment. He flew there on September 10 with his associate, Robert Chastain. They met with Marcos and attended his birthday party the next day. They cultivated this friendship and promised to help him obtain citizenship in another country. In early 1987 Marcos asked if they knew anyone that could supply him with weapons and ammunition.

Although they were not in that line of business, Chastain claimed to have contacts with arms dealers. When discussions began Marcos suggested they use code names when communicating. Marcos chose the name Charlie and Chastain chose Andrew. In one conversation, which took place on May 21, Marcos placed an order to equip his army that included tanks, Huey helicopters, armored personnel carriers, recoilless rifles, rocket launchers, machine guns, 8,000 M-16's, of which a thousand would be equipped with grenade-launchers, and three months' supply of ammunition.

When the method of payment was discussed Marcos asked for $18 million in financing. He added that he had $500 million in bank accounts in Switzerland and $14 billion in gold secretly buried in several different places in the Philippines which could be used as collateral.

When Hirschfield questioned him about the gold Marcos was somewhat vague. At first he implied he got it from the Central Bank through collusion with a former governor now deceased. He said, "It is my money but it, I borrowed it from these people who were buy, who were buying the gold . . ." This scheme of using gold bullion still in the Philippines to borrow large sums of money was also mentioned in papers confiscated from Jose Cruz-Cruzal at the Seattle-Tacoma International Airport in November 1983.

On the tapes, Marcos abruptly changed his story and claimed the gold came from World War II veterans who had belonged to his guerrilla group. Wherever it came from, throughout the taped interview Marcos was adamant about two points. He would never admit having the gold and he didn't want to sell it. "We must never lose the gold. We can lose everything but the gold," he said, and went on to add that Imelda didn't know about the gold because, "she panics." He said Bong Bong knew where it was.

Copies of the tapes were turned over to the Philippine government and the FBI. According to Hirschfield, the copies were edited to delete some remarks by Marcos, who claimed to still have influence over several high-ranking U.S. officials.

Hirschfield claimed he knew the location of about a billion dollars worth of the gold Marcos had mentioned. As a result the PCGG entered into an agreement with him on June 4, entitling him to "5 percent of the value of gold or other precious metals within ninety days of recovery." He never divulged his information about the location and no gold was ever recovered. A few years later he was sent to prison for tax fraud.

The State Department was informed about Marcos' latest fiasco. Once again they warned him about such activities. In addition, the Justice Department wrote and advised him that he must apply in writing forty-eight hours in advance for permission to leave the island of Oahu, which included Honolulu.

Aquino's cousin, Congressman Emigdio Tanjuatco, Jr., flew to Honolulu on January 21, 1988, and met with Marcos to discuss the possibility of continuing with the Sheraton Project. Marcos broke off those talks abruptly.

In February 1988, Francisco Sumulong, an uncle of Aquino, and Roquito Ablan visited Marcos. During the Marcos era he had been a congressman in Ilocos Norte and also served as vice-governor. The governor was Bong Bong. By then Marcos' plans had come apart. A Grand Jury indictment seemed almost certain and with it a high profile trial watched by the whole world.

His only chance was to work out some sort of settlement to end all the litigation in the Philippines and return home, no matter what it cost. He told Sumulong and Ablan to advise Aquino he wanted to make her an offer.

In March, Sumulong and Ablan returned to Honolulu. Marcos presented his proposal. If he and his family were allowed to go home, he would give $15 billion to the Philippine government. Five-billion dollars was to be spent for infrastructure projects in the Philippines; $5 billion would be used to reduce the nation's foreign debt; and $5 billion would be given to Aquino's family for the suffering they endured.

They delivered it to Aquino. She was receptive at first, but when the family met to discuss it they turned down the offer and instead made a counteroffer. This was relayed to Marcos but he didn't respond. Neither Sumulong nor Ablan would say what the counteroffer was. But they did say that Marcos admitted the $15 billion was still in the Philippines. Sumulong was later quoted in the newspaper as saying, "*Sayang, napakinabangan na natin sana 'yung pera*. (It was a pity. We could have used the money.)"

On April 27, Marcos and Imelda were subpoenaed to produce their fingerprints and other items. They appealed. On May

11, Marcos' mother, *Doña* Josepha, died. Marcos appealed to Aquino on humanitarian grounds and asked that he be allowed to attend her funeral. He was turned down.

On June 22 in Washington, the Center for Democracy hosted a breakfast for five Philippine legislators. Ablan and Sumulong were in attendance. They confided to Professor Allen Weinstein that Marcos would return substantial assets to the Philippines if he were allowed to go home, and asked if he would help. He agreed to assist.

Marcos wrote a letter to Weinstein dated July 11, stating he would give $5 billion to the government under the following conditions: 1) He, his family, and his delegation could return to the Philippines and Ilocos Norte; 2) He and his family would have diplomatic and political immunity; 3) The Philippine government would drop all cases presently pending against him in the Philippines and any other country; 4) He would agree not to engage in political activities; 5) He and his family would be issued Philippine passports and could travel freely inside and outside the Philippines. Whether or not this was related to the previous counter offer wasn't known.

There was a follow up letter to Weinstein dated August 5, in which Marcos stated he would prove his sincerity by immediately transferring the Swiss bank accounts under dispute to the Philippine government. Weinstein flew to Honolulu on August 7 to meet with Marcos and discuss the details of the proposal. Consul General Gomez was kept appraised of the situation throughout these discussions. He in turn advised Aquino. The press somehow got word of this development. Aquino issued a public statement that Marcos had to deliver the $5 billion first before negotiations could begin. Marcos reacted by denying he ever made the offer.

On the Hirschfield tapes, Marcos claimed to have $14 billion in gold buried in the Philippines. Then he told Sumulong he had $15 billion hidden there but didn't specifically say the *G* word. Was he bluffing? Depending on the price per ounce, $14 or $15 billion would be 900 to 1,000 metric tons. Despite the occasional telex, rumor, or badly worded contract, no one had reported seeing that much gold in the Philippines. In 1983 Dacus spoke of amounts far larger but he only saw 100 tons on one occasion and 300 to 500 tons on another.

Nandeng Pedrosa, a banker whose father was secretary of finance under President Quirino, was in Taipei in 1988 as a consultant to a Taiwanese group. While there he was asked by one of the group to help in another matter because he spoke English fluently. That is how he met Robert Kerkez.

Kerkez was in Taiwan to try and negotiate a deal involving a gold certificate for 50 metric tons of gold. He wanted five years advance interest at 10 percent a year, for a total of 50 percent of the value of the certificate, discounted by 30 percent. In that way, if the value of the gold fell below seventy percent of its present value then the gold would be sold to pay off the loan. At the time, gold was selling for about $400 an ounce, so the money involved was approximately $246 million. The Taiwanese acting as Kerkez' broker and Pedrosa put together a loan proposal. Soon afterward an agreement with one of the banks was ready to be concluded.

During the negotiations, which took place over a three week period, Pedrosa met with Kerkez four or five times. He described him: "Bob seemed to be a nice man. He wore cowboy boots and his suits were cut in the Texas style. He was well-mannered but outspoken. He said he was just a middleman, that the authority to release the funds would come from the head of a bank in San Francisco. He also said he was there to negotiate as many certificates as the banks in Taiwan could handle. 'How many do you want? Twenty? Thirty?' he said."

While this was going on, the story about Marcos' $5 billion offer came out in the newspapers. Pedrosa read about it and figured that twenty-one of Kerkez' certificates, if they existed, would be worth more than $5 billion if negotiated in this manner. He was anxious to ask Kerkez about this but he didn't show up for their morning meeting. That afternoon the Taiwanese called and said that Kerkez had pulled out of the deal and left for the States. Pedrosa never heard from him again.

Kerkez was from Las Vegas. In subsequent dealings involving gold certificates, others would meet him. Some were invited to his home in the exclusive Spanish Trails subdivision. Several pictures in his study showed him hobnobbing with a smiling President Marcos.

Later in Manila the PCGG invited a retired colonel and two foreigners for questioning. They were allegedly engaged in trading huge volumes of gold bars believed to be part of Marcos' gold hoard. Kerkez was one of the foreigners. The other was Ibrahim Dagher, already known to the PCGG as a friend of another Marcos associate, Michael de Guzman. The colonel's name was Enrique Pimentel. Pedrosa had seen it on the gold certificate Kerkez had with him in Taiwan. Pimentel had been involved in two gold contracts with Michael O'Brien in 1983.

After the Weinstein mission failed, Marcos tried another tack. Harold Ezell was the Immigration and Nationalization Service commissioner for the Western Region which included Hawaii. He had been cordial to Marcos and Imelda during their stay in Honolulu. On August 2 a group called The United Filipino Council of Hawaii honored Ezell with a dinner. The party was held at Marcos' home. He presented a plaque to Ezell in appreciation for his services to the Filipino. Unfortunately the gesture backfired. Ezell landed in hot water with his superiors when news of the party hit the newspapers.

A few weeks later Marcos' hopes were raised when a Philippine court ruled he could come to Manila for Baltazar Aquino's testimony scheduled for November. Aquino (no relation to the president) was cooperating with the PCGG and agreed to testify in one of the numerous civil suits being brought against Marcos. He was Marcos' highways commissioner and had gone to Hong Kong on at least ten occasions between March 1975 and July 1976 to collect "commissions" totalling $4,539,786.60 owed to Marcos by Japanese suppliers of the Philippine highways ministry.

Despite the damming evidence, Marcos was willing to return, perhaps to get out of the U.S. and away from his legal problems. He decided he needed some cash. What with the Philippine government meddling in his bank accounts, he was a little short. Perhaps a quarter-billion would keep him going for a while. Now who did he know that could loan him the money?

CHAPTER THIRTEEN

Umbrella

There were very few men Marcos didn't mess with. Enrique Zobel was one. Scion of the Roxas-Ayala-Zobel clan, his ancestor, Domingo Roxas, founded the family's first trading company in the Philippines in 1834. It grew into a billion-dollar empire. By the time Marcos came to power, Zobel was one of the richest men in the Philippines. He wasn't a crony and he had not made his fortune by pillaging the country. To the contrary, he was a man of enormous vision whose success came from hard work and astute business decisions.

Short, stocky, and competitive, Zobel's first love was polo. One of his polo-playing friends was the Sultan of Brunei, the tiny oil-rich nation to the south. He had rich and powerful friends all over the world. Marcos left him alone.

Zobel could have played the role of landed gentry but that wasn't his style. Chairman of the board, president, and director of dozens of corporations, his financial and managerial prowess could especially be seen in the Bank of the Philippine Islands, which he took over in the mid-seventies and built into one of the nation's largest financial institutions. He also built Ayala Corporation into a billion-dollar real estate and industrial conglomerate.

By the early eighties Marcos and his cronies had effectively destroyed the economy. Zobel agonized over what was happening to the country. He helped organize the Makati Business Club as a forum to critique and comment on government economic policies but soon he realized nobody was listening. In 1985 he told the *New York Times*, "If you had money to invest in Southeast Asia, the Philippines is the last place I would tell you to put it now." He was one of the few that could say something like that and not risk the ire of Marcos.

Upset at Marcos' heavy-handed tactics, Zobel resigned from both Ayala Corporation and the bank and began concentrating his efforts on businesses outside the Philippines through another of his companies, Ayala International. Through all this, he maintained a grudging respect for Marcos, hoping he would come to his senses and turn the country around. He supported Marcos in the 1986 snap election but even powerful friends couldn't help that time.

In October 1988, Marcos asked Doctor Lourdes Pascual, a family friend, to prepare a promissory note and deliver it to Zobel in Manila. The note was prepared but its delivery was delayed by more pressing matters.

On October 21 the Grand Jury in New York handed down an indictment against Marcos, Imelda, Adnan Khashoggi, and eight others. It set off a flurry of legal histrionics that took up most of Marcos' time. It also prevented him from leaving the U.S. He couldn't return to the Philippines for Baltazar Aquino's testimony.

Marcos and Imelda were ordered to report to the FBI in Honolulu on November 18 for fingerprinting, palm printing, and to produce a sample of their handwriting and a recording of their voices. They had been subpoenaed the previous May but they appealed, claiming they were entitled to their Philippine constitutional rights. This motion was denied and they were ordered to comply by August 8. They then claimed head of state immunity. This motion was also denied and they were ordered to comply by August 18. An appeal was filed. The Court of Appeals denied the claim on October 19. The Court also held that the Grand Jury had the authority to order the Marcoses to sign consent directives, authorizing the foreign banks to turn over their financial records. The case was elevated to the Supreme Court. They lost and were ordered to report to the FBI.

Pascual finally flew into Manila in late November and met

with Zobel. She asked if he could loan Marcos $250 million, and showed him the note. It had been antedated to October 17, before the indictment was handed down, to protect Zobel. Signed by Marcos, it stated, "In consideration of this loan I promise to deliver three-million ounces of gold within three years after I return to the Philippines." That was more than 85 metric tons, worth about $1.3 billion, not a bad return. Zobel checked his calendar and told Pascual he would meet Marcos in December.

Marcos encountered more setbacks before Zobel arrived. On November 29 the court-appointed doctor announced Marcos was well enough to travel to New York for his arraignment. On December 1 the Court of Appeals upheld the decision to freeze his assets worldwide. A few days later his own doctors issued a report that described him as chronically ill with multiple abnormalities of the kidney and heart.

On December 8, Zobel met Marcos for dinner. Marcos hardly ate and looked very tired and weak. He asked for the promissory note that Pascual had delivered. Zobel had to go back to his residence ten minutes away and retrieve it.

On returning, he told Marcos he didn't have $250 million available, but he asked how the loan would be repaid if he could arrange it. Marcos asked his nurse, Teresita Gallego, to fetch a folder. Zobel leafed through it. It was about an inch and a half thick and full of deposit certificates for gold stored in various banks all over the world – Switzerland, Monaco, the Vatican, the Bahamas, and other places. He mentally calculated that, at $400 an ounce, the price of gold at the time, the value was approximately $35 billion.

Some of the certificates were dated in the forties after World War II. Marcos explained that he began accumulating gold toward the end of the war. He found some treasure and also bought gold bars from soldiers who found them in the debris of Yamashita's retreating convoy. He reminted the bars in Hong Kong in 1946 and accumulated more through various treasure hunts. The reason he kept it secret until now, Marcos said, was other countries might have a legal claim to it until 1985 because of the statute of limitations.

To most people that knew Marcos, this story sounded a bit

odd. He came from a poor family and he made his first million as a first-term congressman in 1949 and 1950 selling import licenses. He bought a Cadillac to celebrate his new status. Before then, there was no outward indication of any wealth. When he courted Imelda in 1954, he brought her to a bank vault and showed her stacks of hundred-dollar bills but no gold bars. He didn't even open his first bank account abroad until 1967.

Over dinner, Marcos told Zobel he wanted to help the Filipino people. Zobel suggested he set up a foundation. Marcos agreed and asked him to head it. Zobel demurred and suggested instead that the Vatican or its representative head it.

Marcos had voiced his dislike of the church many times, accusing priests and nuns of being communist, but now he readily agreed with Zobel. He said the Roman Catholic church would receive 10 percent of the gold for use in its foreign missions; 10 percent would be retained by his family; 79 percent would go to the foundation set up for the benefit of the Filipino people; 1 percent would go to pay his debts and the balance would go to his loyal staff and his doctors and nurses.

According to Zobel, Marcos rattled off the percentages without hesitation, as if he had planned the whole thing in advance. He may have. Zobel was the god-father of Greg Araneta, who married Marcos' daughter, Irene, in June 1983. Since the early eighties, when the economy went into a tailspin, he had pressured Araneta to convince Marcos to return the treasure and help the country. Zobel knew Marcos had been flying gold out of the country since 1972. As a pilot in the air force reserve, qualified in fixed wing and rotary, he had a lot of friends that flew. Some of the Ilocano (Marcos preferred to trust military from his own province of Ilocos Norte) pilots had talked about flying C-130 aircraft loaded with gold to Zurich.

Marcos said that in future communications he would use the code name Gandhi, and asked that they meet again after he had discussed the plan with his lawyers. He suggested December 23 or 24 but Zobel said he couldn't make it until after Christmas.

Zobel left around eleven-thirty that evening. A few hours later Marcos was taken to St. Francis Hospital complaining of chest pains. On December 18 he was allowed to leave and spend Christmas at home. On the twenty-eighth he was rushed back to the hospital with a high fever. The December meeting was called off. He went home again on January 4, 1989.

From Honolulu, Zobel went to San Francisco and then Europe. He returned to Manila on January 3, in time to celebrate his birthday on the seventh. On January 12, he invited Pedro Cojuangco, President Aquino's brother, and Mrs. Dely Castillejo, Cojuangco's sister-in-law, to his residence. He told them about Marcos' desire to set up a foundation and asked that Cojuangco tell President Aquino.

Marcos was taken back to the hospital on January 15. He fell into a coma four days later. From then on he would only have brief moments of consciousness. On January 16 in Manila, Zobel had breakfast with Vice President Laurel at Laurel's residence and told him about the proposed agreement. To try and convince Aquino that Marcos was only coming home to die, they devised a plan to send two doctors to Hawaii to independently verify his state of health. Laurel said he would ask Aquino to approve it. Later that evening he called Zobel to say it was okay.

Zobel flew into Hawaii on January 18. The next day he heard that one of Marcos' lungs collapsed but doctors were able to inflate it. Around midnight, Laurel called and said the two doctors had been stopped at the Manila airport and prevented from departing by Aquino's secretary of health.

Marcos was too sick to see Zobel. On January 22 he met with Imelda instead and told her about Marcos' wishes for a foundation. The next day he met with Pascual, his lawyer, and one of Marcos' assistants to discuss how the trust agreement should be drawn up. They decided the Papal Nuncio in Manila, Bruno Torpigliani, would serve as principal trustee. The other trustees would be Father Rogelio Alarcon, Rector of Letran College, Pascual, and Zobel. Zobel agreed to serve on the condition that no compensation would be paid to the trustees for their work.

Before leaving, Zobel contacted John Fulks, head of the FBI in Hawaii. He wanted it known that all his dealings with Marcos and the Philippine government were above-board, and asked that the FBI make sure no one saw him and Marcos together when they met. A few days before, a television reporter had come to his house and asked if he were in town to negotiate a deal with Marcos. He denied it, but worried that the plan might be jeopardized if it were made public. Fulks said he would take care of it.

Zobel then called a friend, Frank Yturria, in Washington and asked him to brief Secretary of State James Baker on the situation.

A lot of very important people knew what Zobel was doing. They were not that surprised. Long before meeting with Marcos, he had taken an interest in finding a way to pay off the foreign debt of the Philippines and had discussed the matter with friends in high places. Being a banker himself with worldwide connections, he occasionally met with some of the country's creditors. When the talk came around to that subject Zobel would ask, "How much discount would you give if I could pay off all the debt?" They replied that they would accept forty-eight cents on the dollar. That meant the government only had to repay about $13 billion instead of more than $27 billion.

Zobel flew to San Francisco on January 27 and met with Danding Cojuangco, Aquino's first cousin, Eduardo Romualdez, an uncle of Imelda, Greg Araneta, and two of Imelda's lawyers, John Bartko of San Francisco and Richard Hibey of New York. After the plan was explained to them, Cojuangco, Romualdez, and Araneta expressed their own desires to serve as trustees. Zobel said the final decision would have to come from Marcos.

He returned to Honolulu on the twenty-ninth and went to the hospital at noon but was still unable to see Marcos. That evening he met with Imelda and Bong Bong at the hospital, and showed them a draft of the trust agreement. Bong Bong remarked, "See, mother, father never told us these things."

Zobel didn't know what Bong Bong meant by that statement. It could have meant he was unaware of Marcos' gold hoard, which was unlikely, or that he was unaware of the foundation that Marcos wanted to set up. That Imelda had known for a week and not told her son was just another curiosity in a family known for its intrigues.

The next afternoon Zobel went back to the hospital. Marcos

opened his eyes once and seemed to smile at him, but he went back to sleep. No documents were signed.

The next day Zobel gave Imelda and Bong Bong four copies of the trust agreement. Bong Bong agreed to get his father to sign them when he was able. Zobel departed Honolulu on February 1. When he arrived in Manila he heard that Marcos had undergone a tracheotomy. On February 3 he met with the Papal Nuncio and Alarcon and gave them a copy of the trust agreement.

Marcos' medical condition was rapidly deteriorating. In April the court-appointed doctor reversed his decision and announced that Marcos was medically unfit for travel to New York. In June the doctors removed the kidney that had been transplanted in 1984. From there it was all downhill. Marcos turned seventy-two on September 11. He died seventeen days later shortly after midnight. The trust agreement was never signed.

In deference to Marcos' death, Zobel did not bother the family in mourning. He heard from Pascual that Bong Bong retrieved the folder containing the gold deposit certificates from Marcos' nurse. Later Imelda showed some gold certificates of the same description – yellowed with age and dated 1946 to 1948 – to journalists on two separate occasions.

Zobel believed the certificates were real and quietly pursued the business Marcos never finished. He hoped Imelda and Bong Bong would follow through with Marcos' plans and set up the foundation.

In November 1989 he attended the Volvo Golf Tournament in Spain with Rainer E. Gut, chairman of the board of Credit Suisse. He asked Gut if the Swiss banks would release the gold if the foundation presented two letters of authority – one signed by President Aquino and one signed by the Marcos heirs. Gut replied it could be done. This heartened Zobel. He was a busy man with a vast business and financial empire to oversee. Still, he took the time and did everything he could to see this project through to its fruition. He could not know of the terrible tragedy he would soon face.

As the PCGG went about the task of attempting to locate and recover the hidden wealth of Marcos, they waded through mountains of documents and interviewed hundreds of people. Marcos was suspected of having gold deposited in banks in the U.S, Hong Kong, Singapore, Switzerland, and several other European countries but nothing could be traced to him because the accounts were set up differently.

There was mention of an organization known as Umbrella, which he had set up along the line of communist cells. Each gold account was controlled by a group of trustees, usually three. Each group was unknown to the other. To access an account required approval of all trustees to that account.

Marcos and Bong Bong were the only two people who knew the entire Umbrella structure. After Marcos died, Bong Bong told Imelda. They decided to dismantle the organization but there was a problem. Some people in these groups were loyal to Marcos, not Imelda or Bong Bong, and were out to protect their own interests. The PCGG was aware of this. Imelda had told them as much. They knew that, even when they had the account number, the vault number, and the serial numbers of the bars, the bank would deny the gold's existence to protect its clients.

Marcos had set it up well. His brilliant legal mind combined with the financial skills of the Swiss could make any gold in his possession seemingly disappear.

He wasn't so lucky in other areas. Before he died, an old nemesis returned to haunt him.

One of the first to get a close look at the 2,068 pages impounded by the Bureau of Customs in Honolulu in February 1986 was Bonifacio "Boni" Gillego. In 1982, he was the first to write about and expose the Marcos war medals as fake. A furious Marcos ordered his arrest but he managed to escape to the U.S.

In the States he worked as a hotel clerk to support his family. He kept up the fight by joining the Movement for Free Philippines (M.F.P.), a U.S. group devoted to peaceful lobbying against the corruption and human rights abuses of the Marcos regime. Marcos' agents in the States were aware of the group and continued to hound him and other members.

After Marcos was overthrown, Gillego returned to the Philippines. Aquino asked him to serve as executive director of the PCGG to investigate Marcos' illegal accumulation of wealth. Later he would be elected to congress, but it was while working in the PCGG that he made his discovery.

It seemed only fitting that someone persecuted by Marcos would be the one to find proof that the murders of Gene Viernes and Silme Domingo could be traced all the way to the palace and expose Marcos' regime as cold-blooded killers. He also found something else – the U.S. government was a willing accomplice.

CHAPTER FOURTEEN

Orders from the Palace

It was four-thirty, Monday afternoon in Seattle, Washington. Thane Holm, eighteen, was a cook at Swannie's Restaurant & Bar on Pioneer Square. The weather was pleasant – in the sixties – so he decided to take his break outside. That's when he noticed the drunk across the street crawling on his hands and knees. At least he thought he was a drunk. Then he saw the blood and the man waving his arms and yelling, "Can't you see me? Help me."

Within minutes paramedics and police were on the scene. The wounded man, Silme Domingo, had been shot four times in the chest and stomach. He was able to identify his assailants before the ambulance took him away.

Domingo was a member of Cannery Workers Local 37. Its headquarters was at 213 S. Main Street, the old two-story building where the shooting occurred. Inside was another man, Gene Viernes. Shot in the chest, he had died instantly. Domingo died the next afternoon. Both were twenty-nine.

At the onset of martial law, Marcos wanted to attract foreign firms to the Philippines. He guaranteed low wages and a compliant work force. He did this by controlling all unions through the Trade Union Congress of the Philippines (T.U.C.P.). Strikes were not allowed and wage levels were kept low so exports would earn top dollar. Inflation was rampant. People could not live on the wages they earned. Something had to be done.

Another union was secretly formed. More than a million strong, its first rally was held on May 1, 1980, and thus its name – the Kilosang Mayo Uno (K.M.U.), or May 1st movement.

Most of the unions announced they were quitting the T.U.C.P. to join the K.M.U., which demanded the right to strike, an increase in the minimum wage, and the nationalization of all industries controlled by foreigners. Their thinking was that Marcos had nationalized most local industries, why not the foreign corporations. He brutally suppressed the movement.

In the U.S. in the spring of 1981, Viernes and Domingo belonged to Local 37 of the Alaska Cannery Workers Union, a largely Filipino labor organization headquartered in Seattle. Workers were sent by the union to the canneries in Alaska during the salmon season.

Domingo won election to the important post of secretary-treasurer and Viernes to the position of dispatcher, a tough job which traditionally was the focus of bribe attempts.

They immediately came into contact with Local 37's brusque autocratic president, Constantine "Tony" Baruso, an Ilocano and friend of Marcos. Baruso had not worked in an Alaskan cannery since 1956, and held a full-time job as a machinist at the Boeing Company. A popular figure in the Filipino community, he was often the emcee at Philippine consular events.

After his election, Viernes travelled to the Philippines in March and April 1981 and met with the K.M.U. Ver's intelligence apparatus reported this to Marcos.

On his return to the U.S., Viernes, along with Domingo, attended the International Longshoreman's and Warehouseman's Union (I.L.W.U.) convention in Hawaii. The Alaska Cannery Workers Union was affiliated with the I.L.W.U. They criticized the Marcos administration for alleged brutalities against labor organizations and engineered the passage of a hotly contested resolution critical of the treatment of Filipino workers. The I.L.W.U. authorized an investigative team to look into labor conditions in the Philippines. Baruso also attended the I.L.W.U. convention and fought against the resolution.

On June 1, Viernes and Domingo were gunned down. Domingo named his killers before he died. Jimmy Ramil, twenty-eight, and Pompeyo Guloy, Jr., twenty-two, were arrested. They were members of the Tulisan Gang, a Filipino group. The gang's leader, Tony Dictado, was also arrested. All were charged with first-degree murder.

Testimony during the trial showed that Viernes and Domingo had campaigned to get rid of the gambling activities at the canneries and to change the dispatching system from one of favoritism to seniority. The Tulisan Gang controlled the gambling operations in the canneries. In exchange for "protection," the gang took a cut of the proceeds. The gang was also against changing the dispatching system because they didn't have seniority.

The suspects admitted they were hired by some people but refused to identify them for fear of retaliation on their families in the Philippines. The ownership of the murder weapon – a .45 Mac-10 semi-automatic sub-machine gun – was traced to Baruso but there wasn't enough evidence to charge him.

Also implicated but never charged was Dr. Leonilo Malabed. A boyhood friend of Marcos, he was known in Philippine circles as the "eyes and ears" of Marcos.

Dictado, Ramil, and Guloy were convicted and sentenced to life imprisonment in 1982. But for the friends and families of Viernes and Domingo that wasn't enough. They knew the Marcos regime was behind the murders. The Committee for Justice of Viernes and Domingo was formed. A $30 million wrongful death lawsuit was filed against the Philippine government. There was a motion to include Marcos but he claimed diplomatic immunity as head of state.

The Philippine government tried to claim sovereign immunity but the claim was dismissed. In 1985 the Ninth Circuit Court reaffirmed its decision, stating that sovereign immunity does not prevent foreign governments nor their officials from being brought to court for illegal acts, especially when American citizens were killed.

Throughout this dramatic fight for justice the *Philippine News* in the U.S. kept up a relentless, seemingly futile, battle against the Marcos regime. Through Alex Esclamado, its publisher, the Committee for Justice was given a public forum to keep its case before the public. It was David versus Goliath for so long until Marcos was overthrown.

In February 1986 documents in Marcos' possession were seized by customs in Honolulu. One, marked "Strictly Confidential," was the Mabuhay Corporation, Statement of Expenses as of February 15, 1982. Malabed was president of the San Francisco based corporation.

It listed expenses such as legal fees, finder's fee, and appraiser's fee, all referring to Malabed's attempt to purchase KJAZ radio station in 1978. Malabed's attorney told a television reporter in June 1986 that Malabed discussed this with Marcos, and that it was to be used for pro-Philippine broadcasts. Malabed also owned the pro-Marcos Filipino-American newspaper, *Bataan News*. He said the Mabuhay Corporation was dissolved in 1982.

The document listed "Political Contributions (cleared through PSC-CG)," which was the Presidential Security Command - Commanding General. These were for various local, state, and national elections totalling $175,200, including $50,000 to "Democrat (Carter)," $50,000 to "Republican (Reagan)," and $1,500 to "Carter-Mondale Committee." The mention of "PSC-CG" implied that Ver was behind the contributions. Foreign donations were a violation of federal election laws.

Further down, there was also $19,500 for "special missions" made by Malabed, including two trips to Honolulu – one in April 1980 when Marcos was there to address the ANPA, and another in September 1981 on the way to the Economic Summit in Cancun, Mexico, three months after the murders.

Then it got interesting. The next item was "Advances to C.G. (Special Security Projects)." There were fifteen items, totalling $506,683.68. Item twelve was dated "5-17-81" for $15,000. Item fifteen stated "9-25-81 (Cancun, Mexico) $20,000."

A note at the bottom of the document, in Malabed's handwriting, stated: "I acknowledge having received $1m from PNB for intelligence purposes minus $762,478.52 withdrawn by the AFP by authority of Chief of Staff." PNB was the Philippine National Bank. Another document seized from Marcos was a memorandum signed by Placido Mapa, president of PNB. It indicated more than $9 million would be placed in the "Philippine intelligence fund" out of "PNB profits."

Subpoenaed travel records revealed Baruso purchased a plane ticket and flew to San Francisco on May 16, one day after returning to Seattle from the I.L.W.U. convention. He stayed in the Sutter Hotel near the Philippine consulate. The next day $15,000 was paid by Mabuhay Corporation for a "special security project." Baruso returned to Seattle the same day. The convicted murderers admitted during their trial they were paid $5,000 for the job. The murders occurred two weeks later.

In his 1983 deposition in the civil suit, Baruso answered "I can't remember," to all questions about that trip. He took the Fifth Amendment to all questions about the murders.

Malabed's depositions were taken on May 15 and October 24, 1986. He denied knowing Baruso.

Lawyers for the Committee for Justice flew to Honolulu in July 1986 to take Marcos' deposition. He refused to answer most questions but he admitted that four Philippine government agencies – National Intelligence Security Authority (NISA), Intelligence Section of the Armed Forces of the Philippines, the Presidential Security Command, and the National Bureau of Investigation – collected information on anti-Marcos organizations in the U.S. through the use of military attaches in the Philippine embassy and their consulates.

Paciano F. Dizon, assistant manager of Philippine National Bank, was deposed and produced several documents. Among them was a deposit slip which showed the Mabuhay Corporation opened a bank account at the Philippine Bank of California on July 7, 1977 (7/7/77). Malabed obviously knew about his friend's propensity for the number 7.

The deposition of Marcos resumed on March 4 and 5, 1987. Although Marcos asserted the Fifth Amendment when asked about the payment of $15,000, a lawyer for the plaintiffs pointed out that, unlike a criminal case, the assertion of the Fifth Amendment may be used in a civil case as evidence against the party asserting it.

After seven years of legal sparring, the trial finally began on Monday, November 20, 1989. The Trial Lawyers for Public Justice (T.L.P.) announced that Attorney Richard Ben-Veniste, former chief of Watergate Special Prosecution Force, would join the plaintiffs as lead council. "The U.S. government has been the major block in getting justice for the murders . . . Unlike in the New York indictment where the U.S. has cooperated in every way to prosecute the Marcoses for racketeering, the U.S. has been our main obstacle and adversary . . . by stonewalling every effort . . . to obtain . . . evidence."

Because Marcos had died, his estate was sued. The plaintiffs charged they could not only link the former Marcos regime to the slayings, but implicate the U.S. as well. They claimed that Marcos used Philippine intelligence operatives to monitor anti-Marcos activities in the U.S. and that U.S. intelligence agents aided Marcos by supplying his government with information about Philippine dissidents in the U.S. Eventually the U.S. government was dropped as a defendant but the plaintiffs still intended to prove U.S. involvement in the killings.

Also named as defendants were Malabed and Baruso. The plaintiffs alleged Malabed was used as a conduit through which Philippine government funds were funnelled to pay agents that murdered the union officials and Baruso acted as the middleman between Marcos and the killers.

When testifying, Baruso took the Fifth Amendment seventy-five times and at other times gave inconsistent and conflicting explanations. Malabed denied knowing Baruso or ever meeting him. It was common knowledge within the Filipino community, particularly within the circle of the *Caballeros de Dimas Alang*, a Filipino fraternity, that Malabed and Baruso not only knew each other, they were friends and close associates of pro-Marcos leaders.

Star witness for the plaintiffs, Congressman Boni Gillego, testified in the third week of the trial. He had been a career military intelligence officer and worked at one time with the CIA on an operation in Burma in the late fifties. He discovered the documents that were key to this trial.

Evidence was presented that the Marcos regime established a secret intelligence slush fund operated by Ver and Malabed. The purpose of the fund was to pay for "special security projects," which were intelligence operations against the anti-Marcos movement in the U.S. The murders of Viernes and Domingo was one such project.

Marcos' and Imelda's testimony had been videotaped – Marcos in 1986 and 1987 before he became seriously ill, and Imelda in July 1989. The jury looked perplexed when both Marcos and Imelda rambled on about the number 7.

In her testimony, Imelda stated she greeted many opposition leaders in her hotel suite when she was in New York and that there was a party-like atmosphere. This contradicted earlier testimony by opposition leaders Steve Psinakis and Ken Kashiwahara, Ninoy's brother in law. They said she basically told them that if they caused trouble for Marcos, they would receive trouble in kind.

Using the Freedom of Information Act, lawyers obtained 400 pages of documents from U.S. intelligence agencies related to U.S.-Philippine intelligence dealings. They showed the CIA, FBI, and U.S. government officials had knowledge of Ver's intelligence activities in the U.S.

In December 1989 the jury found the Marcos estate liable for $15 million. "Killing people was a foreseeable result of the network," said plaintiff lawyer Jeff Robinson. Damages amounting to $12,794,000 were awarded to the two children of Domingo – $10 million for the loss of their parent and $2,354,000 to the survivors of the childless Viernes. Imelda's lawyers screamed about miscarriage of justice and promised an appeal, but thirteen months later, in a surprise move, Imelda signed a settlement agreement and paid surviving family members $2 million.

On January 12, 1990, Malabed and Baruso were also found liable in a conspiracy to murder Viernes and Domingo, and ordered to pay $8,396,800 to their survivors. The award could be extracted from the defendant who had the funds. Baruso had no funds, so that left Malabed. At first he tried to elude payment by transferring his real estate properties, bank accounts, shares of stock, notes receivable, and household furnishings and appliances to his wife, but eventually he agreed to settle for $1 million.

In September, Tony Baruso was arrested again, this time for two counts of aggravated first degree murder. President Aquino's foreign affairs secretary, Raul Manglapus, testified at the trial. Manglapus was head of Movement for Free Philippines (M.F.P.) in the U.S. during the Marcos era. He said that military agents were posted in Philippine diplomatic and consular offices around the nation to intimidate opponents of the Marcos regime. The agents discouraged Filipinos from joining the M.F.P. by warning that their families back home might be affected.

In 1978 Manglapus found out that Ver had sent a Filipino national, George Torre, to kill him. Manglapus used his own network to locate Torre and confront him in Chicago. Torre admitted he was sent by Ver. In return a murder charge against him in the Philippines would be dropped.

A pattern of intimidation by the Marcos regime was confirmed by Steve Psinakis. Early one morning in the seventies, he was driving his car in San Francisco. Another car pulled up beside him and a man pointed a gun at his head, then drove off. In 1981 he wrote a book, *Two Terrorists Meet*, about the tactics used by Marcos and about a meeting he had with Imelda in her Waldorf Astoria Hotel suite.

Gillego testified again. Commenting on the expenditures for "special security projects," he said they "were used, in part, to counter the influence of anti-Marcos opposition in the United States, and to monitor and operate against them and for other propaganda and political purposes."

He said Marcos had agents in the U.S. threatening people and the U.S. government knew about it. Placement of military operatives in diplomatic offices other than the country's embassy was a violation of U.S. law, but this was tolerated by the American government because of its then prevailing policy of support for Marcos.

Fidel Ramos, secretary of defense under Aquino, released to Gillego a partial list of military officers detailed in the U.S. between 1972 and 1986. Excluding the embassy, forty-two military officers were assigned to various consulates around the U.S. Eighteen of these agents came from the PSC and NISA, both under Ver.

A witness testified he saw Baruso meeting with Tony Dictado, the gang leader, two days before the murders. Baruso's bank records showed cash deposits between June and November 1981 in amounts between $200 and $1,000. They totalled almost $10,000. Baruso also made a trip to Los Angeles in August 1981, just prior to the start of the murderers' trial. The Mabuhay Corporation document showed that in the same month, another $15,000 was expended for "special security projects" just prior to the start of that trial.

In March 1990, Baruso was found guilty of plotting the murder of Gene Viernes, but acquitted in the slaying of Domingo. He was sentenced to life imprisonment without parole.

Another gold deal surfaced. On Tuesday evening, March 27, 1990, Geoffrey Greenlees, a British national living in the Philippines, appeared before the PCGG for questioning. They wanted to know about a sale involving 2,000 metric tons of gold in Munich. Greenlees had just returned from Munich. He said he was an attorney and had gone to Munich for a client on a legal matter, nothing more.

The PCGG knew there was more. Their information came from Bienvenido Tan, Philippine Ambassador to Germany. A Dr. Seinfeld of the U.S. State Department in Munich had received the information from an Arab, Achmed Uda, who was in jail in Israel for swindling. But Uda also had a reputation as a reliable gold expert and was in the loop when it came to large gold transactions. This one, for 2,000 metric tons, was considered large and was being arranged by the Hongkong Shanghai Bank in Munich. Seinfeld informed Munger, Tolles and Olsen, the law firm in Los Angeles which handled PCGG matters, and also informed Ambassador Tan. In the ensuing investigation, Greenlees' name surfaced. The PCGG had a subpoena waiting when he landed.

When he refused to cooperate, the PCGG informed him a hold order had been issued – he could not leave the country. That was enough to change his mind. He admitted he was arranging a purchase of gold and produced a three-page Memorandum, which called for a Preliminary Purchase Agreement involving not 2,000 metric tons but "1000 M/T rolling over up to 190000 M/T (AU)."

The Memorandum also noted the weight – "12.5 kg. per bar (24K);" the purity – "99.5% or better;" and the hallmark and assay – "J & M [Johnson & Matthey] or any int'l gld member acceptable to Buyers." The price would be based on LME (London Metal Exchange) second fixing in the afternoon one day prior to delivery. There would be a 2.5 percent discount to the buyer. A commission of .625 percent would be paid to buyer's and seller's agents. It was dated February 1990 and signed by Greenlees for the buyer and Victor G. Santos for the seller. Greenlees also produced a letter from Credit Lyonnais Rouse Limited, dated August 17, 1989, certifying his credentials as an agent.

He said the deal was initiated in Manila when a lady, Margaret Tucker, introduced him to a Filipino attorney, Victor Santos, who represented the sellers. The name Margaret Tucker grabbed their full attention. That was the alias used in Europe by Edna Camcam, Ver's girlfriend. At current prices that amount of gold would have been worth approximately $25 billion. That was the same amount Dacus had mentioned in 1983.

Greenlees contacted a consortium of buyers led by Credit Lyonnais Bank and the deal was arranged. Tucker witnessed the signing of the Memorandum. The first sale would be for 5 to 10 metric tons. It would take place in Singapore, not Munich, said Greenlees.

The PCGG allowed him to leave the Philippines and go to Singapore a few days later. They hoped Greenlees could inspect the gold bars to see if they had the Central Bank hallmark, and also obtain the code, the account number, and confirm the names of the trustees.

Badgered by the media, while Greenlees was in Singapore the PCGG released partial names of the three trustees. One was a Marcos relative from Ilocos Norte with the middle name Edralin; another was a certain Candelaria from Paombong, Bulacan; and the third was a certain Maria from Ilocos Norte.

Candelaria V. Santiago's name had appeared on an agreement to sell gold five years before in Luxembourg – involving $800 billion if it were real. And everybody in gold circles in the Philippines knew who Maria was. Better known as Mama Mary, her real name was Maria Gosilitar. A close – some said intimate – friend of Marcos since she was a teenager, Maria was now in her fifties. Imelda called her the "Midnight Lady" for her propensity to visit Marcos at unusual hours. The third lady with the middle name Edralin would surface again later.

Greenlees returned after six weeks and said the other party failed to show up. Almost every other day brought a new announcement. First the sale was called off because Santos no longer wanted to deal with Greenlees. Then the deal was back on. Then off again. The fervor died down. Greenlees left the Philippines. They never tracked down the gold.

Three months after being found liable in the Viernes-Domingo lawsuit, Imelda had to turn her attention to another trial, one that could put her behind bars and take away her frivolous lifestyle for a long, long time.

CHAPTER FIFTEEN

Not Guilty

In March 1990, Imelda was charged in U.S. District Court in New York with taking part in a $345 million racketeering conspiracy. The indictment stated more than $100 million was stolen from the Philippine treasury and brought into the U.S. for purchase of an art collection, jewelry, and real estate in New York. In addition, two American banks and an insurance company were defrauded of $165 million.

Marcos, now dead, was no longer part of the indictment. Only Imelda and Khashoggi were seated at the defense table. One defendant, the California Overseas Bank, had already pleaded guilty to wire fraud. Another defendant, Rodolfo Arambulo, former president of that bank, had pleaded guilty to a charge of racketeering. The others – Glecy and Bienvenido Tantoco and their son, Bienvenido, Jr.; Roberto S. Benedicto; Karl Bock Peterson; and Jaime Alberto Arias – stayed out of the U.S. to avoid prosecution.

Imelda had supporters in the gallery but her primary cheerleaders, the Blue Ladies, were conspicuously absent.

During the trial, the testimony flowed in day after day, showing how Marcos used his dictatorial powers in ordering that money be taken from this institution or that bank. There was plenty of proof Marcos accepted kickbacks and bribes. Not true, said the defense. His commissions from such deals were legal. During his dictatorship he signed Presidential Decree 579, which legalized his right to receive two-and-a-half percent from corporate deals. That was interesting but no one ever heard of that decree, nor had they heard of his accepting a measly two-and-a-half percent.

At first Imelda's defense was that Marcos' wealth came from finding the Yamashita treasure. She asked her lawyers to fly to Manila to obtain the deposition of Orlando Dulay, who was in prison. Dulay claimed he could prove Marcos recovered a treasure. That may have been true but it had nothing to do with Marcos looting his own treasury.

So she claimed that vice president George Bush suggested Marcos invest the so-called Communist Takeover Fund in the States instead of keeping it in the Philippines. Nobody ever heard of such a fund before, and even if it were real that didn't justify the bank accounts hidden beneath all those foundations.

The next tack was more plausible if not any more believable. Investments were made by Marcos during his presidency but he made them on behalf of the country, not merely for his and Imelda's benefit, the defense claimed. But there just wasn't any concrete proof that those investments would inure to the country.

Things didn't seem to go well for Imelda. Like her excuses for having so many pairs of shoes, which she changed weekly – the excuses, not the shoes – her excuses for having so much hidden wealth didn't fly. No matter what she said or did, it seemed to reverberate against her. She tried to play the role of the destitute widow. "I am actually on the welfare of family and friends right now," she said.

The prosecution painted a different picture. Imelda not only wasn't destitute, she had a voracious appetite for spending. Worse, most of her purchases were bought on impulse then set aside when something more interesting caught her eye. Morton Bernstein, who had managed the art and antique collection of Leslie R. Samuels, testified. He was brought by the FBI to the home of Irene Marcos Araneta to identify the objects. Bernstein found them in horrible condition. Precious seventeenth and eighteenth century statues, mirrors, and furniture lay in disarray in a barn. Mirrors were cracked, tables damaged, and some statues had fingers broken off. "It's heartbreaking," said Bernstein. He blamed Imelda personally for the condition of the collection.

In the end, it didn't make any difference. Marcos had obviously raped and pillaged the country, but he was dead and couldn't be prosecuted. Imelda was alive, but spending wasn't a crime. The prosecution failed to connect Imelda to Marcos' misdeeds – a huge blunder.

On her sixty-first birthday, July 2, the jury foreman announced "Not guilty." Khashoggi was also found not guilty of mail fraud and obstruction of justice. Imelda's friends in the court room tried to muffle their squeals of delight. Imelda hugged Gerald Spence, her lawyer. Checking the time, she hurried to St. Patrick's Cathedral on Fifth Avenue. There she crawled on her knees down the center aisle to the altar to give thanks while photographers recorded the event for the six o'clock news.

The following November at New Bilibid Prison in Manila, Dulay called Attorney David Castro. Aquino had appointed Castro a PCGG commissioner in October 1988. He was formerly vice-president of the Philippine Bar Association and member of the Bishops' and Businessmen's Conference (a group of business and church leaders who met to discuss issues of national concern). After serving as a commissioner for two years, he was appointed chairman in 1990.

Castro already knew Dulay. He had been his lawyer on another case in the late seventies. After receiving the message, he called Solicitor General Francisco Chavez. The following afternoon they visited Dulay in prison.

Dulay was an enforcer, one of Marcos' favorites. As a reward for his services, he was appointed governor of Aurora province. On February 6, 1986, the day before the presidential election, Dulay and his henchmen grabbed Francisco Laurella, Fernando Pastor, and his son Fernando, Jr., and forced them into a van. The three were supporters of Aquino. Their bodies were found a few days later.

The autopsies revealed Fernando Pastor and his son had their genitals in their stomachs. They had been forced to eat them after they were cut off. Their bodies bore other signs of mutilation and torture while they were still alive.

Aquino won. Witnesses came forward. Dulay was arrested

but he escaped while in detention. Caught in the States a year later, he was sent back to the Philippines for trial. He ran for congress while on bail. In 1987 his luck ran out. He was found guilty of murder and sentenced to life imprisonment.

Dulay told Castro and Chavez that Marcos found the treasure and had already dug up half of it, worth about $40 billion, and shipped it out of the country. Dulay claimed to be one of three people who knew where the other half was buried. He wouldn't name the other two. He claimed that he helped in the recovery of the site at Teresa, Rizal – the site Leber Group had worked on – but wouldn't talk about other sites. He agreed to lead them to a reburial site but first hc had to go to Japan to see someone. He was told before they would even consider that, he had to produce at least one gold bar to prove himself. He couldn't so he stayed in prison.

On December 21, 1990, the Swiss Federal Tribunal (the equivalent of the U.S. Supreme Court) affirmed the sequestration request of the PCGG. All bank accounts that could be identified as belonging to Marcos or Imelda remained frozen. With accumulated interest, the amount now totalled $356 million.

With Imelda's ongoing legal problems, Zobel had not bothered her with the plans to set up the foundation. In January 1991 he had lunch with Cardinal Sin and four Jesuit priests and told them about the foundation Marcos had planned to set up.

Tragedy struck in May. Zobel was thrown from his horse while playing polo in Spain. He was paralyzed from the neck down. It took a long time to get over the emotional trauma of going from a dynamic human being to a quadriplegic. While Zobel recuperated, in May 1991 Castro called a press conference.

He announced that 325 metric tons of gold valued at $3.5 billion, which had been smuggled out of the Philippines by Marcos, had been found in Switzerland. The bars bore the Central Bank of the Philippines hallmark and were kept in the storage vault of a bonded warehouse managed by Union Bank at the J.M. Kloten airport near Zurich.

He said his information came from a confidential informant

later identified as Reiner Jacobi. Jacobi, a German-born Australian, was a man of high intrigue. On one occasion he claimed to be working for the CIA. On another he claimed to be the half-brother of Klaus Jacobi, deputy chief of the Swiss Foreign Ministry. Neither was true. He had worked as an undercover agent for the U.S. Bureau of Customs at one time until his connections with drug dealers got more cozy than adversarial. He had a talent for promoting himself. He also had a talent for the scam, collecting millions of dollars from investors while promising he was about to do a deal with Imelda "any day now," which would reap him billions of dollars in gold.

One of his associates at Bureau of Customs described him: "You sit there listening to him with your mouth hanging open, and you think he's got to be for real . . . He's a genius at debriefing people . . . then he takes the info and sells it."

Jacobi's involvement with the gold began in Hong Kong in November 1987 when he was introduced to Ibrahim Dagher, the same businessman who had accompanied Michael de Guzman to Zurich in 1986. Dagher introduced his associates – Robert Kerkez and Col. Enrique Pimentel – two names already well known in other gold deals. He offered Jacobi some gold certificates for sale. Jacobi took this information to the Philippine consul general in Hong Kong and wangled a meeting with Castro in Manila.

Now he was just one among many on the trail of the Marcos gold. In Manila in November 1990 he met the infamous Mama Mary. She claimed to know a lot. She said the Blue Book was once in her possession but she had to give it back. The Blue Book allegedly contained a record of all the Marcos gold shipments to various banks and their account numbers. She had bragged to a number of gold buyers about this book but no one ever saw it. Now it was Jacobi's turn to court her. One day she brought along a friend, Adoracion Edralin Lopez, a relative of Marcos.

Lopez claimed to be one of the three signatories when gold was deposited in the bonded warehouse at Kloten airport in 1983. That way, it wouldn't have to go through customs and be registered. The other signatories were a Filipino and a foreigner, both living outside Switzerland. She wouldn't divulge their names. She said Marcos had rented the space for ten years.

After Marcos died, Lopez flew to Zurich to check on the account. She found her name had been removed as signatory. Her objections at the bank fell on deaf ears. She knew the power of the people she was dealing with so she came home to Manila to think of a way to reclaim her rights. Eventually she and Mama Mary crossed paths.

Mama Mary took her to Jacobi. Lopez told her story. She described how the gold was laid out in the vault and, in one tantalizing detail, said that passengers arriving at the airport on Concourse B were literally walking over the gold.

Jacobi told Castro. They devised a plan. In early 1991, Jacobi invited Mama Mary and Lopez to Switzerland to verify the gold's existence. They brought along a friend, Zosimo A. Banaag. After they arrived at their hotel in Zurich, Castro walked up and Jacobi introduced them. At first they were surprised – they didn't know Jacobi was working with Castro – then they agreed to cooperate with the PCGG.

Castro already knew the two ladies. Their names had crossed his desk once before, listed as trustees of the gold Greenlees attempted to purchase. On February 5 in the Zurich office of Franz Reichenbach, one of the Philippine government's Swiss lawyers, Lopez issued a Deed of Assignment to Castro. It stated the gold was in vault number 88-RW-RP and that the account number was G-72570367-d-UBS.

In July, Jacobi was arrested in Munich, Germany. While in Switzerland he had bragged that he had a computer expert, Friedrich "Fritz" Walser, who cracked the bank's computer codes. This set off an investigation. An arrest warrant was issued to Interpol. He and Fritz were charged with violating Swiss banking secrecy laws. He managed to talk himself out of that predicament and was released. He flew to Hong Kong and was arrested again. This time he and an associate had been indicted in Miami for conspiring to import and distribute drugs. The U.S. government requested his extradition to the states.

Because of Jacobi, Castro's credibility was in serious jeopardy. He decided it was time to go public with more information and called a press conference. He produced documents showing the serial numbers of gold bars which were released by the Central Bank's minting plant for shipment in 1983 and 1984. These bars were not part of the Central Bank's official inventory, he announced, and showed a copy of the receipt for the bars signed by Tomas Rodriguez, operations manager of Tamaraw Security Agency. Rodriguez had come forward and admitted that Tamaraw, which was owned by Ver, picked up the gold and took it to the airport. Not only that, Castro said, he had met one of the pilots who flew the bars to Switzerland after Ninoy Aquino was murdered in 1983.

Castro had known about the existence of those gold bars before Jacobi and Lopez entered the scene. The first leak about the shipment came from the wife of an army officer close to Ver who knew Guillermo Carague, secretary of budget and management under Aquino. The lady had given the Tamaraw documents to Carague, who turned them over to Adolfo Azcuna, Aquino's legal adviser. Azcuna, in turn, gave them to Castro. They remained in the PCGG files until some individuals approached him with copies of the documents seeking a reward.

They had one additional piece of evidence – Rodriguez himself. He admitted his role in the matter and testified as to the authenticity of the documents. Now Castro knew some gold bars existed but he didn't know where they were. Then Jacobi appeared with Lopez.

Lopez got into trouble a month after Castro went public with her name. She was arrested in Manila by the National Bureau of Investigation and charged with writing bad checks. After posting bail she went into hiding. She sent a message to Castro, claiming she was being harassed and pursued by friends of Marcos and Imelda who wanted to do her harm. Castro promised to protect her. He didn't know if she was telling the truth but he was aware of instances where people wound up dead or missing after criticizing the Marcoses.

The PCGG filed an application for legal assistance to verify the existence of the gold deposits at Kloten. In the application they estimated as much as 5,000 metric tons might be stored there. Union Bank denied they held such a deposit. The district attorney said this was an old rumor that prompted an official inquiry during the eighties. It yielded no evidence of gold smuggled out of the Philippines. Besides, he said, "that amount was beyond the capacity of the Philippines to produce."

Castro thought the remark a strange rebuttal to the PCGG's request. But there was one flaw in his logic. Lopez had said the bars belonged to the Central Bank of the Philippines but neither she nor anybody else had actually matched the serial numbers of the bars taken out of the Central Bank to the bars in the Union Bank vault at Kloten. Jacobi admitted as much when he later tried to raise $300,000 to bribe a guard so they could get inside the vault to verify the gold was there. An investor put up the money but nothing happened.

Castro met Jacobi and the others in Zurich but they did not visit the Union Bank or the bonded warehouse at Kloten. He sent another PCGG official, Sonny del Rosario, to gather more information but del Rosario went to Geneva. Shortly afterward Castro received a fax verifying the gold bars were at Kloten but it was unsigned. He never did get confirmation that the serial numbers matched.

Attorney Antonio Coronel, Imelda's lawyer in the Philippines, got into the act. That gold doesn't belong to the Central Bank, he told the PCGG. It was privately minted and exported. The government had no basis for demanding it back.

So what, the Philippine government countered. If the Central Bank refined it, then where did it come from? Besides, the burden of proof of ownership rested with Imelda.

The battle over the 325 tons continued. Hong Kong refused to extradite Jacobi. He was subsequently released.

On Sunday, November 4, 1991, the circus came to town. That's how one newspaper described Imelda's return to the Philippines. The Swiss Federal Tribunal's ruling in 1990 stated the Philippine government must comply with the European Convention on Human Rights, especially due process. There had to be a lawsuit filed within one year. Thus, tax evasion and other charges were filed against her by the solicitor general's office and she was allowed to return to answer the charges. She always said she would come back and she did. She wasn't allowed to bring her husband's body home but it was still a triumphant return of sorts after the not guilty verdict in New York.

She rented sixty rooms of the Philippine Plaza Hotel for her entourage, which included four American lawyers, twenty American security guards, and several members of a Washington-based public relations firm. "I come home penniless," she tearfully said on arrival, then repaired to her suite which cost $2,000 a day.

Two months later she declared her intention to run for president in the May elections. Her picture was in the papers almost every day, either being fingerprinted or giving a campaign speech.

She never bothered to contact Zobel so he wrote her on April 20, 1992, and asked that she set up the foundation and "never let [Marcos'] dream die with him." He ended the letter by stating, "I hope that we can begin to work something out within a week after the elections."

The elections were held on May 11. Imelda lost. Zobel waited for a reply but one never came. On Thursday, June 4, 1992, he called a press conference and told the public about his meetings with Marcos, the gold, and Marcos' wish to set up a foundation.

When first asked, Aquino denied knowing anything, then later admitted she was aware of the discussions between Marcos and Zobel. Her overall reaction seemed to be of disinterest. This led Zobel to comment that her main agenda in matters concerning the return of Marcos' gold was that if it would make him look good then she was against it no matter how much the country benefitted.

Imelda chose not to respond. She sent several messages to Zobel saying she would meet with him but she never did.

One day Castro received a surprising phone call. It was Imelda. She was willing to cooperate. He wondered why the sudden change of heart. Before he had met with her privately on four or five occasions to discuss the possibility of a settlement. She admitted Marcos found some treasure but she never got too specific and no agreement ever materialized. Aquino would be out of office in less than a week. Fidel V. Ramos, the newly elected president, was set to be sworn in on Tuesday, June 30, 1992. There was a rumor the PCGG might be dissolved. It only had a six-year mandate.

The meeting was held on Friday, June 26, with her and newly elected Congressman Bong Bong Marcos. After a marathon twelve-hour session, a main agreement and two sub-agreements were signed between the Philippine government, represented by Castro, and the estate of Ferdinand Marcos.

The main agreement stated the government would return all the residential properties of the estate and all personal properties such as jewelry, paintings, clothing, and other personal effects. All other assets of the estate, wherever located, in the name of Marcos or in the name of nominees, agents, or foundations would be divided between the estate and the government, the proportion to be mutually agreed upon. In case the assets in question were held by trustees, nominees, agents, or foundations, the estate would make every effort to convince them to surrender the assets. Failing that, the estate would join with the government in taking legal action to recover.

The sub-agreements included an agreement regarding the transfer of all the paintings to the government; an agreement regarding the transfer of venue of the human rights case ongoing in Hawaii; and an agreement on the sharing of the gold at Kloten. The first two sub-agreements were signed at the same time as the main agreement. The Kloten sub-agreement was still being negotiated. One of Imelda's lawyers had already begun discussions with a Ramos official. Former national security director Emanuel V. Soriano had been chosen as the go-between. They met once, in a Manila Hotel suite, and agreed on the fine points but nothing was signed.

On Saturday morning, Castro was called by Tony Carpio, legal adviser to Ramos. He was advised that on Monday a new chairman, Magtanggol Gunigundo, would take over his duties at the PCGG.

Gunigundo assumed his position as the new chairman. Part of the main agreement signed by Castro stated it was not effective unless approved by the president and the PCGG *en banc*. This had not been done. Gunigundo announced the agreements would not be recognized. The primary reason was that Imelda and Bong Bong had not itemized their assets.

A lot of people were glad to see this happen. The Castro agreement gave the Marcos family immunity from legal action arising from ill-gotten wealth cases. This was not acceptable. There was still a lot to be accountable for. Too much money had been stolen and too many people tortured and murdered. If the public wondered how Imelda and Bong Bong felt about all this, they didn't have long to wait.

CHAPTER SIXTEEN

Quiet Diplomacy's Victims

Gunigundo began negotiations with Imelda as soon as he took office. In August 1992 he reached a tentative agreement for the return of the funds in the frozen bank accounts covered by the sequestration order affirmed by the Swiss Federal Tribunal. With interest they were worth more than $400 million.

He also reduced the foreign debt. After the overthrow, $30 million in Treasury Notes were found in the Central Bank, all that remained of the $125 million in Notes issued in 1983. The rest had been redeemed upon maturity. After a concerted and prolonged legal effort, the PCGG's claim was deemed valid. In addition to reducing the foreign debt by $30 million, that amount was added to the national treasury and turned over to the Comprehensive Agrarian Reform Program.

In September, Marcos was found guilty of violating the human rights of 10,000 victims. This was the culmination of a class action suit that began while the Marcoses were in the air on the way to Hawaii on February 26, 1986. Flamboyant San Francisco attorney Melvin Belli filed a suit on behalf of eight U.S. based Filipinos who were tortured in the Philippines. Another set of victims represented by Robert Swift filed a separate action. In 1991 in Honolulu, U.S. District Court Judge Manuel Real directed all of them be consolidated into a class action suit.

The ruling occurred just after Judge Real found Imee Marcos-Manotoc guilty of the torture and murder of Archimedes Trajano.

In 1977, Marcos-Manotoc was head of the Kabatang Barangay, a national youth group. She was giving a speech to about 2,000 members at the Pamantasan ng Lungsod ng Maynila in Intramuros when she was interrupted by someone shouting from the audience. A young man wanted to know, "Must the KB be headed by the president's daughter?"

For a few minutes she lost her composure. Her bodyguards ordered the man to sit down. The meeting continued. A few days later Archimedes Trajano, a twenty-one year old engineering student at Mapua Institute of Technology, disappeared. His friends said he was the one that interrupted her at the meeting.

His body was found a few days later. It bore evidence of cigarette burns, skull and jaw fractures, and a fatal blow to the head. An autopsy showed he was tortured for at least thirty-six hours before he died. After fifteen years, justice was finally served. Marcos-Manotoc was ordered to pay the Trajano estate $4.11 million.

The ruling against Marcos on behalf of 10,000 human rights victims was unprecedented. Human rights cases had been filed against other dictators, but it was the first time 10,000 had been filed against one person. And it was the first human rights case in the world to be decided for the litigants. It was a long time coming.

Marcos showed his true colors in 1965, the first year of his presidency. The Philippine government signed the United Nations sponsored International Covenant on Civil and Political Rights. Later it backtracked. While stating it fully subscribed to all rights enumerated in the Covenant, the government did not wish to ratify it. The reason given was that it considered provisions allowing states' parties to the Covenant to bring petitions against one another constituted a derogation of national sovereignty. The strong-man did not wish to weaken any of his powers, especially when it came to human rights.

In 1975 the Philippines was a sponsor of the Declaration Against Torture adopted by the United Nations General Assembly but someone forgot to tell certain members of Marcos' military. Human rights abuses continued.

In November 1976, Jimmy Carter was elected president. At

first hopes were raised. His views on human rights were well known. The following year Imelda wangled a meeting with him. The local press exploited the meeting for all its propaganda value, noting how the champion of human rights greeted Imelda warmly. But the reason he saw her was she carried a letter from her husband about the American bases in the Philippines.

In May 1978, Vice President Walter Mondale made a goodwill visit to several countries, including the Philippines. He assured Marcos of U.S. support and signed four aid agreements totalling $41 million. The ceremony was on all the front pages and on television.

Imelda had just defeated Ninoy the month before for a seat in the Interim National Assembly. Everyone was still complaining about the fraudulent election. Opposition leaders requested a meeting with Mondale. He met with them but only in secret so as not to offend Marcos. He even refused to issue a statement. They were surprised and offended. They knew Carter knew about the oppression. The State Department and Amnesty International had the proof. What they didn't know was geopolitics. Military bases were more important than torture victims.

The U.S. government adopted a stance of "Quiet Diplomacy" that harkened back to President Franklin D. Roosevelt's philosophy when talking about another dictator. "He may be a son of a bitch but he's our son of a bitch." Such a policy would have tragic results.

Imelda was aware of the U.S. stance but one time she pushed a little too far. When U.S. congressmen complained about the Philippines' dismal record, she came to Washington to tell them their views were based on hostile sources. She shouldn't have. One of the nicer questions put to her was, "Why should the United States give the Philippines military aid when the money only goes to you to buy jewelry and to the military to torture people?"

She was grilled unmercifully. Congressman Peter Stark noted: "It was like talking to the Tooth Fairy. She never heard of the charges."

Marcos gave the appearance of making amends. In 1979 the Philippines was among the few governments to make the so-called Unilateral Declaration, stating its intention to implement the provisions of the Declaration Against Torture through national legislation and other measures.

In 1980, during the thirty-fifth session of the United Nations General Assembly, it was a sponsor of Resolution 35/170 on a Code of Conduct for Law Enforcement Officials. This was an impressive show of support for human rights but that is all it was – a show. Human rights abuses continued.

Marcos was invited to attend the American Newspaper Publishers Association (ANPA) in April 1980 in Honolulu and address its annual meeting. Protocol required some response from the White House. Carter chose not to meet with him. Instead he sent former Secretary of State Dean Rusk and Assistant Secretary of State for East Asian and Pacific affairs Richard Holbrook with a letter that studiously avoided any mention of human rights.

On January 16, 1981, the day before Marcos lifted martial law, he signed Presidential Decrees 1834 and 1835. The infamous Death Decrees authorized trials in absentia of his political opponents and confiscation of their property if convicted. Anti-government agitators and publishers who allowed their facilities to print propaganda could be executed if convicted. The decrees were kept secret. They came to light two years later. Only after several years of pressure from human rights groups in the Philippines and abroad did he amend them.

When the Pope visited the Philippines in February, he lectured Marcos in the palace. Marcos apologized for what he called "petty and small" church-state differences. But the persecution of priests, nuns, and lay workers continued, and the human rights abuses escalated.

Following its mission to the Philippines in 1981, Amnesty International published a report on September 22, 1982, detailing evidence that members of the armed forces and paramilitary groups acting with official sanction had committed human rights violations and that "disappearances" and extrajudicial executions were becoming increasingly common.

During his state visit to Washington, when asked about the report, Marcos criticized AI's findings and methods. In a speech in San Francisco on September 26, Marcos said, "We can answer, and will answer, the report word by word."

In a letter dated March 23, 1983, the Philippine government replied. The first paragraph set the tone, calling the report a "masterpiece of black propaganda and deception on a grand scale." It then proceeded to present the government's version of some of the cases AI had cited. It responded negatively to AI's recommendations and accused AI of interfering in matters outside its mandate.

It was a sad retort. The evidence was overwhelming that the military were torturing and killing people. But their actions were consistent with a policy set by Marcos – deny, deny, deny.

In 1984 the American Committee for Human Rights sent a mission to the Philippines to observe conditions firsthand. Their preliminary report noted: "It was the overall impression of the mission that one-third to one-half of all individuals arrested by the military are subject to torture, as defined by the United Nations Declaration on Torture."

On May 14, 1984 – election day – eleven people from the hamlet of Langoni, Negros Occidental, were stopped by members of the Philippine Constabulary (PC) a few hours after voting on suspicion of being NPA members. They were marched, their hands bound, through the village of Inayawan to the headquarters of the 338th Company of the PC, where, according to an eyewitness, they were beaten and kicked. Then they were all reportedly taken to a nearby field where nine were shot dead. The following day, the nine bodies were returned to Langoni by truck. Several bore marks of torture. On May 31, one day after local residents testified before a military commission, the eyewitness was charged with murder. Residents subsequently became unwilling to testify. Although criminal proceedings were started, charges against the PC officers were later dropped because of lack of evidence. The fate of the other two arrested that day was still unknown.

The detailed records of the Task Force for Detainees of the Philippines documented 5,531 cases of torture, 2,537 cases of summary execution, 783 cases of disappearances, and 92,607 arrests. These records, presented at the trial, were part of the reason Swift decided that 10,000 people would be the upper limit of the suit.

At the human rights trial nine victims or their kin were chosen to tell their stories. Celsa Hilao, the mother of Liliosa Hilao, was one. On April 4, 1973, her daughter was picked up by the Philippine Constabulary and taken to Camp Crame. She was pistol whipped and injected with what investigators said was truth serum. Two days later she was executed. Soldiers poured muriatic acid down her throat to make it look like a suicide.

Rodolfo Benoza, an organizer for the Urban Poor coalition, was arrested in 1982. He was stripped naked and beaten. The hairs on his face and body were pulled out one at a time. He was held for three years without charges before he was released.

And on and on.

Marcos' lawyers argued that he wasn't directly involved. But former U.S. Ambassador Stephen Bosworth testified he had talked with Marcos over the phone about such matters, and Marcos had replied, "I'm aware there is torture and everything happens, but that is part of the interrogation process and these people are communists."

It wasn't the first time he had publicized his views. On October 20, 1985, Marcos told Ed Barnes on the U.S. television program "60 Minutes," that the religious workers, priests, and nuns were "communists supplying his enemies with guns, food, and medicine."

Human rights abuses were terrible during martial law. Afterward they grew worse. There were several high profile cases which, everyone knew, were just a reminder not to go against Marcos. The murders of Gene Viernes and Silme Domingo in June 1981, Ninoy Aquino in August 1983, and Doctor Potenciano Baccay in 1985 are three of the more celebrated cases. Somehow that term – human rights abuse – did not adequately describe the emotional impact of a veiled threat or warning made by Marcos, Imelda, or their associates. A palpable aura of fear kept most people in place.

Like the dog that didn't bark in a Sherlock Holmes mystery, the witness that didn't testify at Imelda's trial spoke volumes. In Europe, Glecy Tantoco finally reached an agreement with the U.S. Justice Department. She would cooperate and testify against Imelda. In return certain charges pertaining to her and her husband would be dropped. Her testimony was important. One of Khashoggi's lawyers said, "Had Mrs. Tantoco stepped into the courtroom, she could have changed the complete face of this case for both Adnan and Mrs. Marcos. That's how vital a witness she can be for the prosecution."

Tantoco was about to board a plane for New York to testify when she received the news that a kidnapping attempt on her grandchild had occurred in Manila. That did it. She fled and went into hiding. When chief prosecutor Charles LaBella was asked who may have planned the kidnapping, he replied, "I will leave that to your imagination. It has to be a party who knew she was going to testify and who knew her testimony could have nailed those two defendants."

Tantoco knew first hand about such matters. Thomas Bryan of Sotheby's testified at Imelda's trial. At the time the estate of Leslie R. Samuels was up for sale, Tantoco tried to buy the Samuel's apartment at 660 Park Avenue but the cooperative's board rejected her. When this hit the newspapers, Bryan said Tantoco called him and said that if any additional information became public, he should fear for himself and his family.

On January 5, 1993, Imelda didn't show up for the scheduled signing of the new PCGG agreement. A new deadline was set for February 9, which she also missed. She kept vacillating on the terms and conditions. First she wanted approval of the agreement she made with Castro and protection from the U.S. judge handling the claims in the human rights case. Then she added another condition – the return of Marcos' body to the Philippines and burial with honors. Later she withdrew that demand.

She also requested she be allowed to travel abroad for thirty-three days to confer with bank officials in Switzerland, Australia, Hong Kong, and Morocco to work out the transfer of the frozen funds.

While the government was considering her request, they discovered she was attempting to withdraw some of these funds through a power of attorney, dated December 19, 1992, made out to a certain Jose T. Calderon. It gave him authority "to negotiate, transact, withdraw, transfer, sell, or otherwise deal with any rights and interest which I may have with respect to deposits, valuables, securities, precious metals, and other accounts held by Union Bank of Switzerland and Credit Suisse . . . particularly enumerated in the attached list of accounts and inventory furnished by Mr. Zosimo A. Banaag . . ." Banaag had accompanied Mama Mary and Adoracion Lopez to Zurich in 1991.

Her travel request was turned down. All negotiations with Imelda were halted and her requests for travel suspended. Responding to the allegation, Imelda tearfully denied signing any letter of authority or power of attorney. "I am well aware there is a worldwide injunction (on the Marcos assets)," she said.

Coronel, Imelda's lawyer, responded: "She has not executed any power of attorney . . . there would be no sense in executing an authority on behalf of anybody to withdraw the frozen Swiss account because she herself cannot do it. If a principal cannot do it, how can a mere agent do it? There appears to be a conspiracy . . ."

There was no conspiracy, only a plan that might have worked if the power of attorney had not been discovered. In order to transfer the funds to Manila, the Philippine government had to lift the order freezing the accounts. Imelda had hoped that Calderon could move the funds just as the order was lifted, before the government had a chance to transfer them to Manila.

President Ramos responded: "I think the Marcos side will have to prove there was no such special power of attorney. In other words, our view is that the burden of proof is on them."

Before she could offer any proof, other documents popped up. It was revealed that a ninety-four year old lawyer, Elpidio T. Clemente, notarized a special power of attorney on December 16, 1992, issued to Joe Svenson for the transfer of the Marcos Swiss bank accounts to a Caribbean offshore bank.

Then a letter of authority dated January 10, 1993, was made public. It instructed Engracio Pesebre to coordinate with a certain Eduardo Moran "in the implementation of the financial arrangements verbally discussed, as follows: to transfer the proceeds of these financial arrangements to the United Mizrahi Bank, Zurich, and any other financial institutions named by them or any other which you may learn of, to an offshore BVI (British Virgin Islands) company for purposes of trading in financial instruments nominated by this BVI company."

The palace announced she must agree to transfer the frozen funds to the Philippines before any further discussions could be held. By then it was obvious. Imelda was doing everything she could to keep the government away from those funds and to hide them from the human rights lawyers.

Just before ten in the morning on Thursday, January 14, 1993, a van wound its way through the narrow streets of San Juan, Metro Manila. Inside were Robert Swift and the lawyers who had handled the Philippine side of the human rights case since its inception five years before: Romy Capulong, Rod Domingo, Ruben Fruto, and Rene Saguisag.

The driver spotted the Marcos home and pulled into the driveway. They had arrived to take Imelda and Bong Bong's depositions. Waiting in the front yard were hundreds of Marcos supporters shouting, "Marcos, Marcos, Marcos *pa rin.* (We're still for Marcos.)" A hail of tomatoes and rotten eggs hit the vehicle and a stink bomb was set off.

They were ushered inside. In a small room sat Imelda and Bong Bong, with James Linn, Imelda's American lawyer, Antonio Coronel, her Philippine lawyer, and several assistants. Everybody was fanning themselves in the heat. Due to a brownout, there was no electricity or air-conditioning.

The standoff began. There was no lunch break. In a country known for its hospitality, the visitors were offered nothing but water. At one o'clock electricity was restored but still there was no progress. Imelda answered some questions but denied knowing the amount of the Swiss deposits as well as the nature and locations of various properties.

After five hours they left without a deposition. As soon as they were inside the van, another hail of eggs, tomatoes, and mud hit the vehicle, and the chanting began again, "Marcos, Marcos, Marcos *pa rin.*"

Imelda told the press "They want to give away the Marcos estate to card-bearing communists who claim to be victims. Instead of going to the poor and the development of our country, the money will go to the enemies of the state for whom power comes from the barrel of a gun."

It was a strange statement coming from the wife of a dictator who ruled just that way. The irony was that she was doing everything she could to keep as much as she could.

It was Bong Bong's turn the next day, and the venue was switched to a more neutral site, the Mandarin Hotel, but he was no more cooperative than his mother.

In his denial, he was not exactly the smoothest of tongue either. "Everybody wants the money," he said. "This is no longer a case of justice. This is a case of greed."

The press reacted. Manuel Martinez of the *Manila Times* noted: "Now we have come full circle to the point where it is the Marcoses who are pointing to their victims as greedy. Sick, sick, sick." He named a few of Bong Bong's greedy people: "Fernando Nacor, tortured; Wilfred de la Fuente, disappeared; Elizalde Maillar, summarily executed; Pepito Rodriguez, summarily executed; Reynaldo Borbe, summarily executed . . ."

In 1994, the human rights jury awarded the victims $1.2 billion in exemplary damages, then $766.4 million in compensatory damages a year after that, for a total of $1.9664 billion.

Two days after the $766.4 million was awarded, another $7.3 million was awarded to twenty-one Filipinos in a separate lawsuit. In 1995, the U.S. Supreme Court upheld the $1.2 billion judgment. In 1996, the U.S. Court of Appeals upheld the total verdict. In July 1996, $22 billion was awarded to the Golden Budha Corporation, in part because of the torture of Roger Roxas.

Murder, torture, disappearance. That was part of the legacy of Ferdinand Marcos. But only a part.

CHAPTER SEVENTEEN

Central Bank Gold or Treasure?

The international reserves scandal in 1983 did not slow Marcos down. He continued to manipulate the Central Bank. Fernandez, the new governor, didn't mind. He had his own agenda.

In 1984 after the international reserves scandal died down, Marcos issued Presidential Decree 1937, eliminating the ten-year limit on the amortization of losses at the Central Bank. Before the decree, it wrote off one-tenth of its losses every year. Now they could be amortized "over a period at a rate which shall be based on the adequacy of the Central Bank's profits." In other words, forever. There would be no more profits, at least not under the existing regime.

When Marcos signed the decree, the Central Bank's losses were fast approaching ₱100 billion (approximately $5 billion), more than four times the amount known to be missing from the international reserves. Now one-tenth of these losses would no longer have to be written off annually. Incredibly, they were listed as assets.

The Central Bank's original charter provided for two Special Accounts. The Monetary Adjustment Account (MAA) was responsible for the cost of printing notes and minting coins, extraordinary costs in the issuance and servicing of evidence of indebtedness, interest on deposits of the national government, interest on reverse repurchase agreements, as well as payment of gold trader's commissions and handling fees.

The Revaluation of International Reserves Account (RIR) was a special frozen account debited or credited for profits or losses arising from the revaluation of the Central Bank's assets and liabilities in gold or foreign currencies due to: a) changes in the gold value of the peso; b) changes in parities or exchange rates of foreign currencies vis-a-vis the peso; c) changes arising from any other transactions of the Central Bank in gold or foreign exchange.

Laya added another account in 1981 – the Economic Stabilization Account (ESA). The ESA paid extraordinary expenses on foreign borrowing so that the Bank's operating income was not overburdened during a particular year.

Is that clear?

Did it matter?

There is that word *definition* again. One must wonder – at the Central Bank did a *definition* define what something really meant? Or was it an Alice In Wonderland strategy, with Marcos playing Humpty Dumpty and telling Alice, "When I use a word it means just what I choose it to mean, neither more nor less."

The ESA was set up primarily to protect corporate borrowers who were unable to make payments on their foreign loans because of the shortage of dollars. The Central Bank devised a program whereby it assumed the loan and allowed borrowers to deliver to it the peso equivalent of their payments at prevailing exchange rates. If the peso decreased in value, the extra cost was borne by the Central Bank and written off in the ESA. The peso lost half its value during the financial crisis. Marcos allowed his cronies to avail of this facility.

No one had ever heard of a "reverse repurchase agreement" before until the term was made a part of the MAA definition.

That's how the interest on the so-called Jobo Bills was written off. "Jobo" was Fernandez nickname. Under him, the Central Bank offered interest rates on short-term bills as high as 40 percent. Several excuses were given for the unprecedented high interest rate. It was done to reduce liquidity in keeping with guidelines set by the IMF was a nice one. The truth was the Central Bank desperately needed pesos to keep afloat.

When Marcos departed the Philippines in February 1986

the losses in the three accounts surpassed ₱122 billion (more than $6 billion). Of this amount, according to the Central Bank, ₱87 billion, or 72 percent, was attributed to losses in the RIR account, and most of these losses were due to two items: forward cover, which referred to foreign exchange provided by the Central Bank at a fixed exchange rate to importers of oil, grains, and other essential commodities; and swap contracts, which allowed the Central Bank to receive foreign exchange from banks in exchange for pesos at the prevailing rate, with a promise to deliver the foreign exchange back to them at an agreed future date. The low level of reserves made it difficult to return the foreign exchange so the contracts had to be renewed again and again while the peso depreciated.

The Central Bank did not mention losses due to "changes arising from any other transactions of the Central Bank in gold or foreign exchange," which also fell under the RIR.

With the election of President Aquino, the buzzword of the moment was *transparency* – the people had the right to see how their government operated. Apparently this rule did not apply to the Central Bank. Fernandez remained the governor. Its bureaucrats were not replaced. The Central Bank as set up by Marcos remained intact.

In April 1986, Julie Amargo, columnist for the *Malaya* newspaper in Manila, obtained a duplicate copy of the KLM cargo airway bill dated September 9, 1983. She asked the PCGG to investigate and pinpoint the persons behind the shipment.

Two months later, in response to Amargo, the Central Bank published an article in the *Central Bank Review*. It stated the shipment was a location swap that resulted in a sale, and was done to "beef up liquidity at a time when the Central Bank was having difficulty meeting its foreign exchange payments."

It provided the dates and quantities of all location swaps. There were a total of thirty shipments. The first was on December 21, 1981. The last was on July 30, 1986. A total of 6,081 bars was shipped. Twenty-seven of the swaps occurred during the Marcos era, the last on September 18, 1985. A total of 5,390 bars, amounting to 56.6 metric tons, was shipped. The swaps were done to earn interest. Some resulted in actual sales but the article did not specify which ones. The only sale known for sure was the September 9, 1983, shipment, and the press, not the Central Bank, reported that.

The title of the article was "CB's Gold and Silver Reserves Management: Clearing the Doubts." Somehow the title didn't fit with the information. When asked, the Central Bank admitted that, in addition to the location swaps, there were other gold shipments during Marcos' time but they wouldn't clear the doubts about those. They refused to provide further information.

Aquilino Pimentel (no relation to Col. Pimentel) was secretary of interior and local government under Aquino. He resigned to run for senator and won. In November 1987 in a privelege speech, he questioned the way the Central Bank kept its accounts. Using a double-entry accounting system, the losses in the Special Accounts were reflected as assets in the Central Bank's monthly statement of its condition. He said this ran counter to accepted accounting principals, and accused Fernandez of "cooking the books."

He also wanted to know why Fernandez allowed the overprinting of paper money, including the printing of peso bills with the same serial number, which led to massive overspending during the snap presidential elections in 1986. No one knew how much exactly had been printed except the Central Bank and Fernandez wasn't saying.

After the revolution there was almost unanimous approval by bankers and economists alike to demonetize. Fernandez said no, it cost too much to print new money. Yet, within a year, new five-hundred peso notes were printed with the picture of Ninoy Aquino. It would have been no more expensive to demonetize and print one-hundred peso notes with Ninoy's picture.

Fernandez was also criticized for not divesting himself of his shares in the Far East Bank, which he was required to do by law. Since he became governor the assets, deposits, and overall profit of Far East Bank had risen dramatically.

There was also that other matter. Fernandez had the habit of closing down a bank at the slightest infraction of banking regulations. He closed eighty-two rural banks and some commercial banks. Far East Bank acquired many of these banks' assets at bargain basement prices.

Fernandez was already being investigated by several government agencies. Still, under the Central Bank Charter, as governor he was in charge of the gold. He could sell it at any price, at any time, to any buyer, and no one could question him, not even members of congress.

Despite Pimentel's protest, Fernandez was not replaced. In 1989, Senator Ernesto Maceda asked the senate to conduct an inquiry to determine how much gold was bought and produced by the Central Bank in the last ten years, how much gold was sold, at what price, and what persons were involved in the transactions. The public had not been apprised of these dealings which were matters of public interest, he said.

Proposed senate resolution 568 was recommended for approval by the Committee on Banks, Financial Institutions, and Currencies. But nothing happened. It never reached the senate floor and was never passed. Fernandez was finally replaced in 1990. He died in 1994.

Jose L. Cuisa was appointed the new governor. In senate hearings held in 1990 he refused to answer when Senators Alberto Romulo and Rene Saguisag asked how much the country owed its top thirty lenders. On being questioned further by Saguisag, Cuisa admitted that not even the president, much less the cabinet, was informed about certain details of the foreign debt.

There were other matters he didn't inform them about. In August 1990 the government commissioned a United Nations study. Four economic experts were picked by the National Economic Development Authority (NEDA) to make recommendations on how to sustain a positive economic growth. When the team issued its report, it detailed all the wrong policies adopted by the Aquino administration. NEDA Secretary Cayetano Paderanga asked that the harsh language be toned down. A final report was submitted in March 1991. Paderanga provided copies to Secretary of Finance Jesus Estanislao and Governor Cuisa. They decided to shelve the report and didn't bother to tell Aquino. Disgruntled employees at NEDA leaked it to the press. Among other findings, it reported the Central Bank was bankrupt. By December 1991 it had accumulated losses of ₱324 billion ($12.7 billion) in the Special Accounts.

A confidential World Bank report dated February 24, 1992, was leaked. It described the Philippines two biggest problems as "the external debt overhang and the financial crisis of the Central Bank." By November 30, 1992, the losses were ₱561 billion and climbing.

Something had to be done. Cuisa asked that the Central Bank be restructured. The Senate Committee on Banks, Financial Institutions, and Currencies held hearings to consider his request. Romulo, a lawyer and certified public accountant and also the secretary of budget and management under Aquino from 1986 to 1987, was committee chairman. He asked to see the 1983 audit of the international reserves. He was told it was "restricted," that he couldn't get a copy.

Romulo said this wasn't right. There should be full disclosure. The Filipino people had been kept in the dark too long about mysterious happenings at the country's flagship bank. The committee requested a copy. The hearings continued.

On June 14, 1993, Republic Act 7653 created the *Bangko Sentral Ng Pilipinas* (BSP). The old Central Bank became the Central Bank-Board of Liquidators, in order to wind up its affairs. The BSP assumed ₱280.8 billion of the old Central Bank's total liabilities of ₱612 billion.

After all these years, the question still remained. Did Marcos steal any gold from the Central Bank? The Central Bank always refused to comment but there were other intriguing bits of evidence to be considered.

On March 16, 1986, the *Los Angeles Times* reported that 6.325 metric tons of gold was unaccounted for in the Central Bank. In 1978 Marcos signed the decree ordering all gold producers to sell their gold to the Central Bank Gold Refinery and Mint. The Bureau of Mines reported that 124,234 pounds of gold were refined between that time and the end of 1984, the last year for which statistics were available at the time. But the Central Bank reported receiving only 110,319 pounds during this same period. That left a difference of 13,915 pounds (6.325 metric tons). At $390 per ounce (the average price of gold from 1978 to 1984) that amount would be worth more than $86 million.

The director of the Bureau of Mines denied the gold was unaccounted for, and stated that those figures were based on incomplete Central Bank data. True or not, with the findings about the Central Bank's creative accounting of its reserves, it was difficult to accept such statements at face value.

On August 28, 1986, an informant for the National Bureau of Investigation, Christina Concepcion Ismael, posed as a buyer and saw ninety 75-kilogram gold bars in an apartment building in Quezon City. Ismael was given a polygraph test a few days later and passed.

The building, owned by Jonathan Dela Cruz, a friend of Bong Bong, was heavily guarded by a private security force owned by Roquito Ablan, also a friend of Bong Bong. Whether or not the building was ever searched isn't known. The head of the NBI at the time was still a Marcos appointee. He refused to comment. Ninety 75-kilogram bars was about 6.76 metric tons.

The comment about incomplete data raised another question, not about gold shipments but about production. Could there have been other gold produced but never entered on the books?

– In 1973, reserves dropped from 1,857,000 ounces (52.75 metric tons) to 1,057,000 ounces. The Central Bank claimed 800,000 ounces was sold. Assuming an annual production of 30 metric tons, what about the gold produced that year?

– From 1974 through 1977, gold reserves stayed at exactly the same figure of 1,056,000 ounces. Again, what about the four years of production totalling approximately 120 metric tons.

– Gold reserves began another steady annual rise in 1978. From then until 1980 they gradually increased to 1,900,000 ounces, or an average of about 8 metric tons a year. What about the other 22 metric tons annually totalling 66 tons?

– In 1981, reserves took a dip, to 1,650,000 ounces, a drop of 7.1 metric tons, which was sold. But another 30 metric tons should have been produced.

– Reserves rose by 6.1 metric tons in 1982, to 1,866,000 ounces. That left 23.9 metric tons unaccounted for.

– In 1983 they dropped to 289,000 ounces, a decrease of 44.8 metric tons from the year before, which was sold. What about the 30 metric tons produced?

– In 1984 they rose to 786,000 ounces, an increase of 14.1 metric tons. That left 15.9 metric tons unaccounted for.

– In 1985 they rose to 1,478,000 ounces, an increase of 19.7 metric tons. That left 10.3 metric tons unaccounted for. Marcos departed in February 1986.

Not counting the shortage of 6.325 metric tons due to so-called incomplete data in 1984, and not counting the 74.6 metric tons which the Central Bank claimed was sold, an estimated 326.1 metric tons of gold could have been produced, paid for through one of the Special Accounts, and then written off. And the gold would never have officially entered the Central Bank system.

The only proof that Marcos reminted gold at the Central Bank was provided by Castro. This was for 325 metric tons, and it was never officially part of the Central Bank system either. It was recast into standard-size 12.5-kilogram (four-hundred ounce) bars with the Central Bank hallmark. Three-hundred-twenty-five metric tons was 325,000 kilograms, or approximately 26,000 bars. (Central Bank standard-size bars were rectangular with sloping sides. The size was approximately 10.2 by 3.1 inches on top, 9.1 by 2.4 inches on the bottom, and 1.4 inches thick.)

The 325 tons and the 326.1 tons look like they could be one and the same. But only a third of the gold production was refined locally into bars by the Central Bank. The rest was exported as unrefined copper ore. Any bullion recovered was minted and left abroad in Central Bank gold pool accounts in London, New York, or Zurich, or sold for dollars and remitted back to the Central Bank as reserves. Supposedly.

Some of the amounts Marcos talked about were larger than this. Some believed he found the legendary Yamashita treasure. Others scoffed at that. Marcos propagated the Yamashita myth to hide the fact that he looted the Central Bank, that its gold bars were melted down and recast in odd-size bars to make them look old. There was no record that the Japanese plundered any banks or financial institutions, they claimed.

That was an odd argument. The Japanese plundered the

occupied countries of everything – raw materials, money, precious metals, jewelry, art, everything. Also, there was no way to make gold look old. It never lost its lustre.

If Marcos did find a treasure, it should be called the legendary Kuroda treasure. Lt. Gen. Shigenori Kuroda was commander during the Japanese occupation. If any large amounts of treasure were buried, it would have been him, not Yamashita, who would have known about it.

Some of the gold allegedly for sale was marked Sumatra Lloyd and stamped AAA. It was not unusual for gold dealers in Asia to receive an odd-shaped bar with funny markings. The bars might have come from a Chinese money changer in Hong Kong or a heroin dealer in Bangkok, who received gold in various forms – bullion, jewelry, even tooth fillings – and cast it into a size they could handle and a shape they could identify, then add their personal stamp. That had been done long before World War II and long after. The bars marked Sumatra Lloyd could have been treasure but that was pure speculation.

Most of the gold seen or contracted for by private parties during the Marcos era was of the standard size but there were odd-size bars seen. In 1983 Tony Grant in Hong Kong mentioned eighty-five 50-kilogram bars for sale and Dacus saw a roomful of 25-kilogram bars estimated at 300 to 500 metric tons. The bars Ismael saw were 75-kilogram.

Knowing how the Central Bank operated during the Marcos era, anything was possible. The odd-size bars could have been recast Central Bank bars but if someone wanted to sell large amounts of gold on the international market, the first step would be to refine it into standard-size bars acceptable the world over. The London Five set the daily price of gold. If the gold didn't have a recognized hallmark, in order for it to be sold on the international market it would have to be reminted by an approved refinery. There were dozens, in Japan, Canada, the U.S., Germany, Africa, Switzerland, France, United Kingdom, and the Philippines to name a few. The refinery stamped its hallmark on the bar, along with the quality, such as 995 (99.5 percent pure). In the last ten years most traded bars have been 999.

Richard Hirschfield, who secretly tape-recorded Marcos, said

Marcos mentioned specific gold bars taken from the Central Bank, recast and reminted with different markings, and then flown to Hong Kong. Hirschfield may have believed Marcos was talking about Central Bank gold but that wasn't necessarily true.

In the taped interview Marcos said, "... What really happened is that most of this gold was sold and there was something left. Now, but because the gold prices are moving up, Balao and Governor Licaros refused to finalize the contract."

Balao was the Marcos confidant that handled kickbacks from war reparations in the seventies. Licaros was Central Bank governor at the time. The statement implied he and Licaros helped to dispose of gold for Marcos. Balao died in 1977 and Licaros in 1983. Assuming Marcos wasn't lying, any gold he was referring to had to be sold while Balao was alive.

Hirschfield thought Marcos deviated in his story when later in the conversation he stated, "I was the source of the gold ... for a lot of [World War II] veterans." This story might give some credibility to the gold certificates Zobel and others saw.

It also might have meant Marcos would say anything to convince Hirschfield he had gold hidden somewhere. Marcos was a desperate man in 1987. The stories he told about his gold hoard have to be questioned, but he could tell a story. What was that he wrote in his diary? "History should not be left to the historians."

CHAPTER EIGHTEEN

Propagating the Myth

Marcos led a spartan life. He ate simple foods and did not smoke or drink. He did not wont for much in the way of material caprices. His opiate was power. He wanted to build a dynasty. But that wasn't his ultimate goal – he wanted to be immortal.

He believed he had to be Mr. Everything, a hero of biblical proportions, and a supreme statesman who exercised leadership wisely and benevolently. As a result, the Marcos most people thought they knew was an illusion. He never existed. He spent a lot of time hiding his true identity. Imelda did not go to the same extreme but she also attempted to reinvent her past.

By the time Marcos became president in 1965, his propaganda was so successful in covering up his checkered past and delivering to the public his contrived hero-savior persona that relatively few people were aware this image was a cleverly woven tale of myth mixed with fact that began when Marcos was in college.

Marcos' fame started and ended with a murder. In 1939 he was a young man about to finish law school at the University of the Philippines when he was arrested.

In 1935, his father, Mariano, had been defeated in an election for congressman of the Second District of Ilocos Norte. He had been elected in 1924 and 1928, but lost in 1932. In 1935, in its new status as a self-governing commonwealth, the people of the Philippines had to choose its first president. In addition, all assemblymen had to face reelection. Mariano, a member of the Aglipayan Party, decided to run again. Manuel Quezon of the Nationalista Party was elected president. Julio Nalundasan, also a Nationalista, beat Mariano. Both were from the village of Batac and lived a few hundred yards apart.

Nalundasan could never be considered a gracious winner. A mock funeral cortege paraded through Batac carrying a coffin with Marcos' name. The night of September 20 was moonless and rain lashed the village. Delayed by friends congratulating him on his victory, Nalundasan took his supper later than usual. He was standing by the dining room window brushing his teeth when a shot rang out. He fell mortally wounded.

Four years later, young Ferdinand was arrested for the murder, tried, and found guilty. He had taken his bar examinations during the trial and scored the highest. He was the bar topnotcher in 1939. This event, plus his murder trial and conviction, made Marcos front page news.

A year later, in 1940, the Supreme Court overturned the conviction. The justice that penned the decision was Jose Laurel, who may have been somewhat impartial. In 1912, he had also been convicted of murder. At the age of eighteen he stabbed a man in a fight over a girl. His conviction was later reversed by the Supreme Court. Marcos had turned eighteen just nine days before Nalundasan was murdered. Laurel also attended the University of the Philippines law school.

Marcos was somewhat of a celebrity when war came to the Philippines in 1941. He joined the army and was commissioned as a third lieutenant.

After the war, Marcos was elected to congress, then to the senate. By the time he ran for president in 1965 he was a master politician. In preparation for his campaign, a biography by Hartzell Spence was published in 1964, entitled *For Every Tear A Victory* (re-released in 1979 under the title *Marcos of the Philippines*) He had a biographical film, *Iginuhit ng Tadhana (Marked By Fate)*, produced at the same time. In the film, he was shown defending himself in the Supreme Court case that reversed his murder conviction. That never happened.

Both the book and film portrayed him as the Philippines' greatest hero of World War II. That wasn't so either. The medals he claimed to have won were all based on affidavits after the fact. Half of them were awarded in 1963, seventeen years after the war.

Years later, a thorough investigation revealed his claims to be full of discrepancies and inconsistencies. His citations did not reconcile with the facts. They were part of an elaborate hoax perpetrated by someone who couldn't settle for being brave. He had to be the bravest.

Still, he won the election. Emboldened by success, he embellished the myth even more. In 1971, in the September 12 issue of *Asia* magazine, Marcos claimed he "received the surrender of Gen. Yamashita" after a battle with his guerrilla outfit. History has recorded that Yamashita surrendered to Lt. Col. Aubrey Smith Kenworthy and that there was no battle. Yamashita's peaceful surrender had been arranged at least two weeks before the event.

Doubts about the authenticity of his guerrilla outfit, the Maharlika, go all the way back to the end of the war when he and his outfit were turned down for recognition. Even worse, he was suspected of being a collaborator. His father, Mariano, was executed in early 1945 by the guerrillas for collaboration with the Japanese.

Marcos' biography also portrayed him as a sort of student Superman at the University of the Philippines which he entered in 1934 at the age of seventeen. It claimed he was a student leader and active in sports, "winning a place on the all-university wrestling, boxing, and swimming teams." There was no record, however, of Marcos lettering in any sport at the university, according to Ambrosio Padilla, who was the most popular college athlete during Marcos' time. Padilla was on the Philippine Olympic basketball team and went on to become a senator and then president of the Philippine Amateur Athletic Federation. Marcos also claimed, in an interview that appeared in the September 29, 1975, issue of *Sports Illustrated* that he won the small-bore rifle and pistol championship of the Philippines after spending two summers hunting in Davao in 1933 and 1934.

Padilla disclaimed this also, stating that not only is there no record of Marcos competing in or winning such a championship, it was Teddy Kalaw that actually won that title.

Marcos was a good university student but he just wasn't "Number One" in everything like he claimed to be. In oratory no one could match Raul Manglapus at Ateneo University back then. Manglapus went on to become a senator and then secretary of foreign affairs under President Aquino.

At the University of the Philippines, no one could match the likes of student leaders Wenceslao Vinzons and Arturo Tolentino. As a student Vinsons formed the *Malaysia Irrendenta*, a confederation whose goal was to unite all Malay people. His "Young Philippines" campus group was politically influential enough for him to be considered presidential material even as a student. And it wasn't Marcos but Tolentino, the scholar-athlete who was on the wrestling and weight-lifting teams at the university, that President Quezon invited to attend cabinet sessions as student representative.

The Marcos biography and film were all fantasy. How he could fabricate such an enormous fraud and expect the people to believe it is a further insight into his character. Even then Marcos was known as a man to be feared. Anyone who dared to question his background was asking for trouble of the most serious kind.

Marcos' mania for rewriting things didn't stop with his biography. His next, and biggest, challenge came when he convened a Constitutional Convention in June 1971 to rewrite the constitution.

Imelda was caught distributing envelopes full of cash to influence some of the delegates. Marcos halted the Convention and declared martial law. He jailed some of the delegates and threatened the others. The new constitution was rewritten exactly as he wanted.

His next project was history textbooks in the schools. He felt the information they contained wasn't adequate so they too were rewritten to include the great accomplishments of the "Hero From The North." (He was from the northern province of Ilocos Norte.) And then, as if that were not enough, he hired historians to assist him in the last phase of his ultimate propaganda scheme – to rewrite the history of the Philippines, but not in the normal sense. Entitled *Tadhana* (*Fate*), the history would portray him as the country's greatest statesman. His overthrow occurred before it was finished.

Now one may begin to get an idea of what drove the man. He couldn't settle for just being a hero. He had to be the most decorated soldier of the war. He couldn't just be a president. He had to be the best there ever was. He couldn't be just great. He had to be the greatest. Move over, Muhammad Ali.

In many countries a former head of state is usually remembered by naming a park, government building, or highway after him. Marcos altered the process slightly. Since he didn't expect to leave office anytime soon he allowed his name to adorn any appropriate edifice while still president. Soon enough so many streets, rivers, parks, buildings, and towns bore the Marcos moniker that the honor was cheapened.

In 1985 typhoon winds knocked down the scaffolding that had been protecting and hiding a construction site next to the Marcos Park at Pugo, La Union, 120 miles north or Manila. There on the side of a hill gazing sphinx-like out over the park was a huge concrete Mount Rushmore-like bust of Marcos almost a hundred feet tall. The government brazenly announced the purpose of the monument was "to make Filipinos proud of their history and culture."

Marcos was superstitious. His favorite number was seven. His automobiles carried 777 tags and one of his companies was the 777 Corporation. Many of his bank accounts contained the double sevens. He actually signed the declaration of martial law on the twenty-second, but backdated it to September 21, because of his penchant for the number 7 or its multiple. Other more ominous dates were also on the twenty-first. The Plaza Miranda disaster, in which nine of Marcos' political opponents were killed and scores injured, occurred on August 21, 1970. Also the assassination of Ninoy Aquino occurred on August 21, 1983.

Such a propensity for numbers and an interest in superstition is not unusual in Asian cultures but Marcos carried it a little further. It might have pleased him to know the rebellion that brought him down lasted 77 hours, and ended on February 25 (5 + 2 = 7).

He readily admitted to a belief in the supernatural and that sometimes he "heard voices." In October 1972 he addressed the Philippine Historical Association. In defending martial law which he declared a month earlier, he confided that he received several signs from God to act. Imelda even alluded to the notion that Marcos had certain "powers." In 1984, as part of her testimony before the Agrava Commission, investigating the assassination of Ninoy Aquino, she stated "the president is sort of a clairvoyant."

Perhaps Marcos believed all this. When he departed the palace in a hurry in February 1986, papers were left on the top of his desk. One of them was a note from a member of a religious cult predicting that Marcos would be the vehicle for the second coming of Christ.

After his overthrow, in a *Playboy* interview from Honolulu, Marcos commented he was ready to return to the Philippines but was waiting on a sign from God.

There were other hints. The ceiling of Marcos' bedroom had pyramid shapes, hoping to take advantage of such mystical forces. And he boasted about his *anting anting* (amulet) given to him before going to war by a friend of Marcos' father, Gregorio Aglipay. Aglipay was a Catholic priest in 1898 when he joined the revolutionary forces of Aguinaldo, first to fight the Spanish and later the Americans. For this he was excommunicated. He formed his own church in 1902.

Marcos claimed the sliver of wood had been bequeathed down through the ages and gave the owner magical powers. Aglipay inserted this amulet into Marcos' back with an incision made by his own hands. This protected Marcos from harm in battle.

On several occasions Marcos brought a faith healer into the palace to cure his kidney problems by "psychic surgery," in which a faith healer supposedly entered a patient's body with his bare hands and removes diseased organs.

Such were the Marcos beliefs. He never tried to hide the fact that he was "gifted," and professed to have a mystical power to manipulate nature through mediumistic means in order to control events. All this may sound strange to a foreigner but Filipino provincials have practiced animism in one form or another for centuries. Marcos may have thought he really was a Shaman, a person who possessed such powers.

His government printing presses worked overtime to insure the proper image and propagate the myth of the hero-savior. At the same time he was busy taking control of the country. And again it was control in the extreme, total and absolute. This would insure the Marcos dynasty would rule forever.

Life could be good for those who toed the line. The Grand Coalition lived in splendor, beyond the law, almost beyond reality. Those that wouldn't kowtow were threatened, intimidated, or worse. Marcos knew the value of propaganda. At the beginning of martial law all radio and television stations were shut down, as were all newspapers and print media. Journalists critical of his regime were arrested. Only a few were allowed to reopen, and those were pro-Marcos. From then on, the only debate on public issues was for show. There was no creative exchange of ideas except for a few brave enough to defy him and their tenures were short-lived. John Doherty of the prestigious Ateneo University was deported for publishing realistic economic data. Mahar Mahangas was forced to resign from the Development Academy of the Philippines after publishing negative findings on Imelda's social projects.

Marcos attempted to control all information which the public received. If *Time*, *Newsweek*, or any foreign publication carried a derogatory story, that issue would be banned in the Philippines. The writer might even be in for a rough time.

The worst case of intimidation of the foreign press occurred in 1984. The *San Francisco Examiner* printed an interview with Dante Santos, a member of the panel investigating the killing of Ninoy Aquino, in which Santos said the military was to blame. Phil Bronstein, who won an award for his reporting on the Philippines, conducted the interview. After that, he wrote another story about alleged mishandling of funds by the military.

Bronstein and *Examiner* photographer Kim Komenich were staying at the Manila Hotel. Wrote Bronstein, "The men following his (Ver's) orders were everywhere. In blue uniforms on every floor of the hotel. In the lobby wearing plain clothes. Skinny guys with bad complexions, waiting outside in the dark." Two in plainclothes were stationed in a room down the hall. "Not allowed to use the hotel beds, they had set up cots in the room. Their door was open 24 hours a day, and they either stood staring into the hallway or sat on the edge of their cot, bathed in the eerie light of the TV."

The agents followed him everywhere. They tapped his phone, read his mail, snuck into his room and rifled his files while he was out. The driver hired by Bronstein was threatened and forced to inform on him.

When Bronstein confronted Col. Arsenio Tecson, Ver's aide, about the harassment, he said Ver was no longer the Chief of Staff and couldn't do such a thing. Then he invoked Ver's name in an ominous warning. "The General said to me, 'My God, if something should happen to that guy, for instance if he should get run over by a car driven by a drunk driver or something . . .'" Even veteran reporters were surprised at the harassment. It lasted until September 28, when they left Manila for other islands.

It wasn't just the media. All forms of expression came under the scrutiny of Marcos. Theater groups could not put on plays critical of the regime. Imelda banned *Evita* from being performed in the Philippines. It was a play about Eva Peron, a former prostitute who became the influential wife of the Argentine dictator and rose to power.

Another group Marcos feared were the students. He banned student councils during martial law. Emanuel V. Soriano, president of the University of the Philippines and the future national security director, was told "You're dead," when he defied Marcos and allowed student council elections to be held in 1980.

Martial law ended in January. Marcos made a few announcements that suggested sweeping changes in government. But nothing really changed except human rights abuses got worse. When Ninoy was murdered on August 21, 1983, it was the beginning of the end for Marcos. The people couldn't take it anymore. It would take another two and a half years, but he would leave the Philippines in disgrace.

He fed the public a steady dose of propaganda for more than twenty years. There were young men and women with families of their own who had grown up knowing no other president. It must have been difficult for him to accept that they didn't want a hero-savior, that all they wanted was to be able to feed themselves and their children. In the end, he brought about his own downfall by his inability to divine the will of the people.

Another entry in Marcos' diary noted, "I often wonder what I will be remembered for in history? Scholar? Military hero . . .?"

In a supreme irony, he did achieve what he so vainly sought – lasting fame – but not in the way he envisioned:

– The largest human rights case in history – 10,000 victims.

– *Guinness Book of Records* – the world's greatest thief.

– The largest monetary award in history – $22 billion.

After he was overthrown the Marcos myth unravelled like a loose thread in a badly woven tapestry. But another myth, also propagated by Marcos with the help of a few officials, survived.

The government of President Aquino went about the task of rebuilding the economy and searching for the hidden wealth. It also began an investigation. Marcos had exercised complete control of all governmental institutions for at least the last dozen years he was in power. Now they came under intense scrutiny. All, that is, except one.

CHAPTER NINETEEN

The Buddha, the Gold, and the Myth

There have been estimates of what Marcos stole, ranging from $2 to $10 billion. In the Philippine government's case against Marcos (SBNo. 0141), the properties, investments, and bank accounts it identified were worth approximately $5 billion. No gold accounts were found.

The known losses he left behind at the Central Bank included $1.2 billion in missing reserves and $6 billion in the Special Accounts. There were also losses in other government institutions.

The Philippine National Bank (PNB) was in the red ₱72.1 billion. Imelda charged off most of her spending sprees to the PNB, which wrote off her debts as "unresponded transfers." Ver also used PNB funds to finance his intelligence operations.

The Development Bank of Philippines (DBP) losses totalled ₱85.2 billion; Philippine Guarantee Corporation (Philguarantee) – ₱6.2 billion; National Investment and Development Corporation (NDC) – ₱2.8 billion.

These losses were primarily due to behest loans to cronies. The Commission on Audit developed criteria for determining a behest loan: the loan had little collateral; the borrower corporation was undercapitalized; the presence of marginal notes of high government officials on the loan application; the stockholders of the borrowing corporation were closely identified with the Marcoses; the loan proceeds were not used for the intended purpose; and the use of corporate layering (the use of two or more companies with the same incorporators and officers, whereby one company which gives the loan owns the company which obtains the loan, or similar arrangements).

The losses of PNB, DBP, NDC, and Philguarantee totalled ₱160.1 billion ($7.62 billion). In addition, the Philippine Nuclear Power Plant (PNPP) was in the red ₱29.8 billion because Marcos bought one nuclear power plant for the price of two. And Philippine Airlines was in debt $13.8 billion because of gross mismanagement and the free rides taken by Marcos, Imelda, the cronies, their relatives, and various hangers-on.

The total for these governmental institutions amounted to ₱203.7 billion ($9.995 billion). Most of those institutions should have earned a profit or, at the very least, not lost any money. But they were pillaged.

The Grand Total amounted to $17.1 billion in losses. Some of this undoubtedly went through the 7700 accounts on the way to Standard Chartered in Hong Kong, then to Switzerland. Some went into the cronies accounts, then to bank accounts abroad. Some went to Imelda for her spending sprees. The bottom line is, Marcos was responsible for the $17.1 billion. The foreign debt of $27 billion could have been $10 billion or less.

The estimates of what he stole does not include any gold bullion he may have taken from the Central Bank, such as the 326.1 metric tons that could have been produced but not reported by the Central Bank; or the 325 metric tons picked up by Tamaraw and shipped out of the country; or the golden Buddha treasure he stole from Roger Roxas; or any other treasure he found and did not turn over the government's share.

The golden Buddha disappeared. Psychic Olof Jonsson of Leber Group offered a possible clue as to its fate. Marcos told him he intended to melt down all artifacts, including golden Buddhas and other statues, into gold bars so as to hide the country of origin.

The gold bars disappeared also but there was ample proof they existed. PCGG Chairman David Castro accounted for 325 tons. Three Americans in Leber Group – Olof Jonsson, Norman Kirst, and Bob Curtis – saw a roomful on March 11, 1975, at Marcos' summer palace at Mariveles. The bars were stacked from floor to ceiling in a room about thirty feet square and had what appeared to be Chinese markings. These bars bore a strong resemblance to what Ron Lusk described in 1982. Lusk didn't testify at the golden Buddha case, but Attorney Dan Cathcart convinced a jury the gold Marcos' soldiers recovered at the golden Buddha site was the same that Jonsson, Kirst, and Curtis saw in 1975, and Dacus saw in 1983. Other, bigger amounts were also mentioned. Marcos could have found another treasure. Or else . . .

In 1993, six months after the Senate Committee on Banks, Financial Institutions, and Currencies requested a copy of the international reserves audit by SGV, the Central Bank submitted four spiral notebooks with clear plastic covers. The first page was emblazoned with the SGV logo and stated "Central Bank of the Philippines, Executive Summary, Volume I, April 1984."

In November 1996 I was writing this book and requested an interview with Senator Romulo. A 1993 magazine article – "The Case Of The Missing Gold Bullions" – implied he had seen the audit. I was anxious to ask if it revealed any missing gold.

Romulo was by then the Majority Leader and no longer chairman of the Committee on Banks. He said no, he had not seen the audit but he informed me about the four notebooks. Did I want to take a look?

I asked a C.P.A. to examine the data, then got a second opinion before making any conclusions. Romulo was correct, he had not seen the audit. In fact, no one had. There had never been an audit.

The Introduction in Volume I stated, "This report provides the Central Bank of the Philippines (CBP) with the results of our review undertaken in accordance with the terms of reference dated January 9, 1984 and subsequently expanded as detailed in our letter to Central Bank Governor Jose B. Fernandez Jr. on February 15, 1984."

There was no copy of the terms of reference so it was unknown who issued them or what they were. But why did SGV advise the Central Bank governor when they expanded the terms? The Central Bank was the one under investigation.

Under Review Coverage and Limitations, it stated, "We wish

to point out that a special review is not a regular audit, such that, while the review may provide a reasonable basis for expressing limited assurance that there are no material modifications that should be made to the CBP foreign assets and liabilities and the selected domestic accounts as at the cut-off dates mentioned in the preceding paragraph, it *does not provide assurances that all significant matters that would be disclosed in an audit have been uncovered.*" (Italics are the author's.)

Volume I was an Executive Summary of the Special Review; Volume II was a Philippine National Bank Executive Summary; Volume III – Central Bank Details of Special Review; Volume IV – Philippine National Bank Details of Special Review. The four notebooks were not an official report. There were no signatures of any officials. It can only be assumed the PNB was reviewed because the Central Bank had allegedly window-dressed its accounts with the aid of PNB deposits.

A few of the significant matters that were not uncovered were Imelda's spending – her name never appeared – and Ver's intelligence fund. So, how accurate was the review? And how easy would it be to steal or spend a million or a billion dollars then write it off?

There was no hint of theft or missing money. But there were, in the dry language of accounting, "downward adjustments" reported in the Statements of Condition as of the end of the three fiscal years examined.

Under "Gross International Reserves," the Statement of Condition as of June 30, 1983, reported "Proposed Adjustments: (US$1,148.1 million) and (₱12,473.8 million)." The parenthesis indicated a negative number.

The two previous years also reported "Proposed Adjustments." As of June 30, 1982 – (US$831.3 million) and (₱8,790.7 million); and as of June 30, 1981 – (US$133.1 million) and ₱30.9 million.

A total of ₱55,485.8 million ($3.3 billion) was listed under Central Bank Loans and Advances. The review stated, "Our work on this account was limited to the review and confirmation of loans and advances granted under the Consolidated Foreign Borrowing Program (CFBP) of ₱26,308.4 million. We noted a number of deficiencies . . ."

They did not audit the account; they "worked" on it. And this work was limited to less than half of the total. Still, they found "deficiencies," which, in accounting parlance, meant shortages of money.

And what about the Special Accounts? The Revaluation of International Reserves (RIR) and the Monetary Adjustment Account (MAA) were reviewed, but in a very narrow context. The report stated the review of the MAA was limited to 1983, "as records and documents were not given to us despite our persistent follow-ups with the Accounting Department."

The review was not geared toward the gold reserves. It provided some data on its holdings, and in Appendix A, Review Procedures On Foreign and Domestic Assets and Liabilities, under "Gross International Reserves – Gold," it stated:

"Conducted an inventory of all gold bar deliveries at the refinery and reconciled results with recorded balances. Also, observed the inventory-taking procedures followed during the annual stocktaking (sic) at the gold refinery."

It went on to state, "Verified purchases of gold bullions (sic) against computation sheets and supporting documents . . . Verified outward deliveries from refinery against deliver receipts . . . Checked postings . . . Verified outstanding deposits . . . Verified swap arrangements . . . Tied-in transfers of gold from one financial institution to another . . . Checked valuation of gold disposals."

Like the rest of the review, there was no signature, nor was there any supporting documentation. And there was no mention of the 325 tons the bank had reminted, as if this were an everyday occurrence.

The gaps and holes in the report, rendered while Marcos was still in power, were big enough to drive a truckload of gold through. Everything of unimportance was examined in great detail; the rest was a paragon of obfuscation. Still, it had to find something amiss since the Central Bank had no dollars. So, in addition to "deficiencies" in the loans, it found $1.2 billion missing. Only later did Senator Pimentel find liabilities disguised as assets.

The review had to fall far short of the expectations of the IMF and the Bank Advisory Committee, representing the commercial lenders. But they were in an awkward position. Economist

John Maynard Keynes said it first. If you owe the bank a thousand dollars, you have a problem. If you owe the bank a million dollars, the bank has a problem. The lenders couldn't scream too loud. They might never get their money back.

Marcos was in power two more years. What happened during that time? A computer printout found in the palace after he left showed that beginning on December 3, 1985, and continuing until February 19, 1986, a few days before he fled, there were twenty wire transfers totalling $94 million to three Swiss banks – Banque Hoffman, Societe de Banque Suisse, and Union de Banque Suisse; one Swiss company – Transammonia AG; five foreign banks in Zurich and Geneva; and the Commerzbank in Luxembourg.

Here was a possible "smoking gun." Did these monies come from the gold accounts abroad? Despite numerous requests from the PCGG, the Central Bank refused to answer the inquiry. It remained unanswered.

There were three Central Bank governors during the Marcos era. Each allowed Marcos to flaunt the law and steal millions. Some were guilty of bad judgment. Others were greedy. All attempted a coverup.

Marcos reinvented the Central Bank to satisfy his own needs. The Central Bank that people thought they knew – the one created to maintain price stability – no longer existed. It was a myth. It still survives.

The succeeding governors have attempted to bury the Central Bank losses along with the past by restructuring the old debt. To date there has been no contrition. No one has admitted any wrongdoing.

There has never been an investigation or audit. If what Cuisa said was true – that neither the president or the cabinet was informed about certain details – there doesn't seem to be any system of checks and balances.

In light of all the changes in definitions, adjustments to ratios, assorted double entries, and outright theft, this somehow doesn't seem right.

The questions that have been asked for more than ten years remain unanswered. How much was actually stolen and written off under the Special Accounts? And how much gold, if any, did Marcos steal from the international reserves? There is no doubt he looted the Central Bank. There just hasn't been a final tally.

Over at the Batasan, people scream and shout and hurl insults instead of brickbats. A legislature elected by the people engages in the grand sport of politics. Democracy has returned to the Philippines, and with it political stability, the main ingredient toward full development.

The Philippine economy grows by leaps and bounds. Soon it will join the other economic Dragons of Asia. But there is one piece of unfinished business. A nation that does not know its past does not know itself. And the Filipino people know very little about their own Central Bank. It still harbors dark secrets. One more ghost needs to be exorcised. The government has been pushed around by the nation's premier financial institution far too long.

There's an old Chinese proverb: *To err is human; to forgive divine; but to get even – ahh, that's paradise.*

Notes

Preface

I met Roger, his wife, and children, in 1988, while excavating the Fort Santiago treasure site. He worked for us for two years as a treasure consultant. Roger was interviewed numerous times over a two-year period. He described the torture methods his captors employed to get him to sign a confession, which stated Marcos' people were not involved in the theft of the Buddha.

Dan Cathcart and John Tucker provided the background of how the lawsuit started. Documents and trial testimony were also provided.

Cathcart also wrote the book on aircraft accident litigation: *Aircraft Accident Litigation Techniques.*

Chapter 1

Cesar Parlade was assigned to the legal department of the PCGG when I first met him in 1986. He, along with Bonifacio "Boni" Gillego, deputy director of the PCGG, provided access to the library from its inception. Parlade went on to become a commissioner and Gillego was elected to Congress.

During the Aquino presidency, the palace museum offered daily tours (except Wednesdays when her Cabinet met) of Malacañan Palace. You could see where General Ver planted the bombs in President Marcos' office, the bedrooms of Marcos and Imelda, and their vaults. They no longer contained the filing cabinets or jewelry but there were pictures of the way they were found after Marcos left. You could also see the vast room where Marcos' and Imelda's clothes and shoes were still on the racks.

The details of Marcos' abrupt departure and flight to Honolulu via Clark Air Base and Guam are contained in a report prepared by the Readiness Subcommittee of the Committee On Armed Services, House of Representatives, dated May 1986, and entitled "Investigation of the Costs Involved in Moving Former President Marcos and His Party from Manila to Hawaii."

The raid on Imee Marcos-Manotoc's office was also well publicized at the time since it was one of the first to yield quite a bit of information. Journalist Phil Bronstein, reported the story for the *San Francisco Examiner*, entitled "Jackpot for 'Raiders' of the hidden holdings," March 9, 1986.

Although his selective memory presents a distorted version of many events, Colonel Arturo Aruiza, a military aide to Marcos, wrote an interesting book, *Ferdinand Marcos: Malacañang to Makiki*, that provided background information about Marcos' last days in the palace.

The details about Imelda's jewelry being found in suitcases in the palace and in large envelopes at the airport were well documented in newspapers and magazines. One example is *Mr. & Ms.* magazine, dated March 20–26, 1987, "A Gem of a Story."

The sentencing of two municipal treasury employees to prison terms of sixty-four and twenty-six years respectively was reported in the *Filipino Times*, "When Solons Get ₱15,000 Dole Each," March 20–29, 1985.

In the Philippine government's case against Marcos, the properties identified were worth approximately $5 billion. [Republic of the Philippines vs. Ferdinand E. Marcos (represented by his estate/heirs) and Imelda Romualdez Marcos. Civil Case SBNo. 0141.] The petition excluded assets, monies, and all other properties involved in civil cases 0002 – 0035.

Far Eastern Economic Review, 50th Anniversary Issue, "The Sixties – Nationalism and Chaos," 1996, compared the Philippines to other southeast Asian economies.

Guinness Book of World Records, 1991. "Theft: The government of the Philippines announced on April 23, 1986, that they had succeeded in identifying $860.8 million "salted" by the former President Ferdinand Edralin Marcos (1917–1989) and his wife Imelda. It was asserted that the total since November 1965 was believed to be between $5 and $10 billion."

"Convergence of International Law and Domestic Law in the Recovery of the Plundered Wealth," by Jovita R. Salonga, July 20, 1993.

Chapter 2

Intelligence Memorandum. "Philippine Elections." Directorate of Intelligence. Central Intelligence Agency, October 28, 1965.

The quote, "I'll have your head," came from Raymond Bonner's interview with William Bundy, assistant secretary of state for East Asia, in *Waltzing With A Dictator.*

Bonner discovered the quarterly payments to Marcos in a classified GAO Report: B-168501, "Review of Assistance to the Philippine Government in Support of the Philippine Civic Action Group, June 1, 1970. A censored summary of this report was released in 1970. In his Sources and Notes, Bonner noted, "The author was permitted to read and take notes from the still classified version."

Most of Imelda's medical problems seemed to occur at critical periods of Marcos' political career. A typical story appeared in the *Philippine Herald*, on May 29, 1968. "Doctors Set More Tests For Imelda" was the title of the article. It was on page three. That a story about the First Lady only made page three is indicative of how serious the press took such announcements.

Copies of Marcos' and Imelda's signature cards for their Swiss bank accounts were found in the palace after the revolution. Marcos' use of the name William Saunders dates back to World War II. That name came up while researching Marcos' war record. A letter dated July 26, 1944, addressed to Major Bernard Anderson, an American guerrilla, was found in the Whitney Papers, MacArthur Memorial Archives. It requested arms, ammunition, money, and other items, and was signed "William Saunders." It was written on *Ang Manga Maharlika* stationery. That was the name of the guerrilla group which Marcos claimed to have led. On the back of the letter was handwritten, "14 Aug 44, Req. fr Col. Fertig, Dec 43, Ferdinand E. Marcos w/Gen Capinpin." Capinpin was Marcos' commanding officer in the Twenty-first Infantry Division.

The tracing of the Vaduz foundations was detailed in Republic of the Philippines vs. Ferdinand E. Marcos (represented by his estate/heirs) and Imelda Romualdez Marcos. Civil Case SBNo. 0141. Additional information was provided in *Some Are Smarter Than Others*, by Ricardo Manapat.

"I discovered Yamashita's treasure." *Far Eastern Economic Review*, "Quest For Yamashita's Hoard Still Haunts Manila," June 25, 1987.

Roger took me to the site to explain how the digging and the recovery took place. In the course of our interviews Roger was regressed to recall specific points about the excavation and the discovery in order to accurately recall his experience. This story is slightly different from the deposition Roger gave in his civil suit but the details reconciled.

Roger also provided a copy of the statement he made to the Baguio police on April 7, 1971.

Ken Cheatham testified at the civil action in 1966. He provided the photos he took in 1971. Louie Mendoza also testified. (Circuit Court, First Circuit, State of Hawaii, Civil Case Number 88-0522, Roger Roxas and the Golden Budha Corporation vs. Ferdinand Marcos and Imelda Marcos.)

Chapter 3

Philippine historian Teodoro A. Agoncillo published several books about the wartime situation in the Philippines that were helpful: *The Fateful Years*, volumes 1 and 2, and *The Burden of Proof.*

The war in the Pacific was documented in *American Caesar*, by William Manchester, and *Eagle Against the Sun*, by Ronald H. Spector.

Yamashita's retreat was described in *Tiger of Malaya*, by Aubrey S. Kenworthy.

Yamashita's execution was described in Manila newspaper accounts of the period: "General Yamashita Met Slow Death in Black Gallows," *Manila Chronicle*, February 26, 1946, and "Yamashita's End," *Philippine Free Press*, March 3, 1946.

The trial of Yamashita was documented in *The Yamashita Precedent: War Crimes and Command Responsibility*, by Richard L. Lael, and *The Case of General Yamashita*, by A. Frank Reel.

Philippine animosity toward Japan after the war was described in *War Reparations & Peace Settlement: Philippine-Japan Relations, 1945–1956*, by Takushi Ohno.

Minoru Fukumitsu's claim that there was no Yamashita treasure has appeared in numerous periodicals over the years: "There Is No Yamashita Treasure," in the Panorama magazine of the *Philippine Daily Express*, July 17, 1982, and "War Treasure Still Sought In Philippines," *Los Angeles Times*, May 28, 1978.

Ernesto Rodriguez' book, *The Bad Guerrillas of Northern Luzon*, described Marcos' experiences as a guerrilla during the war, and how he was arrested by the U.S. forces.

Houston Turner, Sheldon Empol, and Andy Aquila, three survivors of the Bataan Death March were interviewed on May 12, 14, and 15, 1992, at the fiftieth anniversary convention in Burlingame, California.

Chapter 4

Three books provided the information for the nostalgic glimpse of Manila just before the war. Florence Horn's *Orphans of the Pacific*; Lewis Gleeck's article, "American Life Styles In Colonial Philippines," In *Pammadayaw: Philippine Studies by International Authors, In Honor of Dr. Marcelino Foronda, Jr.*; and Beth Day Romulos's *The Manila Hotel.*

Soldiers of the Sun: The Rise and Fall of the Imperial Japanese Army, by Meirion and Susie Harries, provided excellent insights into the Japanese military before and during World War II.

The story of the silver pesos being dumped in Manila Bay off Corregidor is well known. William Manchester mentioned it in *American Caesar*. Ben Waldron, a Corregidor veteran, also mentioned it in his book, *Corregidor: From Paradise to Hell*.

Col. John R. Vance was 88 years old and living in Corte Madeira, California, when he was interviewed on November 29, 1985. He was General MacArthur's finance officer, and also recalled the dumping of the silver pesos. He recounted how he dutifully read off the serial number of each dollar bill, which was recorded and then radioed to Washington. The bills were then dumped in a fifty-five gallon can and burned.

The British government and the Permanent Secretary, Republic of Singapore, both denied the story about shipping Her Majesty's treasures to Singapore.

The information about the *Awa Maru* was taken from a book, *The Awa Maru Incident*, by Minoru Fukumitsu. It was published in Japan, and no English version is available.

In 1976 several newspapers carried articles about the *Awa Maru* when Commander Loughlin and several others applied for permission to salvage the vessel: "Sunken Ship May Hold $5 Billion Treasure," *San Francisco Chronicle*, November 18, 1976, and "A Treasure Hunt for $5 Billion," *San Francisco Examiner*, November 19, 1976.

Three Filipino eyewitnesses were interviewed and regressed numerous times over a three year period. They were Pedro Lim, Ben Valmores, and Pol Giga. Pedro died in 1995. They provided most of the information about the treasure burials.

Copies of the progress reports on Presidential Security Command stationery found in the palace were provided by a confidential source.

The members of Ver's treasure hunting group were confirmed by several sources: Col. Orlando Dulay, who was interviewed several times in prison before he died in 1997; Reverend Simeon Lepasana, who served with Col. Villacrusis on one of the Task Forces; Johnny Wilson, who served as the historian of the Task Force; and Tabo Ingles, who was a friend and classmate – Philippine Military Academy, Class of 1945 – of Villacrusis.

Chapter 5

A copy of the letter to Marcos, dated May 2, 1973, which told about Task Force Restoration, was provided by a member of Leber Group. A copy also appeared in Jack Anderson's column on July 12, 1978, during the time he was writing about Leber Group. Simeon Lepasana confirmed the letter and his participation on the Task Force.

Numerous interviews with Roger provided the details of his time in prison and how he hid from Marcos after his release.

Zeitlin's story was recalled by Primitivo Mijares in his book *The Conjugal Dictatorship*. Also *Far Eastern Economic Review*, "After Zeitlin, Assurances," November 19, 1976.

The Bernard Wideman incident was reported in *Far Eastern Economic Review*, "Journalist Vindicated," March 11, 1977.

The PCGG provided copies of statements that many of the cronies gave after Marcos fled. These included Rolando Gapud, Jose Y. Campos, Oscar Cariño, and Baltazar Aquino.

The testimony of witnesses at Imelda's trial included Rolando Gapud, Jaime Laya, Enrique Razon, Ricardo Silverio, Andres Genito, Jr., Jesus Tanchanco, and Rodolfo Arambulo. Gapud testified that in 1984 Marcos' daughter, Irene, compiled a twenty-two page list of sixty to eighty companies showing Marcos' interest in each company. (District Court, Southern District of New York. Case Number 86-9729. United States of America vs. Imelda Marcos, Adnan Khashoggi, et al.)

The equipment purchases on which Marcos received 15 percent commission and the official receipts from Berlin and Co. were produced as evidence at the trial.

Other sources were:

A Preliminary Study of Interlocking Directorates, by John F. Doherty, S.J.

Who Controls the Philippine Economy: Some Need Not Try As Hard As Others, by John F. Doherty, S.J.

Some Are Smarter Than Others, by Ricardo Manapat.

War Reparations: Marcos-Honolulu Papers, Oscar L. Rodriguez Papers, Baltazar A. Aquino Papers, Teofisto T. Guingona Jr. Papers, Francisco I. Chavez Papers: from *Japan Inc. In Asia: A Documentation On Its Operations Through The Philippine Polity*, by Mamoru Tsuda and Masaki Yokoyama.

The comment Imelda made about her relatives in "High Flying First Lady of the Philippines," by Roy Rowan. *Fortune*, July 2, 1979, is sometimes paraphrased as "Some are smarter than others."

Foreign debt in 1965 was $360 million. Source: Central Bank of the Philippines.

Chapter 6

Olof Jonsson was interviewed in Las Vegas and Manila. He testified at Roger's golden Buddha trial. *The Psychic Feats of Olof Jonsson*, by Brad Steiger, detailed his amazing abilities.

The Leber Group story was told first by Steve Psinakis in the *Philippine News* in 1978. About the same time the *Las Vegas Sun* picked up the story and reported it. Bob Curtis was interviewed in August 1987 and he recounted the story.

Copies of the letter from Kirst to Curtis dated February 22, 1975, and the Leber Group agreement, which detailed the sharing arrangement, were provided by Curtis.

The first meeting of Leber Group was described by Olof Jonsson, Bob Curtis, Cesar Leyran, and eyewitnesses Ben Valmores and Pol Giga.

In separate interviews, Jonsson and Curtis described their meeting with Marcos in 1974 and the visit to the summer palace where the golden Buddha was seen.

Simeon Lepasana took me to Teresa to see the weed-covered excavation site on the property of Raymondo Francisco.

Lieutenant Ramon Cannu and Lieutenant Bonifacio Gillego served together as platoon commanders in the Korean War in the early fifties. Later, when Marcos was president, Gillego exposed the his war record as fake. Cannu remained in the service and worked for Ver on several projects regarding the treasure.

Primitivo Mijares' defection and bribe was described in Jack Anderson's column in the *San Francisco Chronicle*, "A President Who's Above Criticism," June 29, 1976, and in *Two Terrorists Meet*, by Steve Psinakis.

The Conjugal Dictatorship of Ferdinand and Imelda Marcos, by Primitivo Mijares.

General Singlaub was interviewed by phone. He explained how the Nippon Star operation was set up.

I was asked by Emanuel V. Soriano, national security director, to assist International Precious Metals in their treasure hunt in the Philippines. I wrote a book about the experience: *Asian Loot*.

The Federal Archives and Records Center in San Bruno, California, provided a complete record of Curtis' indictment and trial. (District Court, Second Judicial District of Nevada, Case Number 77-00066, United States of America vs. Robert Curtis and John W. McAllaster.)

The Court Clerk at the Federal District Court in Reno, Nevada provided summaries of Curtis' other two lawsuits. (District Court, Second Judicial District of Nevada, Case Number 307152, Eureka Trust, Liberty Trust, et al. vs. Robert Curtis et al.; District Court, Second Judicial District of Nevada, Case Number 313689, Samuel J. Agnew vs. Robert Curtis et al.)

Chapter 7

Jaime Laya, in his testimony at Imelda's trial, described the functions of the Central Bank as being equivalent to the Board of Governors of the Federal Reserve, etc. (District Court, Southern District of New York, Case Number 86-9729, United States of America vs. Imelda Marcos, Adnan Khashoggi, et al.)

Laya also testified that Imelda took an active role in international monetary affairs. It was standard procedure to provide Imelda with a copy of any letter from the Central Bank that went to Marcos.

The information on the International Gold Pool was provided by John M. Lucas in several interviews, and from the Annual Report of the U.S. Department of the Interior, Bureau of Mines, entitled *Gold*, by John M. Lucas.

The annual production has been quoted at various times to be between 20 and 30 metric tons. Mining executives said that gold panners may smuggle up to 150 metric tons a year. From hearings held by Committee on Banks, Financial Institutions, and Currencies, Chairman: Sen. Albert Romulo, October 3, 1990.

International Financial Statistics, March 1988, published by the International Monetary Fund, provided the information about the annual status of gold reserves at the Central Bank.

Imelda's comment about the internation reserves apeared in *Newsweek*, August 12, 1974, "The Iron Butterfly."

Philippine Public Internal and External Debt, 1949–1982. Source: Central Bank of the Philippines.

Purification Pedro's arrest, torture, and murder was described in Task Force Detainees File 77-BTN-001. Interview with Agnes de Mesa, Task Force Detainees, November 16, 1996.

A Position Paper On Proposed Improvements to the Promotions, Regulatory, and Infrastructure Framework Affecting Philippine Business. Submitted to The Hon. Min. Luis R. Villafuerte, Ministry of Trade, Makati, Metro Manila, August 11, 1980. Submitted by European Chamber of Commerce, Japanese Chamber of Commerce and Industry, American Chamber of Commerce, Australian Business Group.

A Commentary on the Report Entitled "Multinational Corporations in the Philippines" Prepared by the Technology Resource Center, April 16, 1979, was prepared by the American Chamber of Commerce. I wrote the first eight chapters. George Suter, who was president of the Chamber at the time and also head of Pfizer, wrote the last chapter which was about the pharmaceutical industry. Suter knew Marcos personally. Some called him a "known Marcos apologist." He sent the telegram to Marcos.

Central Bank Governor Gregorio Licaros told the president he would like to rest. *Bulletin Today*, Manila, January 13, 1981.

Over the next two years Marcos ordered the government financial institutions to provide ₱30 billion ($3 billion) in bail-out funds to the crony companies. Memo For Concerned Citizens, # 4, Manila, December 1983.

Daily Express, Manila, "Offices Entangled In Red Tape Listed," November 4, 1982.

The information about the 525 tons of gold, Michael Young, and Mr. Au was first brought to light in April 1982 by the *Far Eastern Economic Review* in its article, "Golden Fleece." Michael Young was interviewed by Guy Sacerdoti and Gary Coull.

The data on Ron Lusk was found in an undated confidential memorandum obtained from U.S. government sources. Another confidential source confirmed the information.

Statement of Senator Edward M. Kennedy on Corruption In The Philippines, November 7, 1985.

Statement of Senator Edward M. Kennedy On The GAO Report On U.S. Economic Assistance To The Philippines, May 2, 1986.

The Philippines: Accountability and Control of U.S. Economic Assistance, United States General Accounting Office, Briefing Report To Senator Edward M. Kennedy, May 1986.

San Francisco Chronicle, "Manila's Spending of Aid Criticized," December 6, 1985.

The telex from Bill Erbe was found in the palace after the overthrow.

Seattle Times, "30-M Lawsuit vs. FM, FL," September 18, 1982.

Report of an Amnesty International Mission to the Republic of the Philippines, 11–28 November 1981, An Amnesty International Publication, September 1982.

The Extradition Treaty Between the Philippines and the United States: Facts and Implications, by Jovita R. Salonga. Philippine Studies Occasional Paper No. 5, Philippine Studies Program, University of Hawaii, Center for Asian and Pacific Studies, August 1982.

U.S. Perceptions and Policies Toward the Philippines. Has A Transition Begun? by Larry Niksch. Congressional Research Service, Library of Congress, December 1, 1983. Prepared for the Joint Seminar on United States-Philippine Relations, December 6–7, 1983.

The Luxembourg sales agreement was first reported by the *Philippine Free Press* magazine. The PCGG provided copies of these documents.

Chapter 8

The information about Dacus came from a memorandum published by the Center for Constitutional Rights in the U.S. and from a deposition of his testimony in the trial. (Circuit Court, First Circuit, State of Hawaii, Civil Case Number 88-0522, Roger Roxas and the Golden Budha Corporation vs. Ferdinand Marcos and Imelda Marcos.)

Deposition of Norman Lester Dacus, dated March 27, 1992; deposition of Michael O'Brien, dated December 9, 1992; deposition of John Edward Doel, dated February 5, 1993.

The True Story of the Aquino Assassination, by Gerald N. and Kathleen Thompson Hill, with the cooperation of Steve Psinakis.

San Francisco Examiner, "Imelda Marcos Blames News Media For Unrest In Philippines," September 19, 1983.

In September 1984, a World Bank report, No. 4912-PHIL, was made public. It stated that $3.1 billion of foreign loans contracted for between 1978 and 1982 failed to reach their beneficiaries. *Philippine News* (San Francisco), "$13 billion Philippine Earnings Since 1965 Reported Missing," August 4–10, 1985.

"The only country in the world that published accurate information about its foreign debt." Quote from "The Philippine Economy: Policies and Development, 1975–1982," Published by the Central Bank of the Philippines, 1983.

Laya couldn't fire Balatbat because he "threatened to blow everything skyhigh." Quoted from Senator Albert Romulo's privilege speech, March 15, 1993, "How I Lost My Innocence."

The information about KLM flight 864, the Korean Airlines flight, and the 707 charter flight was contained in an undated confidential memorandum obtained from confidential U.S. government sources.

The information on Cruz-Cruzal's arrest was also contained in the confidential memorandum. Several interviews with Frank Higdon in September and October 1992 confirmed the details.

Brian Lendrum's comments were in the *Far Eastern Economic Review* article, "Golden Fleece," by Guy Sacerdoti and Gary Coull, April 1982.

The letter of Geronimo Velasco to Prime Minister Virata about a $200 to $250 million loan was introduced as evidence at Imelda's trial. (District Court, Southern District of New York, Case Number 86-9729, United States of America vs. Imelda Marcos, Adnan Khashoggi, et al.)

Laya testified at the trial about the Central Bank being no longer able to borrow and about making the appeal to businessmen at the palace.

Some account statements found in the palace detailed the bank accounts of each foundation Marcos and Imelda maintained at Credit Suisse. The date of the statements is given first, followed by the name of the foundation, and the account balance as of that date:

Nov. 13, 1983	– Avertina (two accounts)	– $115,500,000
Jan. 18, 1983	– Palmy	– $ 5,399,588
Apr. 13, 1976	– Scolari	– $ 26,694,002
Nov. 18, 1981	– Spinus	– $ 77,616,043
Dec. 12, 1974	– Trinidad	– $ 2,492,905
Dec. 30, 1980	– Valamo	– $ 65,512,977
Dec. 28, 1980	– Wintrop (two accounts)	– $ 25,883,037
Jul. 4, 1978	– Xandy (two accounts)	– $ 22,486,828

In 1991 and 1992, the Swiss Federal Police turned over to the PCGG the bank statements of all the Marcos bank accounts in Switzerland. These accounts are still classified.

A detailed account of how Marcos used money in three of his Swiss bank accounts to purchase the Treasury Notes was provided by the PCGG in a pamphlet, *Swiss Banks Cracking In!!!* by Dan Richard V. Daniel.

David Castro, PCGG chairman, testified at Imelda's trial that part of the proceeds of the sale of 1.6 million ounces of gold could have been gone toward the purchase of the Treasury Notes.

The televised dressing down of the 350 business leaders was reported in all the media. *San Francisco Chronicle*, "Marcos Blasts Business Leaders," November 11, 1983.

After the overthrow, Roberto V. Ongpin, Marcos' minister of trade and industry and chairman of Task Force Luntian, published *The Binondo Central Bank: The True Story*, in the *Manila Bulletin*, April 25, 1986.

Romulo's statement was made in an interview with *Asiaweek*, "I Am Heartsick," December 16, 1983.

Bulletin Today (Manila), "The Financial Crisis Explained," by the Domestic Information Service. Three part series. December 28, 29, 30, 1983.

Chapter 9

Information on Imelda's shopping trips were taken from testimony at her trial (District Court, Southern District of New York, Case Number 86-9729, United States of America vs. Imelda Marcos, Adnan Khashoggi, et al.) and other documents.

In other trial testimony:

Fe Roa Geminez' notebooks detailing Imelda's spending were presented.

The chart of Imelda's jewelry and clothing purchases was presented by Maria Goreti Jimenez, PCGG.

Oscar Cariño, Philippine National Bank vice president in New York, testified about delivering money to Imelda's hotel suite every time she was in New York.

Enrique Razon testified about the $30 million loan he never received. Laya's testimony recalled the conversation with Gabriel Singson.

Rolando Gapud testified how he supervised the real estate purchases.

The network of shell companies used to purchase the real estate was explained on huge charts by the FBI.

Jaime Laya and Rolando Gapud testified about Cuenca's $8 million being wired to New York for real estate purchases.

Andres Genito testified about the $1 million withdrawal in Hong Kong.

Monica Manalo, PNOC, testified that $60 to $80 million was sold directly to Security Bank and Trust Company from late 1982 to 1983, until the Exoil Handil Swap Arrangement with Pertamina Oil Company (Indonesia) ended. She handled the telexes to Chemical Bank, New York. Eduardo Delfonso, treasurer of PNOC, also testified that Velasco instructed him to sell the dollars to Security Bank and Trust Company.

Jack Tanzer testified about Imelda's jewelry purchases.

Ian Glenn Kennedy, senior vice president at Christie's auction house, testified about the value of the paintings.

Khashoggi's deposition detailed his involvement in the purchase of Imelda's paintings.

The records of real estate purchases were presented. The PCGG also provided documentation on these purchases.

During the trial, Assistant U.S. Attorney Deborah Livingston said, "Imelda treated the New York branch of the Philippine National Bank as her personal piggy bank."

A Cartier representative in Hong Kong said Imelda had put together the world's largest collection of gems: *New York Times*, "Manila Inner Circle Gains Under Marcos," by Fox Butterfield. January 15, 1978.

The tracing of the Vaduz foundations was detailed in the civil case. [Republic of the Philippines vs. Ferdinand E. Marcos (represented by his estate/heirs) and Imelda Romualdez Marcos. Civil Case SBNo. 0141.]

Connie Lowenthal was quoted in the *Far Eastern Economic Review*, "A Fool and her Monet are soon Parted," September 29, 1988. She was an art historian in New York who ran International Foundation for Art Research, which specializes in identifying stolen and fake art. She noted: ". . . they convinced her that in-depth collecting of an artist nobody had ever collected before was what she should do."

There is still some confusion about how many paintings Imelda actually obtained. A good source for a detailed list of the paintings is *Some Are Smarter Than Others*, by Ricardo Manapat. Manapat listed 182 art works Imelda purchased as compiled by government investigators, but mentions the list is not complete. Approximately half are still missing.

People, "The Imelda Marcos Shopping Guide: A Cache 'N' Carry Way To Spend The Fortunes Of A Nation," April 7, 1986.

Chapter 10

William Sullivan described Imelda's ancestral estate in his book, *Obbligato*.

The secret decree appointing Imelda chairperson of a committee with presidential powers was found in the palace after the overthrow.

Imelda's appointment as governor of Metro Manila and Marcos' comments were reported in *Pacific Stars and Stripes*, "Marcos Family – Study Core of Philippine Life," November 9, 1975.

Cosmopolitan. "The Ten Richest Women In the World," December 1975.

San Francisco Chronicle, Herb Caen's column, March 11, 1975.

Imelda's appointment as minister of human settlements was reported in *The New York Times Magazine*, "Creating A Dynasty In the Philippines," May 24, 1981.

Far Eastern Economic Review, "Out of the Muddle, A Promise of Bliss," February 16, 1979.

The white sand escapade was reported in *People* magazine, "The Imelda Marcos Shopping Guide: A Cache 'N' Carry Way To Spend the Fortunes Of A Nation," April 7, 1986.

Life magazine reported on Imelda's twenty-fifth wedding anniversary, and was banned in the Philippines. "Silver Anniversary For the Iron Butterfly," July 1979.

Imelda's formula for development was described in the *Far Eastern Economic Review*, "A Political Factor In the KKK Equation," October 29, 1982.

Commissioner Eufemio Domingo of the Commission on Audit disclosed that more than ₱198 million in Kilusan sa Kabuhayan at Kaunlaran Processing Center Authority (KKK-PCA) funds were paid out from February 1984 to February 1986 to fictitious contractors for non-existent projects. *Daily Inquirer* (Manila), "Fictitious Contractors Got ₱198M," June 28, 1986.

Far Eastern Economic Review, "A Political Base Grows From A Military Base," October 29, 1982.

Imelda's public argument with Cardinal Sin over the Manila International Film Festival was described in *Far Eastern Economic Review*, "MIFF sin miffs Sin," February 17, 1983.

Her propensity for building was reported in the *Los Angeles Times*, "Imelda: The Philippine 'Eva Peron,'" October 24, 1980.

Far Eastern Economic Review, "Life Raft For Manila's Hotels," October 21, 1977.

The University of Life episode was reported in *Newsweek*. "The Iron Butterfly," August 12, 1974.

"I'm like Robin Hood . . ." *Fortune*, "High Flying First Lady of the Philippines," by Roy Rowan, July 2, 1979.

Metro Manila Commission managed to accumulate debts of ₱1.99 billion. *Philippine News* (San Francisco), "Imelda's M. Manila Commission In Hock," December 11–17, 1985.

The growth of the communist party in the Philippines was reported in "The Situation In the Philippines," U.S. Senate Staff Report For the Committee On Foreign Relations," Washington, D.C., October 1984.

The Philippine Revolution: The Leader's View, by Jose Maria Sison, head of the Communist Party of the Philippines, provided the leader's perspective.

The Huk Rebellion, Benedict J. Kerkvliet.

Inside the Philippine Revolution, William Chapman.

The Dead Season, Alan Berlow, provided shocking details of poverty on the island of Negros and how the New People's Army stepped in to fill the void left by a lack of law and order.

Philippine News (San Francisco), "Imelda's 'Philosophical' UN Speech Astonishing," October 23–29, 1985.

Statement of Senator Edward M. Kennedy on Corruption In The Philippines, November 7, 1985.

Statement of Senator Edward M. Kennedy On The GAO Report On U.S. Economic Assistance To The Philippines, May 2, 1986.

The Philippines: Accountability and Control of U.S. Economic Assistance, United States General Accounting Office, Briefing Report To Senator Edward M. Kennedy, May 1986.

Report To The Committee On Foreign Affairs, House of Representatives, "Economic Support Fund Assistance To The Philippines," GAO/NSIAD-84-44, January 27, 1984.

Business Day (Manila), "COA Insists FM Diverted Some US Economic Aid Fund," April 18, 1986.

"In the province, the farmer . . ." I have paraphrased a quote from an Agency for International Development report, "War on Hunger," December 1977.

The World Bank and the World's Poorest, 1980. World Bank brochure, 1980.

Poverty and Basic Needs. World Bank brochure, 1980.

Poverty Profile, Bicol Region, Report by U.S. Agency for International Development, August 1982.

Poverty Profile, Eastern Visayas, Report by U.S. Agency for International Development, September 1982.

Poverty Profile, Western Visayas, Report by U.S. Agency for International Development, January 1981.

Number of Filipinos living below the poverty line reported in *Business Day* (Manila), "Determining Poverty Thresholds," May 25, 1984.

The information on the rain forest came from the Philippine government's Office of Southern Cultural Minorities, Quezon City.

Philippine News (San Francisco), "Tale of Imelda and 'The Toilet King,'" December 11–17, 1985.

Chapter 11

Business Day (Manila), "Reserves Overstated Since 1981," August 9, 1984.

Lew Simons wrote a book, *Worth Dying For*, which detailed the hunt for the hidden wealth, for which they won a Pulitzer Prize for the *San Jose Mercury News*.

Far Eastern Economic Review, "Overbuilt, Underbooked," by Bernard Wideman, January 21, 1977.

New York Times, "5 Years of Philippine Martial law Builds Personal Power of Marcos," by Fox Butterfield, January 9, 1978.

Ibid, "The Marcos Connections in the Capital," by Jeff Gerth, November 12, 1985.

Wall Street Journal, "Ties To the Top; In the Philippines, It's Whom You Know That Can Really Count," by Barry Kramer, January 28, 1978.

Nation, "Marcos's Influential Enemies," by Brennon Jones, October 4, 1980.

The story about Oliver North and Ver was widely reported. William Scott Malone gave a good account in "Greed: The Golden Fleece," *Regardies*, October 1988.

The Interpol cable and secret U.S. Treasury Report was obtained from a confidential source.

Philippine News (San Francisco), "The Mystery of the Baccay Case: Solved But Not Solved," December 4–10, 1985.

The use of USAID money to pay off the Treasury Bills was introduced in evidence at Imelda's trial. (District Court, Southern District of New York,

Case Number 86-9729, United States of America vs. Imelda Marcos, Adnan Khashoggi, et al.) The evidence included a copy of the wire dated December 20, 1985. But the charge was not listed in the indictment. Judge Keenan allowed the evidence but it was not identified as USAID money because it was outside the scope of the indictment.

Information on Rolando Gapud and the 7700 accounts in Security Bank and Trust Company came from his testimony at the trial.

The letter from Fe Roa Geminez to Ms. P.A.L. Vine, requesting that $708,000 be remitted to the law firm of Anderson, Hibey, Manheim and Blair, Marcos' attorneys in Washington, D.C., was introduced as evidence at the trial.

Fe Roa Geminez' fifty-six page ledger listing Marcos' campaign expenditures from September 1, 1985, to February 22, 1986, was introduced in evidence at Imelda's trial.

Investigation of Philippine Investments In the United States: Hearings Before the Subcommittee On Asian and Pacific Affairs. 99th Congress. First and Second Sessions. December 3, 11, 12, 13, 17, and 19, 1985; January 21, 23, and 29; March 18 and 19; April 9 and 17, 1986.

San Francisco Chronicle, "Philippines Diverted U.S. Schools Aid," December 8, 1985.

Philippine News (San Francisco), "U.S. Halts Fund Aid to NEA for Anomaly," January 8–14, 1986.

Phil Bronstein and Kim Komenich of the *San Francisco Examiner* were in Antigue the day after Eveliano Javier was murdered. They told me what happened. Komenich's photo of Javier in the morgue surrounded by his friends and family won a Pulitzer Prize.

The Commission on Audit reported the $150 million missing. *San Francisco Chronicle*, "Marcos Officials Looted Treasury of $150 Million, Auditors Say," April 3, 1986.

The newly printed peso notes in possession of Alfredo Romualdez was reported in the *Philippine News* (San Francisco), "Marcoses, Pals Dipped Hands in Most Government Till," April 9–15, 1986.

A copy of the telex from the Archdiocese of San Francisco was provided by a confidential source.

The *Sunday Telegraph* in Australia reported the story of T.C.B. "Andrew" Tan trying to sell 2,000 tons of gold. It was reprinted in the *Daily Inquirer* (Manila) on April 21, 1986.

A copy of the papers of Great American Management Corporation of Houston were provided by a confidential source.

The English language newspaper in Tokyo, *Yomiuri Shimbun*, reported the twenty tons of gold being sold by Marcos aides. It was reprinted in the *Manila Journal* on January 5, 1988.

The details of Marcos' abrupt departure and flight to Honolulu via Clark Air Base and Guam are contained in a report: *Investigation of the Costs Involved in Moving Former President Marcos and His Party from Manila to Hawaii.* Report prepared by the Readiness Subcommittee of the Committee On Armed Services. 99th Cong., 2d sess., 1986. Committee Print 20.

Information on Operation Big Bird came from De Guzman's testimony to the senate and his sworn affidavit he made to a Swiss notary. Copies of the letters of authority signed by Marcos and Imelda and numerous correspondences between De Guzman and the Swiss authorities, and De Guzman and Philippine authorities were provided by a confidential source.

Chapter 12

Aruiza's book, *Ferdinand Marcos: Malacañang to Makiki*, provided the details of Marcos' search for another domicile outside the U.S. and the constant visits of people willing to help him for a price.

The revolt led by Tolentino was reported in the *San Francisco Examiner*, "What Marcos Told the Coup Leaders To do," July 13, 1986, and the *San Francisco Chronicle*, "Marcos Loyalist Names Himself Acting President," July 7, 1986.

Telephone interview with Mike Whitey, lawyer for the Committee for Justice of Viernes and Domingo.

Emanuel V. Soriano was national security director at the time of the January 1987 coup. He provided first-hand information about what went on behind the scenes. The coup was widely reported in newspapers in Manila and the U.S. *San Francisco Examiner*, "Besieged Rebels Surrender In Manila," January 29, 1987.

Khashoggi's testimony in the rackettering trial mentioned the shipload of gold. (District Court, Southern District of New York, Case Number 86-9729, United States of America vs. Imelda Marcos, Adnan Khashoggi, et al.)

All documents relating to the Sheraton project, including a draft of the agreement dated February 28, 1988, with corrections in Marcos' handwriting, were provided by a confidential source.

The transcript of the interviews which Robert Chastain and Richard Hirschfield taped was provided by a confidential source.

Francisco Sumulong went public with his story about the $15 billion offer in June 1991. The *Daily Globe* newspaper reported the story in an exclusive interview with Sumulong on July 23 and 26, 1991.

Marcos' $5 billion offer was reported widely in the media in the Philippines and abroad. A copy of the letter Marcos sent to Weinstein and a copy of the letter Marcos sent to President Aquino were provided by a confidential source.

Nandeng Pedrosa was interviewed on April 6 and 14, and August 31, 1990. A fourth interview was arranged but his untimely death of a heart attack precluded such a meeting. He provided me with a copy of the gold certificate which Bob Kerkez was trying to negotiate. Kerkez' summons by the PCGG made the newspapers: "PCGG Summons Trio Dealing in FM Gold," *Philippine Daily Inquirer*, September 13, 1990, "3 Marcos Treasure Hunters Being Hunted By Military," *Daily Globe* (Manila), September 13, 1990.

Baltazar Aquino's Second Supplemental Deposition, dated January 9, 1986, identified the receipts for the monies he deposited for Marcos. (Republic of the Philippines vs. Ferdinand E. Marcos, Imelda Marcos et al., PCGG Case No. 1, Filed April 4, 1986.)

Chapter 13

Enrique Zobel and the clan were in *Fortune's* list of billionaires. *Fortune*, September 7, 1992.

I interviewed Zobel numerous times. The first was on July 30, 1992, just after the story came out that he had met with Marcos and seen the gold certificates. He graciously provided more details of his meeting with Marcos and others involved in the attempt to set up the foundation. He provided copies of his notes to Marcos. In one, they changed code-names. Marcos was "Ulysses" and Zobel was "Mars." He also told me about the Ilocano pilots flying gold to Zurich.

Aruiza's book, *Ferdinand Marcos: Malacañang to Makiki*, helped reconcile the dates of Marcos' hospitalization.

Imelda showed a leather bound album containing gold certificates to Jose Mari Velez when he visited her in New York, and later in Manila to a journalist, Luisita Lopez Torregrosa, who interviewed her for *Vanity Fair*, "The Thrilla In Manila," May 1992. Others in Manila spoke of several green folders she always carried with her, which contained the gold certificates.

Conrado Limcauco, head of television Channel Four in Manila in 1992, was empowered by the government to conduct his own private investigation into Marcos' treasure recoveries. He was the first to uncover Operation Umbrella. The PCGG documents and information helped corroborate his findings. The information about Bong Bong and Imelda trying to dismantle the Umbrella organization was provided by a confidential source.

Boni Gillego provided documents and information about his role in the lawsuit regarding the Viernes and Domingo murders.

Chapter 14

Seattle Times, "Union Official Slain, Another Hurt; Hiring Dispute Probed," June 2, 1981.

Ibid, "2 Arrested In Union Shooting; Second Man Dies of Wounds," June 3, 1981.

Seattle Times, "$30-M Lawsuit Against FM, FL," September 18, 1982.

The *Philippine News* (San Francisco) and its publisher, Alex Esclamado, championed the cause of the Viernes-Domingo murders from the start in 1981 until the last trial – of Tony Baruso – in March 1990. The series of articles constantly reminded the public of the injustice.

"The Spy Network Of the Marcos Dictatorship In the U.S.A.," by Bonifacio H. Gillego. Undated.

District Court, Western District of Washington. Case Number C89-1145R. Committee for Justice of Viernes and Domingo vs. Estate of Ferdinand Marcos et al.

Superior Court of Washington. Case No. 81-1-01924-9-SEA. State of Washington vs. Ramil, Guloy, Dictado.

Superior Court of Washington. Case No. 90-1-06199-6-SEA. State of Washington vs. Constantine Baruso.

The details of the Munich gold deal were provided by interviews with former PCGG Chairman David Castro in Manila on March 8 and 11, 1993, and April 17 and 24, 1993, at his office and the Asian Institute of Tourism.

Geoffrey Greenless was interviewed in Manila at the Sheraton Hotel on February 16 and December 15, 1991.

A copy of Greenlees' Purchase Agreement, dated February 1990, in the form of a Memorandum, was appended to Senate Committee Report No. 1443, dated October 16, 1991, submitted by Committee on Banks, Financial Institutions, and Currencies.

A copy of the letter from Credit Lyonnais Rouse Limited, dated August 17, 1989, was also appended.

Business World (Manila). "Gold Sale Confirmed by PCGG," March 29, 1990.

Chapter 15

According to the indictment against Imelda and the other defendants, false and fraudulent representations were made to Citibank, N.A., Security Pacific Bank, and Security Pacific Mortgage Corporation to secure loans to purchase, maintain, and improve real estate purchased in New York City. (District Court, Southern District of New York, Case Number 86-9729. United States of America vs. Imelda Marcos, Adnan Khashoggi, et al.)

Orlando Dulay was interviewed at New Bilibid prison on February 18, 1991, and March 17, 1993. Dulay's mother-in-law, Mrs. Ladra, also helped a great deal delivering messages back and forth. His lawyer, Mario Ongkiko, and Solicitor General Frank Chavez were also interviewed.

PCGG Chairman David Castro was interviewed on May 9, 1991, March 8, 11, 17, April 24, 29, 1993. Castro related how the documents from the Tamaraw Security Agency were first given to the palace and then to him. He interviewed Tomas Rodriguez and others who took part. My requests for interviews were turned down. One witness was interviewed in 1991 but then recanted because he feared for his life.

Jacobi's exploits with Dennis Howard Marks are chronicled in a book, *Hunting Marco Polo,* by Paul Eddy and Sara Walden.

Jacobi's money scams were chronicled in "Las Vegans Fear Losses In Gold Scam," which appeared in the *Las Vegas Sun* on April 6, 1993, under the series of articles, "Search For the Tiger's Treasure."

District Court, Southern District of Florida. Case Number 91-0220. United States of America vs. Reiner Jacobi, a/k/a Rex Johnson, a/k/a Rolf Gerhard Koenig, a/k/a Reinhard Koenig, a/k/a Dirk F. Stoffberg, a/k/a Herbert Solomon.

Philippine News (San Francisco), "Imelda Brings Circus To Town," November 6–12, 1991.

All the newspapers carried accounts of the Enrique Zobel press conference. The most thorough was a three-article series published by the *Daily Inquirer* (Manila) on June 5, 6, 7, 1992.

Joan Orendain, Zobel's public relations manager, provided me with a copy of his statement, the letter to Imelda, and the promissory note.

Castro provided the information about the meetings with Imelda. Copies of the Agreements signed between Castro, Imelda, and Bong Bong were also provided.

Chapter 16

PCGG Chairman Magtanggol Gunigundo provided the details of his negotiations with Imelda.

District Court, State of Hawaii, Multi-District Litigation, Master Docket No. 840. Plaintiffs versus Ferdinand E. Marcos.

The State Department objected to a state visit by Nicaragua's Anastasio Somoza Garcia in 1939. President Franklin D. Roosevelt's reply was, "He may be a son of a bitch but he's our son of a bitch."

The importance of the military bases was reported in *U.S. Perceptions and Policies Toward the Philippines. Has A Transition Begun?* by Larry Niksch. Congressional Research Service, Library of Congress, December 1, 1983. Prepared for the Joint Seminar on United States-Philippine Relations, December 6–7, 1983.

"Like talking to the Tooth Fairy." *Fortune*, "The High-Flying First Lady of the Philippines," July 2, 1979.

Human Rights Violations In the Philippines: An Account of Torture, 'Disappearances,' Extrajudicial Executions and Illegal Detention, Amnesty International USA, undated.

Report of an Amnesty International Mission To the Republic of the Philippines, 11–28 November 1981, Amnesty International Publications, 1982.

Country Reports on Human Rights Practices for 1981, Report submitted to the Committee on Foreign Affairs, U.S. House of Representatives and the Committee on Foreign Relations, U.S. Senate, by the Dept. of State, February 1982.

The Philippine Government's Response to the Report of an AI Mission to the Republic of the Philippines 11–28 November 1981 and AI's Reply to the Government Response, Amnesty International, AI Index: ASA 35/18/83, December 1983.

The Situation In the Philippines, A Staff Report prepared for the Committee on Foreign Relations, U.S. Senate, October 1984.

The Philippines: A Situation Report, Staff Report to the Senate Select Committee On Intelligence, U.S. Senate, November 1, 1985.

Salvaging Democracy: Human Rights in the Philippines, Lawyers Committee for Human Rights, New York, December 1985.

Bantay ng Bayan: Stories from the Namfrel Crusade 1984–86, Kaa Byington.

Political Detention and Military Atrocities in the Philippines 1981–1982, Task Force Detainees of the Philippines, Quezon City, Philippines, 1986.

The May 14, 1983, incident was reported in the 1985 *Amnesty International Report*, covering the period January to December 1984, pp. 237–240.

Thomas Bryan of Sotheby's International Realty testified at Imelda's trial about the threat Tantoco made. (District Court, Southern District of New York. Case Number 86-9729. United States of America vs. Imelda Marcos, Adnan Khashoggi, et al.)

Copies of the Powers of Attorney of Calderon and Svenson, and the Letter of Authority to Pesebre were provided by a confidential source.

Robert Swift's encounter with Imelda and Bong Bong in Manila was described in *Philippines Free Press*, "The Imelda Act," January 30, 1993. Former Senator Rene Saguisag filled in a few of the details.

Chapter 17

Central Bank Deputy Governor Ed Zialcita was interviewed, along with Guillermo Carague, Monetary Board Member.

The definitions of the special accounts were provided by the Central Bank Dept. of Economic Research. Mr. Tony Cintura was especially helpful.

In a Privilege Speech on February 3, 1993, Sen. Albert Romulo revealed that more than $600 million of the Central Bank losses consisted of "private sector" debts. Companies favored by Marcos could borrow abroad with protection against the decline of the peso. If the peso decreased in value, the extra cost was borne not by the companies but by the Central Bank's Exchange Stabilization Account.

Philippine journalist Julie Amargo obtained a copy of the KLM waybill. The Central Bank provided a copy of its article, "CB's Gold and Silver Reserve Management: Clearing the Doubts."

Privilege Speech of Sen. Aquilino Pimentel: "No To Untouchability," November 9, 1987. He detailed fraudulent acts committed by Central Bank Governor Fernandez. He also uncovered the anomalies in the August 17, 1987, Central Bank Statement of Condition.

Senator Maceda provided a copy of proposed senate resolution number 568 and Committe Report No. 829 which approved it.

Far Eastern Economic Review, "The Financial 'Wizards,'" by Jose Galang, March 29, 1984.

World Bank report leaked. *Far Eastern Economic Review*, "Manila's Black Hole," July 23, 1992.

Privilege Speech of Sen. Albert Romulo: "How I Lost My Innocence," March 15, 1993.

Report on the Transfer of Assets and Liabilities from the Former Central Bank to the *Bangko Sentral ng Pilipinas*. Volume I – Main Report, and Volume II – Details of Assets and Liabilities. November 3, 1993.

Daily Inquirer (Manila), "Plugging the Black Hole: How the Central Bank proposes to straighten its multi billion financial mess," by the Central Bank of the Philippines, April 19, 1993.

The information about Ismael and the 7.5 metric tons in the Quezon City house was provided by a confidential source.

Marcos kept a diary. It was found in the palace after he hastily departed the Philippines. His entry about history and historians was made on May 24, 1971.

Chapter 18

Philippine Herald, "Rep. Nalundasan Shot To Death," September 21, 1935.

Marcos' claim that Yamashita surrendered to him appeared in the *Asia* magazine on September 12, 1971. Vicente Barranco questioned this fact in his own article, dated October 23, 1971, in *Philippines Free Press* magazine, "Did Yamashita Surrender to Marcos?"

A book on Marcos' war exploits was published by the Philippine government, Office of Media Affairs, during the Marcos era, entitled *Documents on the Marcos War Medals.*

Ernesto Rodriguez' book, *The Bad Guerrillas of Northern Luzon*, described Marcos' experiences as a guerrilla during the war, and how he was arrested by the U.S. forces.

Documents from the National Archives, provided by John Sharkey of the *Washington Post*, detailed events surrounding the execution of Mariano Marcos.

The courageous story of Quintero's decision to expose Imelda for handing out envelopes full of cash at the Constitutional Convention was documented in *The Weekly Nation*, "The Ordeal of Quintero," June 12, 1972.

Phil Bronstein won the annual Thomas M. Storke International Journalism award, given by the World Affairs Council.

November 4, 1984, *San Francisco Examiner*, "Menacing Philippine Agents Harass, Tail, Threaten Reporter," by Phil Bronstein.

"Artists, Writers And Intellectuals And The Culture Of Crisis," Doreen G. Fernandez, Ateneo de Manila University, Philippines. A paper written for the Association of Asian Studies Annual Meeting, March 22–24, 1985, Philadelphia.

Marcos diary entry on October 8, 1970.

Chapter 19

The data examined consisted of four volumes dated April 1984:

Volume I – Central Bank of the Philippines Executive Summary.

Volume II – Philippine National Bank Executive Summary.

Volume III – Central Bank Details of Results of Special Review.

Volume IV – PNB Details of Results of Special Review.

The computer printout of the $94 million sent to Swiss banks was obtained from a confidential source.

Republic of the Philippines vs. Ferdinand E. Marcos (represented by his estate/heirs) and Imelda Romualdez Marcos. Civil Case SBNo. 0141.

"The Case Of The Missing Gold Bullions," *Philippine Graphic*, April 19, 1993.

The grand total for these governmental institutions amounted to ₱209.9 billion ($9.995 billion). Data from Bureau of Treasury report "Assets and Liabilities Assumed By the National Government." (BTR/EDMD, October 28, 1993). At a meeting in Senator Romulo's office on May 29, 1997, Bureau of Treasury officials explained Proclamation 50 and how the amounts were derived.

Senator Alberto G. Romulo's privilege speech – "The Central Bank Losses & The Public Sector Deficit." January 20, 1992.

Definition of "Behest Loan:" Senate Committee Report No. 58, Submitted by the Committee on Banks, Financial Institutions and Currencies on December 18, 1992, Re: Inquiry in aid of legislation of four-hundred-nineteen (419) accounts from the four (4) government financial institutions (GFI's) namely: the Development Bank of the Philippines (DBP), the Philippine National Bank (PNB), Philippine Export and Foreign Loan Guarantee Corporation (PHILGUARANTEE) and the National Development Company (NDC), some of which are considered "BEHEST LOANS" yet now form part of the country's public sector debt.

Select Bibliography

BOOKS AND PAPERS

Agoncillo, Teodoro A., *The Fateful Years.* 2 vols. Quezon City, Philippines: R.P. Garcia Publishing Co., 1965.

Agoncillo, Teodoro A., and Milagros C. Guerrero. *History of the Filipino People.* 5th ed. Quezon City, Philippines: R.P. Garcia Publishing Co., 1977.

Amnesty International. Annual Reports for 1983, 1984, 1985, 1986.

Ibid. Human Rights Violations In the Philippines: An Account of Torture, 'Disappearances,' Extrajudicial Executions and Illegal Detention. Undated.

Ibid. Report of an Amnesty International Mission to the Republic of the Philippines, 11–28 November 1981. September 1982.

Ibid. The Philippine Government's Response to the Report of an AI Mission to the Republic of the Philippines 11–28 November 1981 and AI's Reply to the Government Response. ASA 35/18/83. December 1983.

Araneta, Salvador. *America's Double-Cross of the Philippines: A democratic ally in 1989 and 1946.* Bayanikasan Research Foundation, Manila, 1978.

Aruiza, Arturo C. *Ferdinand E. Marcos: Malacañang to Makiki.* Quezon City, Philippines: AC Aruiza Enterprises, 1991.

Bautista, Romeo M. *Industrial Promotion Policies In the Philippines.* Makati, Metro Manila: Philippine Institute For Developmental Studies. 1979.

Bello, Walden, David Kinley, and Elaine Elinson. *Development Debacle: The World Bank in the Philippines.* San Francisco: Institute for Food and Development Policy, 1982.

Belote, James H. & William M. *Corregidor: The Saga of a Fortress.* New York: Harper & Row, 1967.

Berlow, Alan. *Dead Season.* New York: Pantheon Books, 1996.

Bernas, Joaquin G. "Some Reflections On Eight Years Under Martial Rule." From *Not By Bread Alone.* Edited by Fr. Pacifico A. Ortiz, S.J., Bishops-Businessmen's Conference Dialogue On Human Development Under Martial Law. Manila, 1980.

Bonner, Raymond. *Waltzing With A Dictator: The Marcoses and the Making of American Policy.* New York: Times Books, 1987.

Burton, Sandra. *Impossible Dream: The Marcoses, the Aquinos, and the Unfinished Revolution.* New York: Warner Books, 1989.

Byington, Kaa. *Bantay ng Bayan: Stories from the Namfrel Crusade 1984–86.* Manila: Bookmark, 1988.

Cathcart, Dan. *Aircraft Accident Litigation Techniques.* Charlottesville, Virginia: Michie Company, 1985.

Central Bank of the Philippines. "The Philippine Economy: Policies and Development, 1975–1982." Manila, 1983.

Chapman, William. *Inside the Philippine Revolution: The New People's Army and Its Struggle for Power.* New York: W.W. Norton and Company, 1987.

Circuit Court, First Circuit, State of Hawaii. Civil Case Number 88-0522. Roger Roxas and the Golden Budha Corporation vs. Ferdinand Marcos and Imelda Marcos.

Daniel, Dan Richard V. *Swiss Banks Cracking In!!!* Manila: PCGG Research Department. Undated.

District Court, Central District of California. Case Number 86-3859. Republic of the Philippines vs. Ferdinand E. Marcos, Imelda Marcos, et al.

District Court, Second Judicial District of Nevada. Case Number 77-00066. United States of America vs. Robert Curtis and John W. McAllaster.

District Court, Second Judicial District of Nevada. Case Number 307152. Eureka Trust, Liberty Trust, et al. vs. Robert Curtis et al.

District Court, Second Judicial District of Nevada. Case Number 313689. Samuel J. Agnew vs. Robert Curtis et al.

District Court, Southern District of Florida. Case Number 91-0220. United States of America vs. Reiner Jacobi, a/k/a Rex Johnson, a/k/a Rolf Gerhard Koenig, a/k/a Reinhard Koenig, a/k/a Dirk F. Stoffberg, a/k/a Herbert Solomon.

District Court, Southern District of New York. Case Number 86-9729. United States of America vs. Imelda Marcos, Adnan Khashoggi, et al.

District Court, State of Hawaii, Multi-District Litigation, Master Docket No. 840. Plaintiffs versus Ferdinand E. Marcos.

District Court, Western District of Washington. Case Number C89-1145R. Committee for Justice of Viernes and Domingo vs. Estate of Ferdinand Marcos et al.

Doherty, John F., S.J. *A Preliminary Study of Interlocking Directorates.* Quezon City, Philippines: Ateneo de Manila University Press. Undated.

Ibid. Who Controls the Philippine Economy: Some Need Not Try As Hard AS Others. Quezon City, Philippines: Ateneo de Manila University Press. Undated.

Eddy, Paul, and Sara Walden. *Hunting Marco Polo: The Pursuit of the Drug Smuggler Who Couldn't Be Caught By the Agent Who Wouldn't Quit.* Boston: Little, Brown and Company, 1991.

Espiritu, Augusto Caesar, Merlin M. Magallona, Lilia R. Bautista, Reuben D. Torres, and Esteban B. Bautista, *Philippine Perspectives On Multinational Corporations.* Quezon City: University of the Philippines Law Center, 1978.

European Chamber of Commerce, Japanese Chamber of Commerce and Industry, American Chamber of Commerce, Australian Business Group. *A Position Paper On Proposed Improvements to the Promotions, Regulatory, and Infrastructure Framework Affecting Philippine Business.* Submitted to The Hon. Min. Luis R. Villafuerte, Ministry of Trade. Makati, Metro Manila, August 11, 1980.

Fernandez, Doreen G. "Artists, Writers And Intellectuals And The Culture Of Crisis." A paper written for the Association of Asian Studies Annual Meeting. Philadelphia, March 22–24, 1985. Quezon City, Philippines: Ateneo de Manila University Press.

Fukumitsu, Minoru. *The Awa Maru Incident* (in Japanese). Tokyo: Yomiuri Shimbun. Undated.

Gillego, Bonifacio H. *The Spy Network Of the Marcos Dictatorship In the U.S.A.* Manila. Undated.

Gleeck, Lewis E. Jr. *President Marcos And The Philippine Political Culture.* Manila: Loyal Printing, 1987.

Ibid. The American Half-Century (1898–1946). Manila: Historical Conservation Society, 1984.

Guinness Book of World Records, 1991. New York: Bantam Books, 1991.

Harries, Meirion and Susie. *Soldiers of the Sun: The Rise and Fall of the Imperial Japanese Army.* New York: Random House, 1991.

Hill, Gerald N. and Kathleen Thompson Hill, with the cooperation of Steve Psinakis. *The True Story of the Aquino Assassination.* Sonoma, California: Hilltop Publishing, 1983.

Horn, Florence. *Orphans of the Pacific.* New York: Reynal and Hitchcock, 1941.

Hunt, Ray C., and Bernard Norling. *Behind Japanese Lines: An American Guerrilla In the Philippines.* Lexington: University Press of Kentucky, 1986.

Innis, Joe W., with Bill Bunton. *In Search of the Awa Maru.* New York: Bantam Books, 1981.

International Monetary Fund. *International Financial Statistics.* Washington, D.C., March 1988.

Ito, Masanori. *The End of the Imperial Japanese Navy.* New York: W.W. Norton: Jove Books, 1962.

Jesswani, Jesus, ed. *A Look At Philippine History.* Manila: St. Paul Press, 1989.

Johnson, Bryan. *The Four Days of Courage: The Untold Story of the People Who Brought Marcos Down.* New York: The Free Press, 1987.

Karnow, Stanley. *In Our Image: America's Empire in the Philippines.* New York: Random House, 1989.

Kenworthy, Aubrey S. *Tiger of Malaya.* New York: Exposition Press, 1953.

Kerkvliet, Benedict. *The Huk Rebellion: A Study of Peasant Revolt In the Philippines.* Quezon City, Philippines: New Day Publishers, 1979.

Lael, Richard L. *The Yamashita Precedent.* Wilmington, Delaware: Scholarly Resources, Inc., 1982.

Lawyers Committee for Human Rights. *Salvaging Democracy: Human Rights in the Philippines.* New York, December 1985.

Letter from William Saunders to Commanding Officer, Luzon, dated 26 July 1944. Norfolk, Virginia: MacArthur Memorial Archives.

Lindholm, Paul R. *Shadows From the Rising Sun.* Quezon City, Philippines: New Day Publishers, 1978.

Lucas, John. *Gold.* Annual Report of the U.S. Department of the Interior, Bureau of Mines. December 1992.

Mamot, Patricia R. *People Power.* Quezon City, Philippines; New Day Publishers, 1986.

Manapat, Ricardo. *Some Are Smarter Than Others: The History of Marcos' Crony Capitalism.* New York: Aletheia Publications, 1991.

Manchester, William. *American Caesar.* Boston: Dell Publishing Company, 1978.

Manila Merchants Association. *Manila: The Pearl of the Orient.* Manila, 1908.

Maurico, Luis R., ed. *Renato Constantino and the Marcos Watch.* Quezon City, Philippines: Karrel, Inc., 1987.

McDougald, Charles C. *A Commentary On the Report Entitled "Multinational Corporations In the Philippines" Prepared By the Technology Resource Center.* Prepared for the American Chamber of Commerce of the Philippines. Makati, Metro Manila, April 16, 1979.

Ibid, Multinational Corporations In the Philippines, 1978. Prepared for the American Chamber of Commerce of the Philippines. Makati, Metro Manila, December 1, 1980.

Morrison, Samuel Elliot. *History of U.S. Naval Operations In World War II.* vol 12. Boston: Little Brown & Co., 1966.

National Economic and Development Authority. *Philippine Statistical Yearbook.* Manila, various years.

Niksch, Larry. *U.S. Perceptions and Policies Toward the Philippines. Has A Transition Begun?* Prepared for the Joint Seminar on United States-Philippine Relations. December 6–7, 1983. Congressional Research Service, Library of Congress. December 1, 1983.

Ohno, Takushi. *War Reparations & Peace Settlement: Philippines-Japan Relations, 1945–1956.* Manila: Solidaridad Publishing House, 1986.

Owen, Norman G., ed. *The Philippine Economy and the United States: Studies in Past and Present Interactions.* Michigan Papers on South and Southeast Asia. Center for South and Southeast Asian Studies. Number 22. The University of Michigan, 1983.

Philippine Chamber of Industries. *A White Paper On Philippine Industry.* Manila, 1977.

Pimentel, Aquilino. "No To Untouchability." Privilege speech. Senate of the Philippines. November 9, 1987.

Psinakis, Steve. *Two Terrorists Meet.* San Francisco: Alchemy Books, 1981.

Quito, Emerita S., ed. "American Life Styles In Colonial Philippines." In *Pammadayaw: Philippine Studies by International Authors, In Honor of Dr. Marcelino Foronda, Jr.* Manila: De la Salle University Press, 1987.

Reel, A. Frank. *The Case of General Yamashita.* Chicago: University of Chicago Press, 1949.

Republic of the Philippines. Bureau of Treasury. *Assets and Liabilities Assumed By the National Government.* BTR/EDMD. Manila, October 28, 1993.

Ibid. Committee of Seven. Created Under Republic Act 7653. *Report on the Transfer of Assets and Liabilities from the Former Central Bank to the Bangko Sentral ng Pilipinas. Volume I – Main Report, and Volume II – Details of Assets and Liabilities.* Manila, November 3, 1993.

Ibid. Office of Media Affairs. *Documents On the Marcos War Medals.* 1983.

Republic of the Philippines vs. Ferdinand E. Marcos, Imelda Marcos et al. PCGG Case No. 1.

Republic of the Philippines vs. Ferdinand E. Marcos (represented by his estate/heirs) and Imelda Romualdez Marcos. Civil Case SBNo. 0141.

Rodriguez, Ernesto R., Jr. *The Bad Guerrillas of Northern Luzon.* Quezon City, Philippines: J. Burgos Media Services, 1982.

Romulo, Alberto G. "How I Lost My Innocence." Privilege speech. Senate of the Philippines. March 15, 1993.

Ibid. "The Central Bank Losses & The Public Sector Deficit." Privilege speech. Senate of the Philippines. January 20, 1992.

Ibid. "Time For Tough Decisions." Privilege speech. Senate of the Philippines. February 3, 1993.

Romulo, Beth Day. *The Manila Hotel.* Manila: The Manila Hotel. Undated.

Salonga, Jovita R. "Convergence of International Law and Domestic Law in the Recovery of the Plundered Wealth." Manila, July 20, 1993.

Ibid. "The Extradition Treaty Between the Philippines and the United States: Facts and Implications." Philippine Studies Occasional Paper No. 5, Philippine Studies Program. Honolulu: University of Hawaii, Center for Asian and Pacific Studies, August 1982.

Senate of the Philippines. *Inquiry in aid of legislation of four-hundred-nineteen (419) accounts from the four (4) government financial institutions (GFI's).* Committee Report No. 58. Submitted by the Committee on Banks, Financial Institutions and Currencies. December 18, 1992.

Simons, Lewis M. *Worth Dying For.* New York: William and Morrow, Inc., 1987.

Singlaub, John K., with Malcolm McConnell. *Hazardous Duty.* New York: Summit Books, 1991.

Sison, Jose Maria. *The Philippine Revolution: The Leader's View.* New York: Taylor and Francis, 1989.

Smith, Robert R. *U.S. Army in World War II: Triumph in the Philippines.* Washington: Government Printing Office, 1963.

Spector, Ronald H. *Eagle Against the Sun.* New York: The Free Press, 1985.

Spence, Hartzell. *For Every Tear A Victory: The Story of Ferdinand E. Marcos.* New York: McGraw-Hill, 1964.

Steiger, Brad. *The Psychic Feats of Olof Jonsson.* Englewood Cliffs, New Jersey: Prentice Hall, 1972.

Steinberg, David Joel. *The Philippines: A Singular and Plural Place.* Boulder, Colorado: Westview Press, 1982.

Sullivan, William H. *Obbligato.* New York: W.W. Norton & Co., 1984.

Superior Court of Washington. Case No. 81-1-01924-9-SEA. State of Washington vs. Ramil, Guloy, Dictado.

Superior Court of Washington. Case No. 90-1-06199-6-SEA. State of Washington vs. Constantine Baruso.

Sycip, Gorres, Velayo & Company. 4 Volumes. Volume I – Central Bank of the Philippines Executive Summary; Volume II – Philippine National Bank Executive Summary; Volume III – Central Bank Details of Results of Special Review; Volume IV – PNB Details of Results of Special Review. Manila, April 1984.

Task Force Detainees of the Philippines. *Political Detention and Military Atrocities in the Philippines 1981–1982.* Quezon City, Philippines, 1986.

Toland, John. *The Rising Sun.* New York: Bantam Books, 1970.

Tsuda, Mamoru and Masaki Yokoyama. *Japan Inc. In Asia: A Documentation On Its Operations Through The Philippine Polity.* Tokyo: Askashi Shoten Publishing Co. Ltd., 1992.

Umali, D. Ahl. *Tracing Marcos' Gold.* Hong Kong. Undated.

United Nations Development Program. *Sharing In Development.* Report of Inter-Agency Team. Metro Manila: National Economic and Development Authority, 1974.

U.S. Agency for International Development. *Economic Profile and Causes of Poverty In Bicol.* Manila, May 1982.

Ibid. Effects of Recent Developments on the Coconut Farmers. Manila, January 9, 1984.

Ibid. Overview of Developments In Public Expenditures, 1978–1983. Manila, 1984.

Ibid. Poverty Profile, Bicol Region. Manila, August 1982.

Ibid. Poverty Profile, Eastern Visayas. Manila, September 1982.

Ibid. Poverty Profile, Western Visayas. Manila, January 1981.

Ibid. War on Hunger. Manila, December 1977.

U.S. Congress. House. *Investigation of the Costs Involved in Moving Former President Marcos and His Party from Manila to Hawaii.* Report prepared by the Readiness Subcommittee of the Committee On Armed Services. 99th Congress. Second session. Committee Print 20. 1986.

Ibid. Investigation of Philippine Investments In the United States. Hearings Before the Subcommittee On Asian and Pacific Affairs. 99th Congress. First and Second Sessions. December 3, 11, 12, 13, 17, and 19, 1985; January 21, 23, and 29; March 18 and 19; April 9 and 17, 1986.

U.S. Department of State. *Country Reports on Human Rights Practices for 1981.* Submitted to the Committee on Foreign Affairs, U.S. House of Representatives and the Committee on Foreign Relations, U.S. Senate. February 1982.

U.S. General Accounting Office. *Economic Support Fund Assistance To The Philippines.* Report To The Committee On Foreign Affairs, House of Representatives. GAO/NSIAD-84-44. January 27, 1984.

Ibid. The Philippines: Accountability and Control of U.S. Economic Assistance. Briefing Report To Senator Edward M. Kennedy. May 1986.

U.S. Senate. *The Philippines: A Situation Report.* Staff Report to the Senate Select Committee On Intelligence. November 1, 1985.

Ibid. The Situation In the Philippines. Staff Report For the Committee On Foreign Relations. Washington, D.C. October 1984.

Waldron, Ben. *Corregidor: From Paradise to Hell.* Freeman, South Dakota: Pine Hill Press, 1988.

Wilcox, Marrion, ed. *Harper's History of the War in the Philippines.* New York: Harper & Brothers Publications, 1900.
World Bank. *Aspects of Poverty In the Philippines: A Review and Assessment.* Volume II. Washington, D.C., December 1, 1980.
Ibid. The World Bank and the World's Poorest, 1980. Washington, D.C., 1980.
Ibid. Poverty and Basic Needs. Washington, D.C., 1980.
Wurfel, David. *Filipino Politics: Development and Decay.* Quezon City, Philippines: Ateneo de Manila University Press, 1988.
Zaide, Gregorio F. *Jose Rizal: Life, Works, and Writings.* Manila: C.P. Villanueva, 1981.

ARTICLES

"3 Marcos Treasure Hunters Being Hunted By Military." *Daily Globe.* Manila, September 13, 1990.
Alibutud, J.R. "The Mystery of the Baccay Case: Solved But Not Solved." *Philippine News.* San Francisco, December 4–10, 1985.
Anderson, Jack. "A President Who's Above Criticism." *San Francisco Chronicle.* June 29, 1976.
"A Treasure Hunt for $5 Billion." *San Francisco Examiner.* November 19, 1976.
Almario, Manuel F. "The Case Of The Missing Gold Bullions." *Philippine Graphic.* Manila, April 19, 1993.
Barranco, Vicente. "Did Yamashita Surrender to Marcos?" *Philippines Free Press.* Manila, October 23, 1971.
Benoza, Nick G. "Marcoses, Pals Dipped Hands in Most Government Till." *Philippine News.* San Francisco, April 9–15, 1986.
Bronstein, Phil. "Imelda Marcos Blames News Media For Unrest In Philippines." *San Francisco Examiner.* September 19, 1983.
Ibid. "Jackpot for 'Raiders' of the Hidden Holdings." *San Francisco Examiner.* March 9, 1986.
Ibid. "Menacing Philippine Agents Harass, Tail, Threaten Reporter." *San Francisco Examiner.* November 4, 1984.
Ibid. "What Marcos Told the Coup Leaders To Do." *San Francisco Examiner.* July 13, 1986.
Butterfield, Fox. "Manila Inner Circle Gains Under Marcos." *New York Times.* January 15, 1978.
Ibid. "5 Years of Philippine Martial law Builds Personal Power of Marcos." *New York Times.* January 9, 1978.
Cannon, Carl M. "Imelda's 'Philosophical' UN Speech Astonishing." *Philippine News.* San Francisco, October 23–29, 1985.
Central Bank of the Philippines. "Plugging the Black Hole: How the Central Bank proposes to straighten its multi billion financial mess." *Philippine Daily Inquirer.* Manila, April 19, 1993.
Ibid. "The Philippine Economy: Policies and Development, 1975–1982." Manila, 1983.
Clever, Dick. "30-M Lawsuit vs. FM, FL." *Seattle Times.* September 18, 1982.

"Cory Silent on Sumulong Revelation of $15B FM Loot." *Daily Globe*. Manila, June 26, 1991.

Deane, Daniela. "Besieged Rebels Surrender In Manila." *San Francisco Examiner*. January 29, 1987.

"Determining Poverty Thresholds." *Business Day*. Manila, May 25, 1984.

"Doctors Set More Tests For Imelda." *Philippine Herald*. Manila, May 29, 1968.

Domestic Information Service. "The Financial Crisis Explained." Three part series. *Bulletin Today*. Manila, December 28, 29, 30, 1983.

Ellison, Katherine. "Tale of Imelda and 'The Toilet King.'" *Philippine News*. San Francisco, December 11–17, 1985.

Florentino, Chay O. "Fictitious Contractors Got ₱198M." *Philippine Daily Inquirer*. Manila, June 28, 1986.

Galang, Jose. "The Financial 'Wizards.'" *Far Eastern Economic Review*. Hong Kong, March 29, 1984.

"General Yamashita Met Slow Death on Black Gallows." *Manila Chronicle*. Manila, February 26, 1946.

Genovea, Miguel C. "Sumulong Tells How RP Lost $15B of Marcos Wealth." *Daily Globe*. Manila, June 23, 1991.

Gerth, Jeff. "The Marcos Connections in the Capital." *New York Times*. November 12, 1985.

Ibid. "Manila's Spending of Aid Criticized." *San Francisco Chronicle*. December 6, 1985.

"Gold Sale Confirmed by PCGG." *Business World*. Manila, March 29, 1990.

Gonzaga, Leo. "Life Raft For Manila's Hotels." *Far Eastern Economic Review*. Hong Kong, October 21, 1977.

Guillen, Tomas and Dave Birkland. "2 Arrested In Union Shooting; Second Man Dies of Wounds." *Seattle Times*. June 3, 1981.

"Imelda's M. Manila Commission In Hock," *Philippine News*. San Francisco, December 11–17, 1985.

"Imelda: The Philippine 'Eva Peron.'" *Los Angeles Times*. October 24, 1980.

Johnston, David. "Philippines Diverted U.S. Schools Aid." *San Francisco Chronicle*. December 8, 1985.

Jones, Brennon. "Marcos's Influential Enemies." *Nation*. October 4, 1980.

"Journalist Vindicated," *Far Eastern Economic Review* . Hong Kong, March 11, 1977.

Kamm, Henry. "Creating A Dynasty In the Philippines." *The New York Times Magazine*. May 24, 1981.

Kramer, Barry. "Ties To the Top; In the Philippines, It's Whom You Know That Can Really Count." *Wall Street Journal*. January 28, 1978.

Lopez, Antonio. "I Am Heartsick." *Asiaweek*. Hong Kong, December 16, 1983.

Losee, Stephanie. "Billionaires, The." *Fortune*. September 7, 1992.

Maidenflores, Jaime. "Our Friend, the Enemy." Panorama Sunday Magazine. *Philippine Daily Express*. Manila, July 17, 1978.

Malone, William Scott. "Greed: The Golden Fleece." *Regardies*. October 1988.

"Marcos Blasts Business Leaders." *San Francisco Chronicle*. November 11, 1983.

"Marcos Loyalist Names Himself Acting President." *San Francisco Chronicle*. July 7, 1986.

"Marcos Unloads Gold Assets." *Manila Journal.* Manila, January 5, 1988.

"Marcos' WWII Gold Hoard Worth $22B." *Philippine Daily Inquirer.* Manila, April 21, 1986.

"Marcos Officials Looted Treasury of $150 Million, Auditors Say." *San Francisco Chronicle.* April 3, 1986.

Moraes, Dom. "The Cool Couple." *Asia.* Hong Kong, September 12, 1971.

Nuguid, Nati A. "The Imelda Act." *Philippines Free Press.* Manila, January 30, 1993.

Nuyda, Doris G. "A Gem of a Story." *Mr. & Ms.* Manila, March 20–26, 1987.

Ocampo, Rosa. "U.S. Halts Fund Aid to NEA for Anomaly." *Philippine News.* San Francisco, January 8–14, 1986.

Ocampo, Sheila. "A Political Base Grows From A Military Base." *Far Eastern Economic Review.* Hong Kong, October 29, 1982.

Ocampo-Kalfors, Sheila. "MIFF sin miffs Sin." *Far Eastern Economic Review.* Hong Kong, February 17, 1983.

Ongpin, Roberto V. "The Binondo Central Bank: The True Story." *Manila Bulletin.* Manila, April 25, 1986.

"Out of the Muddle, A Promise of Bliss." *Far Eastern Economic Review.* Hong Kong, February 16, 1979.

Parial, Ernesto C. "Imelda Brings Circus To Town." *Philippine News.* San Francisco, November 6–12, 1991.

"PCGG Summons Trio Dealing in FM Gold." *Philippine Daily Inquirer.* Manila, September 13, 1990.

Preston, Douglas. "Assault On A Treasure Island." *Readers Digest.* September 1988.

"Rep. Nalundasan Shot To Death." *Philippine Herald.* Manila, September 21, 1935.

Ronquillo, Marlen. "$13 billion Philippine Earnings Since 1965 Reported Missing." *Philippine News.* San Francisco, August 4–10, 1985.

Rowan, Roy. "The High Flying First Lady of the Philippines." *Fortune.* July 2, 1979.

"Quest For Yamashita's Hoard Still Haunts Manila." *Far Eastern Economic Review.* Hong Kong, June 25, 1987.

"Reserves Overstated Since 1981." *Business Day.* Manila, August 9, 1984.

Sacerdoti, Guy. "A Political Factor In the KKK Equation." *Far Eastern Economic Review.* Hong Kong, October 29, 1982.

Sacerdoti, Guy, and Gary Coull. "Golden Fleece." *Far Eastern Economic Review.* Hong Kong, April 1982.

Saguisag, Rene. "When Solons Get ₱15,000 Dole Each." *Filipino Times.* Manila, March 20–29, 1985.

Scott, Margaret. "A Fool and her Monet are soon Parted." *Far Eastern Economic Review.* Hong Kong, September 29, 1988.

Senoren, Samuel V. "Offices Entangled In Red Tape Listed." *Philippine Daily Express.* November 4, 1982.

"Silver Anniversary For the Iron Butterfly." *Life.* July 1979.

Subang, Leticia M. "COA Insists FM Diverted Some US Economic Aid Fund." *Business Day.* Manila, April 18, 1986.

"Sunken Ship May Hold $5 Billion Treasure." *San Francisco Chronicle.* November 18, 1976.

Tasker, Rodney. "After Zeitlin, Assurances." *Far Eastern Economic Review.* Hong Kong, November 19, 1976.

"The Iron Butterfly." *Newsweek.* August 12, 1974,

"There Is No Yamashita Treasure." Panorama Sunday Magazine. *Philippine Daily Express.* Manila, July 17, 1982.

"The Sixties – Nationalism and Chaos." *Far Eastern Economic Review.* 50th Anniversary Issue. Hong Kong, 1996.

"The Ten Richest Women In the World." *Cosmopolitan.* December 1975.

Thompson, Gary and Steve Lanigher. "Las Vegans Fear Losses In Gold Scam." *Las Vegas Sun.* "Search For the Tiger's Treasure" series. April 6, 1993.

Tiglao, Rigoberto. "Manila's Black Hole." *Far Eastern Economic Review.* Hong Kong, July 23, 1992.

Torregrosa, Luisita Lopez. "The Thrilla In Manila." *Vanity Fair.* May 1992.

"Union Official Slain, Another Hurt; Hiring Dispute Probed." *Seattle Times.* June 2, 1981.

Villafranca, Vic. "The Ordeal of Quintero." *The Weekly Nation.* Manila, June 12, 1972.

Villanueva, Felicia Pamela A. "CB's Gold and Silver Reserve Management: Clearing the Doubts." *Central Bank Review.* Manila, June 1986.

"War Treasure Still Sought In Philippines." *Los Angeles Times.* May 28, 1978.

Wideman, Bernard. "Overbuilt, Underbooked." *Far Eastern Economic Review.* Hong Kong, January 21, 1977.

Wolmuth, Roger. "The Imelda Marcos Shopping Guide: A Cache 'N' Carry Way To Spend The Fortunes Of A Nation." *People.* April 7, 1986.

"Yamashita's End." *Philippine Free Press.* Manila, March 3, 1946.

Zeitlin, Arnold. "Marcos Family – Study Core of Philippine Life." *Pacific Stars and Stripes.* November 9, 1975.

Zobel, Enrique. "Enrique Zobel On Marcos Gold." *Philippine Daily Inquirer.* Manila, June 5, 1992.

Ibid. "FM Bares Plan For 'Foundation.'" *Philippine Daily Inquirer.* Manila, June 6, 1992.

Ibid. "FM Didn't Tell Wife About Trust." *Philippine Daily Inquirer.* Manila, June 7, 1992.

Index

The Author

Charles C. McDougald lived in the Philippines for ten years during the martial law turbulence, mostly as a student. He obtained a masters degree from the Asian Institute of Management then went on to the University of the Philippines where he obtained his doctorate. He already held a batchelor of science degree from the University of Georgia.

After Ninoy Aquino was assassinated he wrote *The Marcos File*, which exposed the corruption and excesses of the Marcos regime. It also debunked the Marcos war record as a complete fabrication. McDougald's background and experience as a former captain in the Green Berets in Vietnam helped in this research.

One of his professors at the University of the Philippines was Emanuel V. Soriano, president of the school, who became President Aquino's national security director. McDougald was asked to find the truth about the legendary Yamashita treasure buried in the Philippines during World War II. After hunting for the treasure for two years, he wrote about his adventures and about Marcos' own attempt to find the gold in *Asian Loot.*

No treasure was found but the foundation was laid for his next book, *The Buddha, The Gold, and The Myth.* It reveals further details of Marcos' greed and his quest for riches and shines a spotlight on the shadowy world of the Central Bank. Fast-paced and scintillating, the book reads like an adventure novel. Through meticulous research, sordid never-before-told details emerge of treasure hunts and gold deals, of torture and murder, of dark secrets and a coverup.

McDougald now lives in San Francisco with his wife and two children.